Reprints of Economic Classics

AN ESSAY ON THE
DISTRIBUTION OF WEALTH

AN

ESSAY

ON THE

DISTRIBUTION OF WEALTH

BY

GEORGE RAMSAY

[1836]

AUGUSTUS M. KELLEY • PUBLISHERS
CLIFTON 1974

First Edition 1836

(Edinburgh: Adam & Charles Black; London: Longman, Rees, Orme, Brown, Green & Longman, 1836)

Reprinted 1974 by

Augustus M. Kelley Publishers

Clifton New Jersey 07012

Library of Congress Cataloging in Publication Data

Ramsay, Sir George, 1800-1871.
    An essay on the distribution of wealth.

    (Reprints of economic classics)
    Reprint of the 1836 ed. published by A. and C.
Black, Edinburgh.
    1. Wealth. 2. Distribution (Economic theory)
I. Title.
HB771.R3 1974   330.1'6   72-179344
ISBN 0-678-00884-1

PRINTED IN THE UNITED STATES OF AMERICA
by SENTRY PRESS, NEW YORK, N. Y. 10013
Bound by A. HOROWITZ & SON, CLIFTON, N. J.

AN

E S S A Y

ON THE

DISTRIBUTION OF WEALTH.

BY

GEORGE RAMSAY, B. M.

OF TRINITY COLLEGE, CAMBRIDGE.

EDINBURGH:

ADAM AND CHARLES BLACK;

AND LONGMAN, REES, ORME, BROWN, GREEN, AND LONGMAN,

LONDON.

MDCCCXXXVI.

PREFACE.

In presenting to the Public the following Essay on the Distribution of Wealth, a few preliminary remarks may be considered necessary. Some apology, it may be thought, is required, for entering upon a subject which has already engaged the attention of so many able Political Economists. The very attempt is sufficient to show that I do not consider their labours as altogether satisfactory. Indeed, notwithstanding all that has been written, it had long seemed to me very certain that much still remained to be done. This is not surprising, if we consider how comparatively new the whole science yet is, and that the Distribution of Wealth forms, as RICARDO has observed, the grand Problem to be solved. If this be once thoroughly understood, the rest will be found comparatively easy. The above writer has contributed, probably more than any other since the days of ADAM

SMITH, to the clearing up of this intricate subject. But if he have done much, it seems to me equally certain, that he has also left much to his successors. This I think proved, not only by the works of that eminent Author, but also by those of his followers and professed disciples. Thus, Mr. MILL, whose " Elements" are so well known, and who undertakes merely to give a clear compendium of the labours of his predecessors, of RICARDO in particular, was so little satisfied with what he had first written on Profits, that, in a Second Edition, he materially altered it; and if the former account of this vital question was inaccurate, I think there can be little doubt that the latter is even more so. These remarks may suffice to show that the subject is far from being exhausted.

How much of original may be found in the present Essay, must of course be left to the reader to determine. When one has long read and thought on any branch of inquiry, it becomes no easy matter to determine what is due to others, what to one's own meditations. Often what one thinks to be new, may in fact have been said before, perhaps even have been read at some remote period. Occasionally, also, one may broach original views without being well aware of it at the time. Of course, no person at the present day can pretend to write on Political Economy, without having first perused and reflected on the works of the great Masters of the Science, particularly ADAM SMITH, RICARDO, MALTHUS, M'CULLOCH, SAY, STORCH, TOOKE, TORRENS, &c. My obligations to these distinguished Authors, I beg here to acknowledge, once for all. At the same time, as this Science has been made so much a field of controversy, which has served not a little to discredit it in the eyes of the Public, my object has been to avoid that as much as possible. Thus, I have been led to take less notice of the works of my predecessors than has hitherto been usual; but this was for the reason just given, and by no means from an intention to undervalue their labours, or to deny how much I am indebted to them. But where any thing particular occurs which I know to be derived from their writings, I have taken care to mention it; and I have also been induced to combat some errors supported by high authority.

The theory of Profits being perhaps the most intricate of the science, has, as might be supposed, given rise to numerous discussions. To this accordingly I have been induced to pay particular attention. I cannot but feel a hope that this very delicate question may now be found satisfactorily stated.

But there is one point in particular, to which I must allude, namely, the division of landed property. This occupies so prominent a part in the present work, that some reason for dwelling on it so long may be required. The great importance of the subject, the cursory manner in which it has hitherto been treated, and the totally opposite opinions entertained concerning it in two of the most remarkable nations of Europe, France, and Great Britain, have led me to make it the object of a special inquiry. The importance of the subject no one I suppose will deny, since it is of vast weight in morals and economics, and the very corner-stone of politics. Nor does it seem to me that the question has been done justice to. The only discussions of any length which I have met with, are contained, the one in an early number of the Westminster Review, the other in M. de Staël's "Lettres sur l'Angleterre."* Both of these able writers have argued in favour of equality. The difference of opinion between Great Britain and France is known to all; in the one, the prerogative of primogeniture being very generally approved of, while in the other it is even more commonly consi-

* I have since learnt that there is a discussion on this subject by Mr. Macculloch, in a supplementary volume to his edition of the Wealth of Nations; but this I have not been fortunate enough to see.

dered as detestable. Now, as this is a question which bears not only on Political Economy, but also on Morals and Politics, it is impossible to make up our minds upon it without investigating all its tendencies. The system which is good in one point of view may be bad in the others, in which case our judgment must balance the advantages with the disadvantages, before it can see which way the scale inclines. I shall therefore, I trust, be excused for deviating a little from the proper object of a work of this nature, in order to discuss the Political and Moral Consequences of the opposite systems.* In treating the political question, the two different faults of extreme brevity and prolixity were to be avoided. Herein lay a principal difficulty. A very concise statement could never do justice to such a subject, and a very full investigation would have led too far from the main intent of the Essay. It is for the reader to determine how far I have succeeded in avoiding either extreme. Those who are inclined to prosecute the political question farther, may be induced to peruse " A Disquisition on Government," which grew out of the present work, and gradually

* Distribution of Wealth being the point where Political Economy and Politics touch, an excursion into the neighbouring province was the less to be avoided.

swelled to such a degree, as to render necessary its publication in a separate form.

Whatever may be thought of the inquiry into the division of landed property, to one merit, at all events, I hope to be found entitled, that of impartiality. Due force I think is given to the arguments which militate against my own opinion. In treating a subject in this way, one advantage at least may be expected, namely, that although the conclusion should be found erroneous, the discussion shall not have been thrown away.

Though Distribution of wealth be the proper object of this treatise, yet it seemed to me absolutely necessary to pave the way by some preliminary definitions and explanations. These, if correct, will be found useful, as applied not only to what follows, but likewise to the other branches of Political Economy. And here I have been led to investigate the doctrine of Value, on which so many controversies have arisen. It is likely that this preliminary part may be found the most dry and uninviting, but, if well understood, the reader will probably find little trouble in comprehending the rest of the work. A few clear notions at the outset amazingly facilitate our future progress, and put an end to that disgrace to philosophy—a war of words.

CONTENTS.

PART I.

PRELIMINARY.

CHAPTER I.

PART II.

DISTRIBUTION OF WEALTH.

CHAPTER I.

CHAPTER VIII.

CHAPTER IX.

CHAPTER X.

CHAPTER XI.

CHAPTER XII.

NOTE.

TO

SIR WILLIAM HAMILTON, Bart.

PROFESSOR OF LOGIC IN THE UNIVERSITY OF EDINBURGH,

AS A MARK OF ESTEEM AND ADMIRATION,

THIS WORK

IS RESPECTFULLY DEDICATED,

BY HIS FRIEND

THE AUTHOR.

PART I.

CHAPTER I.

INTRODUCTION.

WEALTH is the object of the science of Political Economy, not the wealth of an individual or class of individuals in particular, but that of a nation at large, nay of the world in general. The first point then ought to be, to obtain accurate ideas in regard to the Nature of Wealth.

Wealth or riches, as forming the subject of Political Economy, embraces material objects only. This is a circumstance of much importance to observe; for though the great father of the science, Adam Smith, as well as most of his ablest successors, have used the term in this sense; yet one or two more recent writers have attempted, by extending its meaning, to give a wider range to their speculations. But such endeavours have merely shewn, that to treat of things essentially different under one denomination, is not only of itself an error in logic, but tends to throw the whole subject into confusion. Thus it is with the *immaterial* products of M. Say.

But all material objects do not constitute wealth. It is necessary for this purpose that they possess utility, so that in some way or other they may be subservient to the various wants of men. Nothing that is absolutely useless can ever be a portion of riches. But of these useful objects, some are provided by Nature spontaneously, that is without the aid of human exertion, in quantities so unlimited, that there is enough, and more than enough, to satisfy the wants of every individual. Such are the air we breathe, light, water, &c. If the same were the case with all other material objects of utility, it is evident that the science of political economy could never have arisen. What purpose could it serve, to increase the quantity or change the distribution of that which already existed, and was distributed to every one in abundance greater than each could require? In such a state of things the ideas of wealth or poverty must have been alike unknown. This science can have to do with those objects alone which are not afforded spontaneously by Nature in unlimited abundance. And since most, if not all of these, admit of some degree of increase by means of human exertion, the science becomes not merely speculative but practical. The other objects above mentioned, not forming in any manner the subject of scientific inquiry, must of course be excluded from our notion of wealth.

According to the view above taken, Wealth may be defined to consist in,

Those material objects necessary, useful, and agreeable to man, which are not provided spontaneously by Nature in unlimited abundance.

Spontaneously means, as I have above stated, without the aid of human exertion.

Thus, the only ideas essentially comprehended in the notion of wealth, are those of Matter, Utility, and some degree of Scarcity.

Wealth being thus defined, we shall be able to form a more accurate idea of the science which treats of the same.

As the material objects necessary to our existence and comfort do not present themselves before us spontaneously, the first point to be known is, how they may be created, or, in the technical language of the science, produced? But what is the precise meaning which we must attach to this term?

Man, it is well known, has no power to create or annihilate one particle of matter; all that he can do is to promote certain changes of various kinds, by co-operating with nature. He who plants a tree tends to favour its growth, so far as this action goes; its future progress must depend upon the quality of the soil and climate, still perhaps assisted occasionally by the watchful care of the pruner or trainer. The hand of genius can change a shapeless block into the almost living image of the human frame; for though the mind may plan, the organ must execute, aided by tools suited to the rough material on which they are to operate; in a word, nature and art must contribute to the wonderful result.

The end of production is, to promote such changes in matter as may accommodate it to the wants of men. Therefore, it may be defined to be, the creation of utility in material objects, through the aid of human exertion. The first part, then, of political economy treats of the general causes which promote and facilitate production.

As in all states of society the least degree removed from barbarism, different classes of individuals concur more or less directly in the business of production; the next question comes to be, how is the whole produce to be distributed among these different sets of persons? What proportion is to go to each? The general causes which regulate the distribution of wealth form then another branch of the subject.

Now, if each individual, or even each collection of individuals, supposed to work in common, produced all the commodities which they might require; after these various articles had been raised and distributed, it would remain for them only to be consumed. But in all more advanced periods of society this is never the case. The different sorts of products which each individual or establishment is employed upon, are generally very limited, and often exceed not a single species. By far the greater part then of the objects which each person may require, must be obtained by exchanging the result of his own industry for that of others. Consequently, the causes which determine the proportions in which commodities exchange, form an important part of the science of wealth.

Lastly, comes consumption, the nature of which, its different kinds, and their respective effects on national riches, occupy the fourth division of the subject.

According to what has now been observed, we perceive that political economy may be defined to be,

That science which treats of the Production, Distribution, Exchange, and Consumption of wealth. These are its four primary divisions.

CHAPTER II.

PRODUCTION.

MAN, it has been said, by co-operating with the powers of Nature, is enabled to procure for himself objects necessary to his well-being, or in a word, to produce.

The next question then is, what are these powers? What are the various sources whence wealth is derived?

The sources of wealth are either original or derived. The original are of two kinds.

The first comprehends the land and waters of the globe, whence are drawn agricultural products, minerals, and fish. But the land may be of the highest fertility, its bowels may abound in the richest ores, the waters may teem with inhabitants, and yet all this be unavailing to the existence and comfort of man. Certain means must be taken before these sources of wealth can be of any advantage. These means constitute the second kind of original sources, which embraces all those agents which concur in production through the medium of sensible motion. These agents are either inanimate or animate. The former are,

1. Wind.

2. Running water.

3. Vapour of water, or steam.

The animated agent is Man, whose labour is indispensable to production.

From these original sources wealth is derived. Now this may be consumed either without leaving any thing behind, or may be itself so employed as to aid a new production. It is then called Capital. Capital, then, is a source of riches, but not an original one.

These then are the sources from which springs the wealth of nations. By their co-operation certain changes are to be effected, so as to render material objects fit to satisfy the wants of men. But what is the nature of these changes?

If we examine attentively the whole range of productive employments, we shall find that the modifications which it is the purpose of these to bring about, may all be included under two general heads, change of *form* and change of *place.** By change of *form*, I mean any alteration effected in the nature of matter, whether chemical or mechanical, whether in its intimate composition or simply in its external shape and appearance. These alterations constitute the business of Agriculture and Manufactures. By means of the former, the soil and waters are transformed by unknown and mysterious processes, into vegetable pro-

* For this truly logical classification, I am indebted to M. Destutt de Tracy, " Traité d'Economie Politique," chap. 11. one of the very best little works ever written on this science.

ducts for the use of man; by the latter, these products undergo still farther modifications, numerous often and complicated; from the first dressing of flax, for instance, to the final application of the scissors which are to fashion out the web into a garment.

After all these transformations, or some of them only have been gone through, it remains that the commodities be transported to those places where they are most wanted. This change is the object of the second great branch of production, or Commerce, as it is usually called.

To prove that commerce or change of place is as much a case of production as change of form, may perhaps to many appear quite superfluous. But such have been the vague and erroneous notions entertained on this subject, that a few words of illustration may not be thrown away. Production, we have seen, is the creation of utility in material objects through the aid of human exertion. That the changes of form which matter undergoes in the processes of agriculture and manufactures are instances of production, every one will allow. But what would be the utility of heaps of commodities accumulated in one place? At most they could contribute to the necessities of those only who lived in the immediate neighbourhood, and who might come themselves to the spot and procure what they wanted. Whatever was not disposed of in this way must remain till it rot. Would not he add a decided utility to this remainder, who should convey it away from the place where it now lies, without benefiting any one, to another locality where it might minister to the wants of many? And would not this utility, though of a different nature, be quite as decided as the change from flax to yarn, or from yarn to a linen web? In one part of a country, the crop of corn may have been so abundant as far to exceed what the surrounding inhabitants can possibly consume; in another, the people may be dying of hunger. Will any one say, that corn would not, at this period, have a much higher utility in the latter situation than in the former? In fact, if it cannot be removed, a great part of the plentiful crop becomes, for the present at least, utterly destitute of this quality, and if of a perishable nature, as potatoes, may be lost for ever.

Commerce, then, or the transport of commodities from one place to another, is quite as much a branch of production, as changes in the forms of matter, that is, as agriculture and manufactures.

As an instance, on a large scale, of the truth of these remarks, I may allude to a circumstance familiar to all those who have travelled by night in a coal district. Whoever has passed after sunset through the country around Newcastle, must have been struck with those vast fires by which the firmament is lighted up on all sides, as if from the craters of an hundred volcanoes. These conflagrations proceed from the coal of inferior quality collected at the mouths of the pits, and which, on account of the expence of carriage, cannot be transported to a distance. Thus a commodity, that in other situations would minister to the health and comfort of a numerous population, becomes where it now is, a mere incumbrance; and what in many places would be hailed as one of the blessings of life, is here considered as worse than useless dross.

Having brought forward an instance on a great scale, I may perhaps be pardoned mentioning another, which, though completely in point, is certainly a comparatively trifling one. The child who climbs the mountain side, to gather wild strawberries for the market below, confers upon them a degree of utility which, in their original situation, they assuredly did not possess. She is therefore, in the language of political economy, a producer, and in this case, the whole production consists in conveying the fruit from one place to another.*

The principal reason, no doubt, of the obscurity often found in writings upon this subject is, that commerce or transport has been confounded with the circulation, or exchange, but these are quite different. It is the conveying of commodities from place to place, not the exchanging them when brought together, which alone is productive.†

---

* Among the mountains of Savoy, I have often seen troops of girls ascend to the tops of mountains four thousand feet high, that is about equal to Ben Nevis, to pull strawberries for sale in the small town at the foot.

† See more on this point under the head of Exchange. In his "Elements of Political Economy," Mr. Mill treats of foreign commerce under Interchange, instead of under Production.

Having mentioned Capital among the sources of wealth, as the only one which is not original, but derived, it becomes highly necessary to form to ourselves accurate ideas as to its nature.

Capital, we have seen, is a portion of the national wealth, employed, or meant to be employed, in favouring reproduction. But in what manner does it so concur? What changes does it undergo previous to the completion of those commodities to the raising of which it is applied? Is it *in the mean time* of advantage to any one, or is its utility to be measured solely by the result? This is a question of the greatest importance. We shall find that capital is of two very different kinds; the one during the business of reproduction undergoes various alterations more or less complete, none of which however are in themselves of the slightest use to any one, the capital thus employed not ministering immediately to the necessities or comforts of a single individual; the other, while it conduces, though more remotely, to the common result, satisfies in the mean time the most indispensable wants of man. The first remains in the possession of its owner or employer until the produce is completed; the second can become serviceable to the end he has in view, only by his parting with it to others. The former of these I call Fixed, the latter Circulating capital. The one is useful from its result only, the other is so both immediately and remotely.

These terms have not always been used in the definite sense here attached to them. They have generally had reference merely to the greater or less durability of the objects, on which distinction no very exact classification could be founded, the degrees passing so insensibly the one into the other, that it would be difficult, if not impossible, to say where to draw the line.   I am aware that most classifications are liable to a similar objection, but not to the same extent.   The terms *fixed* and *circulating*, as I employ them, have a well defined demarcation, do not deviate in any very forced manner from the usual sense, and express very accurately one of their distinctive qualities.   The one remains fixed in the possession of its owner or employer, the other circulates between him and his workmen.   Nor is this all.   The old division into fixed and circulating capital, considered as more or less durable merely, was one of very little use either in speculation or practice ; whereas the present is of first rate importance, full of interesting consequences, which will gradually unfold themselves as we proceed.*

Fixed capital comprehends chiefly, 1. The seed of the agriculturist, and the raw material of the manufacturer, which may be considered as the basis of the product.   2. Implements and machines of all kinds

---

* Mr. Ricardo himself has allowed, that the distinction between these two sorts of capital, as then generally understood, was of little use, for he says of it in a note, " A division not essential, and in which the line of demarcation cannot be accurately drawn."   Principles of Political Economy, ch. i. sect. iv.   Mr. Malthus, however, defines the two exactly as I do, (" Definitions in Political Economy,") but so far at least as I know, he was not aware of the important deductions which might be drawn from their accurate separation.

by which labour is assisted. 3. Buildings necessary for carrying on the work, or for storing its result. 4. Horses, oxen, or any other animals, bred, nourished, and trained on purpose to aid in the raising of wealth. 5. Cattle, sheep, &c. kept with a view to advantage from their increase, or simply from their fattening. There are besides various other elements of fixed capital, which do not admit of a ready classification, such as manure of all kinds, fences necessary for agriculture, and the fuel consumed in manufactories.

Circulating capital consists exclusively of subsistence and other necessaries advanced to the workmen, previous to the completion of the produce of their labour.

Now it is evident, that while the former is consuming, it benefits no one. The seed, when consigned to the ground, can never become the food of man ; the raw material, in its various stages of change prior to the last, serves not as clothing or furniture to any individual; implements wear out, without being used as a defence ; and buildings decay without affording shelter to the people.

It is equally clear that circulating capital, by the very act of its consumption, maintains the existence and supports the strength of a great part of the population.

And here one important conclusion presents itself, which is, that fixed capital alone, not circulating, is properly speaking a source of national wealth. It is of course absurd to talk of capital and labour as sources of riches, and to include at the same time, under the former head, the reward paid for the use of the latter. In this way of stating the case, not labour only, that is the exertion of a man's arms and hands, is an agent in production, but also that portion of the return to which he is entitled as a compensation for his toil. Now this may form an inducement to him, a motive to industry, but clearly is not an *immediate* agent in the work of production. *Remotely*, no doubt, it will contribute to it, by giving a stimulus to his exertions, but that is all. This is so true, that were we to suppose the labourers not to be paid until the completion of the product, there would be no occasion whatever for circulating capital. The above class being able to live on their former earnings till a new creation of wealth was terminated, industry would be carried on on a scale quite as great as if they were obliged to depend for subsistence on advances made to them by a more wealthy order of their fellow-citizens. The sources of national wealth would unquestionably be as great in the former case as in the latter. Nothing can prove more strongly that circulating capital is not an *immediate* agent in production, nor even essential to it at all, but merely a convenience rendered necessary by the deplorable poverty of the mass of the people. Were they richer, it is evident that circulating capital would not be indispensable; for they might then wait to be paid at once out of the finished product, either in *kind*, or in something else obtained in exchange for the same.*

These remarks being premised, we shall now be able to arrive at some idea of what may properly be called Cost of Production.

Cost of production may be defined to be, the sacrifice to which the community is put in order to raise any commodity, a sacrifice really and truly such, containing *in itself* no *immediate* compensation, but submitted to for the sake of that result which is expected to follow. But in what does this sacrifice consist? It can be made up of two elements only, a sacrifice of personal ease, or of a portion of wealth called capital. Every man is fond of his ease, and will not give it up for nothing. If then he consent to abandon it, this can be only from a prospect of remuneration. Labour, in the language of Adam Smith, if not the whole of the purchase-money paid for all things, is at least a principal part of it; that is, of the sacrifice which they cost. But this is not all. As soon as wealth comes to be accumulated, it is evident that any portion of it withdrawn from the consumption of man, that is, from ministering to the necessities of human nature, and either hoarded or expended without, *in the mean time*, benefiting any one, is at least a temporary abandonment of riches; in other words, a sacri-

* See more on this subject in the chapter on Revenue.

fice different in kind no doubt from that of personal ease, but no less real. That it is a sacrifice is certain from this, that but for the hope of remuneration it never would be submitted to. Without such a prospect, the owner of the portion of wealth in question would assuredly greatly prefer consuming it either in gratifying his own wants, or else in maintaining labourers from whose exertions he might expect an increased return. But we have seen, that fixed capital, as above defined, is the only part of wealth consumed without immediately benefiting any one, since that which circulates ministers to the necessities of the labouring population. Therefore the former alone constitutes an element of cost of production in a national point of view, that is, in the light in which it is properly regarded by political economy. For we shall find that a certain class of individuals, namely the employers of capital, estimate it differently. But this shall be shown at length hereafter.*

But are there no other sources of wealth besides these two of which a sacrifice is required with a view to production? To discover this, it will simply be necessary to pass them in review.

---

* See chapter on Gross Profits. This is a distinction of very great importance, and another deduction already drawn from the clear separation of fixed and circulating capital before laid down. Cost in a national point of view must be carefully distinguished from cost as estimated by the employers of capital. They are very different things, as may already in part be seen, and as shall be shewn more at large in treating of Profits and Revenue.

As for wind and water, though these, considered as objects for the immediate gratification of our wants, are, as has been before observed, generally unlimited, the former always, yet when looked upon as agents in the production of wealth, they assuredly are not so. For the one is often still, and the other cannot always be found in sufficient abundance to turn all the machinery required. But as they are not in the slightest degree lessened in quantity by being employed as moving powers; for the water which turns a mill is just as plentiful after as before that operation; therefore the using of them for this purpose cannot be the least loss or sacrifice of riches whatsoever, that is, can form no part of cost. In regard to land, the case is the same. Though not unlimited, except in newly settled countries, yet it cannot be taken away or diminished, and is besides of no use, unless cleared and cultivated. Therefore the giving it up to cultivation is no injury or loss to any one, and consequently has nothing to do with cost.

With respect to steam, which is not a spontaneous gift of nature, but requires labour, the case is different. Were steam capable of being detained and made use of at a future time, it assuredly might form a portion of wealth. But this from its qualities is impossible. If not employed *at the moment* for the particular purpose for which it was created, it is gone for ever, and cannot be realized as riches. Therefore the cost consists not in the steam itself, but in that expense of fuel and labour necessary to its generation.*

From all this it follows, that labour and fixed capital are the only elements of expense of production. But as the latter is not an original source of wealth, but derived from the former, it might appear, and has indeed been often said, that this ultimately forms the sole cost. For a capital must itself have required a sacrifice, say both in labour and fixed capital, and this last in its time must have necessitated a previous sacrifice, perhaps of both likewise, until we mount up to a capital produced by labour alone. Ultimately then, or originally, the sacrifice required for the raising of any commodity, resolves itself, it would appear, into the labour bestowed upon it either proximately or remotely. This, however, we shall find, is not strictly true. The reason of which limitation is, that the longer a fixed capital is kept as such, that is, in a state in which it cannot satisfy any immediate wants, either of its owner or of labourers in his employment, the greater is the sacrifice submitted to, in other words, the cost. The proof of this is, that but for the expectation of an ample remuneration at last, it never would be hoarded up for so long a period. So that cost comes to be measured not merely by the quantity of labour bestowed upon

---

* To some these nice investigations may appear useless, to others too metaphysical. As they are short, however, and may tend to clear up our ideas on this delicate subject, they will perhaps meet with some excuse.

the whole, but also by the length of time elapsed before the produce of that labour is made serviceable to the wants of men. But for a farther illustration of this truth, I must refer to the following chapter.

Before proceeding any farther, it may be well however to determine what is properly meant by Consumption. This is in truth the converse of production. The one being, as we have seen, the creation of utility in material objects through the aid of human exertion, the other is the destruction of the same through the agency of man. This utility conferred, consists, as has been observed, either in change of *form* or change of *place*, the former of which alone is ever impaired in consumption. Thus, when we employ food, fuel, clothing, or furniture to satisfy our necessities, we destroy more or less rapidly so much utility, that is, we deprive matter of that *form* in which it is serviceable to the wants of our common nature. So also, when implements become worn away under our hands, we strip so much matter of its usefulness, that is, we render it unfit in future to aid in the business of the production of wealth. These cases are very clear. But when wool or cotton are converted by the various processes of manufacture into cloth or calico, to some it may not at first appear wherein lies the destruction of utility. The reason of which doubt is, if in truth there should be any, that consumption is here so closely followed by production, that the former is apt to be forgotten in the latter. But cloth or calico cannot be made out of wool or cotton, without the destruction of the latter as such, that is, without depriving them of that species of utility which they possessed in their primary form.

And this leads me to remark, that there are two kinds of consumption. When, as in the two last cases, a new commodity arises immediately out of the destruction of the old, then the consumption is said to be productive; when no such result is obtained it is called unproductive. Now, according to this definition, it would appear that the consumption of fixed capital only is productive, for it alone, in proportion as destroyed, is immediately replaced by a new result. And in strictness of language this would be true. But as the food, &c. which constitute circulating capital, both enable and induce the labourers to work, it has been considered practically advantageous to consider its consumption also as productive, though, if so, evidently in a more remote degree only; for labour, not that which maintains it, is the immediate agent. Still, as this last does lead to production, and that too not *very* remotely, the consumption of circulating capital may be considered as productive when it maintains labourers who by their own hands actually give rise to some material object constituting wealth.

But to show how dangerous it is to depart from metaphysical accuracy in the use of scientific terms, I may observe that this very circumstance of giving the name of productive consumption, not to that only which is immediately productive, but also to ano-

ther species which is more remotely so, has led some
authors to push its signification still further, so as
completely to overthrow the very foundations of the
science. Thus, it has been maintained, by political
economists of no slight eminence, that the consumption of soldiers, sailors, &c. is productive, because the
general security which they maintain is essential to
all prosperity, and, consequently, to the increase of
wealth among other good things. That these classes
of persons are useful in a certain number, no one
would deny, but as their labour is not immediately
worked up in a material commodity, they are in an
economical sense utterly unproductive. For political economy does not treat of every kind of utility,
but of that only which is inseparably connected with
matter. Now, the wealth of a nation, so far from being augmented in proportion to the increase in the
number of soldiers and sailors, is thereby diminished,
so that the fewer it can do with, the better for the
riches of the country; whereas, every addition to the
number of able-bodied labourers, is a source of new
advancement in wealth. But this truth is so obvious,
that had it not been sometimes called in question, I
should not have troubled the reader with its proof.

Now, what is true of soldiers, sailors, &c. equally
applies to physicians, lawyers, actors, singers, musicians, &c. all of whom are considered by M. Say as
productive,* as if the benefit derived from the advice

---

* Mr. Macculloch, I perceive, has adopted the same opinion, " Principles of Political Economy," Part IV.

of a medical man, or the pleadings of a barrister, the pleasure arising from an air or a song were wealth! Oh logic, where art thou flown? A right definition of terms is sufficient to put an end for ever to such disputes.

CHAPTER III.

ON EXCHANGE.

AFTER commodities are produced, they must, previous to consumption, be exchanged and distributed. Now, it is evident that either they may first be exchanged, and what is thus obtained afterwards distributed, or they may be distributed before any exchange takes place. It would seem from this, to be a matter of indifference in what order these divisions of the subject may be treated. Since in all advanced communities however, after the separation of employments has become established, the produce of industry is always exchanged for some common equivalent which is distributed amongst the various classes of persons instead of the original commodity, it becomes impossible in such states of society to trace the operations of the simple principles of the distribution of wealth without being previously acquainted with the general theory of exchange.

I shall commence then with this. But here I must remark, before advancing any farther, that exchange has not commonly been classed, as one of the primary branches of political economy. It has generally been mixed up at one time with production, at another with distribution, though in reality essentially different from both. By being confounded with commerce, erroneous ideas, as we have already seen, have sometimes arisen as to the nature of the latter, which has been rashly supposed to partake of all the qualities of the former. But the conveying of commodities from place to place is an operation totally distinct from that of exchanging them for one another when brought together. The former alone belongs to production, the latter not at all. In truth, it would be quite as correct to say, that agriculture and manufactures are the same thing as exchange, as to pretend that commerce is. This obscurity, I am well aware, is favoured by the common use of language. Thus, when we talk of a trade, we mean some productive employment, but when it is said that trade is flourishing, it is understood that goods sell well and rapidly, in other words, that exchange or circulation is brisk.*

Exchange is different from distribution also, for the sharing of the produce, say of a farm, among the labourers, farmers, and landlords, and the exchanging that produce, whether before or after its division, for money or other commodities, are two events altogether separate.†

---

* The same ambiguity is found in French; *commerce* occasionally signifies transport; but when it is asserted *Le commerce va bien*, this implies that merchandise does not lie long on hand.

† Mr. Storch, in his very admirable " Cours d'Economie Politique," a work to which I confess my great obligations, has made a classification more nearly resembling my own than any other. Though he treats of the circulation under the head of distribution, yet he takes

But this branch of the subject is not only essentially distinct from any other, but is also of an importance and extent quite sufficient to justify its independent position, comprising as it does every thing relative to the Circulation. It embraces the whole theory of money and credit which are its engines, the doctrine of *the* exchange, specifically so called, and the principles of banking, enough assuredly to fill up one leading division of the science. These reasons will, I trust, be found sufficient to establish the accuracy of my classification.

Exchanges may be brought about in three ways,

First, By barter.

Secondly, By the intervention of a common commodity, willingly accepted of by all the members of the society. This is Money. The term *circulating medium* expresses exceedingly well its peculiar function.

Thirdly, By credit.

As it is not the object of this Essay to treat of every branch of political economy, but of that of distribution in particular, together with such preliminary topics as are absolutely indispensable to a right comprehension, not of a single department only of the science, but of all, it follows, that under the present head one point alone is here to be discussed, which serves as a foundation, however, to the whole; a

care to separate the former from the latter by the appellation of secondary distribution, and discusses it apart. Mr. Mill, indeed, makes a leading division of Interchange, but does not seem to me to point out its proper limits.

point moreover which has hitherto proved the greatest stumbling-block of economical writers, the highly
important doctrine of Value. Having fixed the limits
of this division of our subject, I now proceed to examine that on which it entirely rests.

Without the facility of exchanging one object for
another, it is evident that very small progress could
ever have been made in the advancement of material
comforts. Each individual, or at most each family,
must have procured for themselves, by their own
unaided exertions, every article of which they might
stand in need for their existence and conveniency.
So little skill, however, is ever required in any occupation by him who meddles with many, and so much
time is lost in passing from one to the other, that the
progress in wealth made in this manner, could have
been but very small, and wants even the most indispensable, could have been satisfied but very imper-
fectly. Another alternative might no doubt present
itself. Any number of individuals might agree to
form a society in which a division of employments
should be established, and the total produce of their
industry become the common property of all, or be
divided amongst them in equal proportions. This
system would be liable to all the inconveniencies
however, which attend a community of goods. The
want of a sufficient stimulus, the stimulus afforded
by the undisputed and undivided produce of one's
personal labour, and the absence of the fear of immediate penury, would soon incline each man to re-

lapse into that indolence to which we are all naturally too prone, and to depend for his supply of necessaries more on the exertions of his fellows, than on
his own.

Attempts have been made even in the present day,
to establish a system of this kind, but, as we might
well imagine, they have ended only in disappointment.
Neither this plan, then, nor the original and simple
one could have succeeded in raising man much above
the condition of savage life, or have provided even
the most common necessaries, for the support of any
but a very scanty population. It is the introduction
of exchange that after the institution of property, has
contributed more than any other cause to the advancement of the wealth of nations, by allowing each
individual to devote himself to one employment only,
or at most to a very few simple ones, certain of being
able by the produce of his own industry, to procure
whatever else he may require. Without it, division
of labour could never have taken place.

Now, as soon as a commodity will exchange for
any quantity of one or more other commodities, or of
labour, it is said, in the language of political economy, to possess the quality of Value in exchange or
exchangeable Value.

The *degree* of value is estimated or measured by
the general power of exchanging for the mass of commodities and of labour, possessed by the object in
question; in other words, by its general power of
purchasing. The greater the quantity of these for

which *any given portion of it* will exchange, the greater
the value. For, as in computing the specific gravities of bodies, equal bulks are always taken, so
in estimating the values of objects, equal quantities are supposed. Now, quantity, in the language
of this science, sometimes means volume, sometimes weight. Thus, when we compare the value of
a piece of satin with that of a web of linen, we
say, that a yard of the former is worth double or
triple a yard of the latter. Here volumes are
reckoned. But when we affirm that a pound of tea
is more valuable than a pound of coffee, we of course
compute by weight. In all cases, then, where values
are compared, equal quantities are presumed, whether by this we mean weight or volume.

Again, as in calculating specific gravities, some
one body must be taken as a term of comparison,
which is usually water, so in measuring value, one
particular commodity called money is commonly assumed as a standard. Now, since it is well known in
chemistry, that a given bulk of water is itself not
always of the same weight, but varies according to
the temperature ; therefore, care is always taken to
specify the degree of heat, which being once fixed,
remains in all experiments for ever unaltered. Unfortunately for political economists, they do not possess a standard, the value of which, like the weight of
a given volume of water at a certain temperature is
not susceptible of change. The proper measure of
value, as at first observed, is the mass of commodi-

ties and of labour for which any given portion of any object will exchange ; but as this mass is altogether unmanageable for daily practice, it becomes indispensable to fix upon some one, the least variable we can find. The precious metals have therefore been selected. Value then estimated in gold and silver is Price.*

In giving a definition of wealth, I remarked that there are some material objects, highly useful, nay indispensable to the existence of man, yet being afforded to us spontaneously by Nature in unlimited abundance, we are exempted from all care on their account, and therefore they cannot form a subject for practical science, the object of which is to increase what is deficient, not to add to what is already superabundant. Accordingly, we excluded these from our definition of wealth. Now these very same objects are destitute of exchangeable value, as no one would give any thing for that which can be had for nothing.

It is no less evident that the objects which have value must be possessed of some utility, since no person would give any thing for that which was absolutely good for nothing; which did not contribute

* Mr. Malthus has proposed labour as the best measure of value, with what propriety, I confess, I cannot see. So far is labour from being itself invariable, that it is widely different in different countries. Compare, for instance, what a native of the United States of America can procure for himself by a day's labour with that which a poor Irishman can gain in his own country, and how vast is the dissimilarity! For we have no occasion to look to India and China for the truth of this remark.

in some way or other to the necessities, comforts, or merely elegancies of life. Thus, in order that an object should possess value, it is necessary, 1. That it have utility. 2. That it be not provided spontaneously by Nature in unlimited quantity. But is value in proportion to utility?

We have seen that some of the most useful objects have no value at all. Others, though of great value, have very little utility; the precious stones, for instance. Value, therefore, is not proportional to utility. Is then the value of any commodity in proportion to the scantiness in which it has been afforded spontaneously by nature? This certainly would be the case were there no means of increasing this spontaneous supply. Value in such a state of things would depend entirely upon scarcity. But if this scarcity can be relieved by art, if additional supplies can be raised by human exertion to an indefinite extent, the value of the object must then depend upon the sacrifices required in order to produce it. The greater the sacrifice, the higher will be the value of the result. Were it otherwise, the commodity would soon entirely cease to be raised, or at most would be fabricated in a smaller quantity; the consequence of which would inevitably be, either that it could not be procured at all, or if so, only at an advanced rate. In order therefore to discover what regulates value, we must point out what are the sacrifices essential to production.

Now these having already been determined in the

proper place,* it might perhaps be sufficient to refer the reader to what has there been said. But as in a matter of this importance I would rather appear tiresome from repetition, than run the chance of not being fully understood, I shall once more go over some of the same ground.

Among the sources of wealth, we have seen that labour holds a prominent place. This is the only original sacrifice which man is put to in order to procure those material comforts that he requires, a sacrifice of that ease to which all are inclined, and which none are willing to give up without the hope of compensation.

But after that, by means of labour co-operating with the powers of nature, wealth has to a certain extent been created and preserved, this itself, as we have already seen, may be made instrumental in furthering a future production, in which case it assumes the name of Capital. But this portion of wealth cannot be so employed without the owner withdrawing it from his own private consumption. He sacrifices it in the prospect of a more ample return. The sacrifice alone is certain, the return uncertain; and however great this may happen to turn out, it is no less clear that the first must previously have been submitted to. The sacrifices, then, to which man is put in the course of production, are of two kinds, 1. A sacrifice of Ease. 2. A sacrifice of a portion of

---

* See Chapter on Production.

Wealth; that is to say, an expenditure of Labour and of Capital. The greater the amount of these the greater will he expect his return to be, the higher, in other words, the value of the product. And such, in ordinary circumstances, must be the case. It would seem from this, that the degree of value of any commodity must be regulated by the quantity of labour, and the value of the capital expended on the production. But it will be said, this capital itself could not have been created without the aid of labour. If it has been produced by labour alone without the participation of capital, its value will be determined solely by Quantity of Labour. Thus quantity of labour regulating the value of the capital in the first instance, and afterwards this value, together with an additional portion of labour fixing the value of the finished commodity, it would appear that *ultimately* value is determined by quantity of labour alone. If the former capital has itself been produced by the co-operation of labour and a still previous capital, it will make no real difference, for in every case, by going back to the original sources of wealth, we shall find that capital is not included in the number. Therefore the value of that first created must have been determined by something prior, which can be nothing else than the quantity of labour bestowed upon it. Labour is the original sacrifice or " purchase-money which was paid for all things."

It would appear then, from this view of the case, that quantity of labour regulates the value not of those commodities only which have been produced by it alone, but of those also which have been raised or fabricated after the creation and co-operation of capital; that it is, in short, the sole regulator of value.

But however specious this conclusion may seem, it is by no means universally true. The use of fixed capital modifies to a considerable extent the principle that value depends upon quantity of labour.

For some commodities on which the same quantity of labour has been expended, require very different periods before they are fit for consumption. But as during this time the capital brings no return, in order that the employment in question should not be less lucrative than others in which the product is sooner ready for use, it is necessary that the commodity, when at last brought to market, should be increased in value by all the amount of profit withheld. This shews most clearly how capital may regulate value independently of labour. We may take for an instance the commodity, wine. Two casks of this liquor of the very same vintage and vineyard may be supposed to be sold, the one soon after its fabrication, the other not for several years, during which time it has been kept in a cellar to acquire its full maturity. Now this cask of wine constitutes a fixed capital. But the dealer would certainly never have thought of keeping it so long, did he not expect that its value at the end of the period would be considerably increased. And in fact it might be double, triple that of its

brother cask.* But the very same quantity of labour
was expended on each. It is impossible to bring forward a more convincing case in disproof of the univer-
sality of the principle, that labour is the regulator of
value. It is evident that capital is a source of value
independent of the former. The cask of wine might,
we may suppose, owe all its value previous to its being deposited in the dealer's cellar, to the labour bestowed in raising the grape and in fabricating the
liquor, but to what is owing its subsequent value?
Not to labour, for there has been none: to what then
but to a capital withheld?†

Let us now take a view of the progress of wealth
from the rudest ages, and trace the causes of value
as they arise.

In the earliest state of society, capital does not exist. In this condition of things, the quantity of labour expended in procuring any commodity, is the

* Going the other day to purchase some brandy, various samples
were presented to me, all of which were originally of the very same
quality and price, namely, one franc and a half the bottle, but had now
mounted up to four, five, and even six francs respectively, according to
the age.

† An author of deserved reputation has attempted to reconcile this
case with his favourite principle, by talking of the labour of a cask in
a cellar, the labour, that is, of fermentation! A greater instance could
perhaps no where be found, of the determination, so common to philo-
sophers, to force nature into a beloved system. It is sufficient to remark, (if indeed it be worth while, so obvious is the sophism,) that the
fallacy consists in giving to the term labour a new signification quite
different from that in which it has hitherto been universally received
among political economists. Labour, forsooth! All writers, with the
exception of the above, have meant by this word, labour of man, not
of acids and alkalis. After this, are we not tempted again to exclaim,
O Logic! where art thou flown!

only circumstance which can ever bring to a conclusion the competition arising between different classes of persons, each endeavouring to get as much as he can for his own. It is through the medium of this competition that the quantity of all other things for which each will exchange, is determined, or, in other words, its value. No doubt it may happen either from an accidental superabundance of any one article, or from an unexpected falling off in the intensity of the demand, that is, in the sacrifice which the demanders are able and willing to make in order to procure it, that its value may fall below that of other commodities on which the same quantity of labour has been bestowed. But this cannot be of long continuance, for no one will consent permanently to realize less by his exertions than others do. The article in question, will either cease to be produced altogether, or will be raised in smaller quantity until the falling off in the supply has brought up its value to the ordinary level. On the other hand, should any article rise above the usual rate, either from a sudden falling off in the supply, or an increased intensity of demand, an additional quantity of labour, attracted by the extraordinary gains, would soon be turned in this direction, and a greater abundance speedily bring down value to its common state. Previous to the creation of capital then, quantity of labour expended is the only circumstance that can determine value, which it does, by increasing or diminishing the supply according to circumstances.

By and by, some fixed capital, such as implements and raw materials, comes to be accumulated. It is natural to suppose, that at first the owner of this will himself be also a labourer, and combine the two capacities. He will no doubt expect that the product of his labour and capital combined shall be sufficient not only to remunerate him for the former, but also to replace all the latter which has been consumed during the course of the work. But no one would turn away a portion of his substance from ministering to his wants and enjoyments, were he to gain nothing by so doing, which would be the case if the capital was restored to him just as it was. In order to incline him to separate it from that fund destined for his private consumption, he must be led by the prospect of its increase, that is, by the hope of profit. The produce of his labour and capital together, must then, in the ordinary state of things, afford a suitable, in other words, the usual reward for the former, and replace the latter so far as expended, with an increase in *kind*; or, if the product be of a different sort from the materials of the capital consumed, then its value must be somewhat greater than that of the said capital. Consequently, in this state of society, the different producers, in exchanging their commodities, will compete with one another, until their values shall be settled pretty nearly in proportion not merely to the quantity of labour applied, but also to the value of the fixed capital expended. Quantity of labour will still, ultimately, however, be the principal cause, since the value of the fixed capital itself must in great measure depend upon the labour bestowed upon it. The *principal* cause, I say, but not the *sole* cause; for we have seen that the value of things depends in part upon the length of time that must elapse before they can be brought to market. The longer a capital remains engaged, the more will the product when at last completed, deviate in its value from that which it ought to have, were it in proportion merely to the labour bestowed. Because, the greater will be the part of profit in the value of the whole.

In the last and most advanced state of things, capital, both fixed and circulating, comes to be accumulated in the hands of a particular class of men. The labourer now no longer works on his own account, but is employed by others. Instead of looking to the product when completed as that which is to pay him for his trouble, he receives his remuneration in advance in another shape. Let us see whether this new circumstance gives rise to any change in the causes which regulate value.

It is quite evident that the sole *immediate* cause which now can determine the relative values of things, is the total value of the capital, fixed and circulating, either actually expended upon them, or vested and employed without being entirely consumed. To the capitalists, it is a matter of indifference what quantity of labour has been applied, except in so far as this has affected the amount of circulating capital required. All that they care for is, to get back the

value of their capital, with as great a profit as possible. They look to nothing else. The total value
of the capital employed and expended, either wholly
or in part, is now the only circumstance which serves
to bring to a conclusion the competition which takes
place between the various capitalists, each striving to
get as much as he can for his own, and this competition will so regulate value, as to afford every one the
amount of his advances with a corresponding profit.

But it may be said, though it be allowed that after
the accumulation of capital fixed and circulating, the
value of any product is regulated *immediately* solely
by the total value of the capital employed, of both
kinds; yet that this value is itself determined by
quantity of labour, and thus that ultimately the whole
labour bestowed upon any commodity, is the sole
cause of its value. But this is precisely the notion
which has already been shown to be erroneous in the
present chapter, and might have been previously sus-
pected to be so, from what was said in treating of Cost
of Production. But in order to prove the matter
still more satisfactorily, let us again examine it more
narrowly in the instance before us, where both fixed
and circulating capital are supposed to be employed.

There are two circumstances, neither of which can
I think be disputed, which taken together, will prove
that in this case value is not solely regulated by
quantity of labour. These are, first, that where both
fixed and circulating capital are made use of, the sole
immediate cause of value, is the total value of the two

kinds expended, provided, that in the cases compared, the capitals be entirely consumed in the same
time. This has already been proved. Secondly, that
a circulating capital will always maintain more labour
than that formerly bestowed upon itself. Because,
could it employ no more than had been previously
bestowed upon itself, what advantage could arise to
the owner from the use of it as such? That it is used,
is the clearest proof that some profit is thereby derived, and if there be a profit, the quantity of labour
which a circulating capital can command, must be
greater than that which produced it.* Bearing these
principles in mind, let us proceed to examine the
point in debate.

We suppose a commodity raised by the co-operation of the two kinds of capital. Now, let it be
granted, for the sake of simplicity, that the fixed capital owes its value entirely to the quantity of labour
bestowed upon it, though from what has been observed in the former part of this chapter, this is by no
means necessarily true. But let it be admitted. The
value of the product will consequently depend partly
on that remote labour, partly on the labour immediately applied, which is maintained by the circulating capital, and which, we have seen, must be greater
than that formerly bestowed on the same. But it is
evident, that if the portion of capital, which, in the
present instance, is fixed, had, on the contrary, been

---

* This principle was brought forward and applied by Mr. Torrens,
in " An Essay on the External Corn Trade."

also of a circulating nature, it would likewise have maintained more labour than that previously expended upon itself. Therefore, on the whole, the product would have been the result of a greater quantity of labour, than if part of the capital were fixed. But the capitals being on both suppositions of the same value, and being, as is imagined, entirely consumed in the same time, the value of the finished commodity would, in the two instances be identical. Thus, it appears quite evident, that value does not depend exclusively on quantity of labour. But one or two examples will render this still more clear. Let us put the strongest case first.

Suppose two capitals of equal value, each produced by the labour of 100 men operating for a given time, but of which the one is wholly circulating, the other wholly fixed, and may perhaps consist of wine kept to improve. Now, this circulating capital, raised by the labour of 100 men, will, as we have seen, employ a greater number, say 150. Therefore the product at the end of the coming year, will, in this case, be the result of the labour of 150 men. But still it will be of no more value than the wine at the termination of the same period, though only 100 men have been employed upon the latter. This, it is evident, is an extreme case, and puts in the strongest point of view how much value may diverge from quantity of labour.

But, let us now take another example, and one of more frequent occurrence.

Let us suppose, as before, two capitals of equal values, each produced by the labour of 100 men operating for a given time. Of these equal capitals, the one we may imagine consists of fixed capital, the product of the labour of 50 men, and of circulating also resulting from the labour of 50. The other may be made up of fixed capital, on which 80 men have been employed, and of circulating raised by 20. Now, these capitals being of equal value, it follows, from what has been said above, that the values of their products will also be equal, supposing the former to be entirely consumed in the same time. But will these products be the result of equal quantities of labour? The circulating capital, that is, the food and other necessaries raised by the labour of 50 men, will, as we have previously seen, employ a number of men greater than 50. Let us suppose that it will employ 75. Now, the fixed capital was, in this case, the result of the labour of 50 men. Therefore, the total quantity of labour, immediate and remote, applied to the completion of that product on which the greatest proportion of circulating capital has been expended, will be that of 125 men.

The other capital is composed of fixed, resulting from the labour of 80 men, and circulating of 20. Now, according to the ratio adopted above, if circulating capital, raised by 50 men, will employ 75, then that derived from the labour of 20 will maintain 30. But the labour of 80 men was expended on the fixed capital. Therefore, on the whole, the labour of 110 men will have been applied to that product on which the smaller proportion of circulating capital has been spent. Now, I have shewn, that the two products will be of equal value, being the results of equally valuable capitals, supposed to be entirely consumed in the same time. Yet the one has been raised by the labour of 125 men, the other of 110. Thus the product of the labour of 110 men will exchange for the product of the labour of 125.

Hence it is clearly proved, that two objects of equal value, may or may not be results of equal quantities of labour, according as the same or a different proportion of fixed capital has been expended on them.

There is no possible way of escaping this conclusion, except by asserting that the quantity of labour which any circulating capital will employ is no more than equal to that previously bestowed upon it. But this we have seen cannot be, for were it so, no profit could be derived from such capital. This would be, in fact, to say, that the value of the capital expended is equal to that of the product, which is quite out of the question.

Had the proportion of fixed capital, in one of the instances above stated, been still greater, it is manifest that value would have depended still less on quantity of labour.

It will now, I trust, be conceded without further hesitation, that the general principle of value being regulated by quantity of labour is materially limited by the employment of fixed capital. Let us see how the case stands in respect to that which circulates.

In order to discover whether this has any effect in limiting the general principle, it is necessary to compare together products, one of which has been raised by means of circulating capital, the other entirely without it, that is, by labourers working on their own account. Now, this last case is not merely a possible one, and peculiar to the infancy only of society, but actually occurs at the present day in many countries of Europe where much land is cultivated by little proprietors, without any other assistance than that of the members of their own families. In France, Switzerland, and Savoy, such proprietors are very common. There can be little doubt that produce raised in this manner would be of less value than if circulating capital had been employed. For the peasant who tills the land on his own account reckons not the materials of his private consumption as part of his expences, but his labour only. The former is considered simply as the fund for the immediate gratification of his wants, and for which no return is expected. But the capitalist who employs labourers, must have restored to him not the value of the capital only, but a profit on the same. Therefore he cannot sell so cheap as the man who works on his own account. Thus, suppose, that in any country, corn was raised in the manner above stated, but manufactures through the intervention of circulating capital, and that the exertions of 100 countrymen for

100 days could produce grain worth 500 pounds. In
order to employ the same number of manufacturing
labourers, at the same rate, and for the like period
of 100 days, the capitalist must consequently advance
a similar sum. But if his product be worth no more
than 500 pounds, which is the exact amount of his
disbursements, he can of course realize no profit
whatever. Therefore his commodity must be of a
greater value than this, that is, superior in value to
the corn which had been raised by precisely the same
quantity of labour. If profits be at 10 per cent., the
former will be so much higher than the latter. Consequently, it appears, that the employment of circulating capital also limits the general principle.*

But here it must be remarked, that wherever the
use of circulating capital becomes universal, this effect
ceases to be felt, for that which is common to all employments, is the same as if common to none. In
order that any difference be perceptible in the results,
there must be some in the preceding circumstances.
Were all goods, for instance, raised ten per cent. on
account of their being produced through the medium of circulating capital, there would be no change
whatever in their relation to each other, which in
fact proves that the very supposition of an *universal*
rise is absurd. Therefore, in those countries where

---

* From what is here said, it seems to me to follow, that the cultivation of land by little proprietors, must have a tendency to discourage
the business of farming carried on by a separate class of persons, that
is, by capitalists possessing experience in rural affairs. The former
will be able to undersell the latter.

this species of capital is always used, its effects as a cause limiting the more general principles of value may fairly be omitted.

Thus we have seen, that in the earliest stage of society, previous to the creation and employment of capital, value is regulated solely by quantity of labour.

After some fixed capital has been accumulated in the hands of those who toil, so as to facilitate their exertions, we have farther seen that value comes to be determined *immediately*, partly by the quantity of labour directly applied, partly by the value of the capital. It has also been remarked, that the value of this capital must itself depend, *in great measure*, on the quantity of labour necessary to raise it, and therefore that the value of the product of this capital may be traced *ultimately* to the same source. But at the same time, that this principle is liable to great modification, on account of the different periods during which fixed capitals are engaged, before their products can be completed. The capital so engaged must, at last, however, be returned with a profit, which profit may constitute no small part of the value of the whole ; so that products of equal value may have had very different quantities of labour bestowed upon them. This was illustrated by wines of different ages. We were thus led to the conclusion, that capital is a source of value independent of labour.

It further appears, after circulating capital as well as fixed comes to be accumulated in the hands of a particular class of men, and the labourers cease to work on their own account, that the sole *immediate* cause which determines value, is simply the total value of the capital of both kinds employed in production.

That capitals whose total value is the same, but consisting of fixed and circulating in different proportions, if entirely consumed in the same time, will give rise to products also of equal value, but on which very different quantities of labour have been bestowed. And the more the fixed capital, the less the labour. Therefore it again follows, that fixed capital is a cause of value distinct from labour.

The case of circulating capital was lastly considered. It was found that it certainly does tend to raise the value of those commodities on which it is employed, as compared with others produced by independent workmen, but when universally made use of, that its effects become imperceptible.

But these conclusions by no means prove that quantity of labour does not at all times continue to be a cause of value; they merely shew that it is not the only one. In advanced states of society, the *immediate* cause, as we have seen, is the total value of the capital employed, both fixed and circulating. But what determines the amount of these? It is evident, that the total value of capital indispensable to any production, must depend upon two things, the value of the fixed capital required, and the quantity of necessary labour. Any increase or diminution in this last must augment or lessen the amount of circulating capital essential for the purpose, and through this medium must have a corresponding effect on the value of the result. Moreover, the value of the fixed capital itself must depend, in great measure at least, upon the quantity of labour which, at one time or another, has been expended upon it. Therefore, the value of the product will *ultimately* be regulated, *to a great degree*, by the total quantity of labour applied from first to last.

We have seen, that the introduction of capital modifies this original cause in three particular circumstances.

First, When fixed capital alone is employed, and the products of equal capitals require very different periods before they can be completed.

Secondly, When the capitals are also equal, but composed of fixed and circulating in unequal proportions.

Thirdly, When circulating capital is used in some branches of national industry, in others not.

The reason of which modification in the second case is, that a circulating capital will always maintain more labour than that bestowed upon itself, more by the whole amount of profit realized; whereas a fixed capital can represent that labour only formerly given, and yet must afford to its owner as great a remuneration as if it had departed from him, and employed a greater number of people than those who first produced it.

But the first and second cases are fundamentally

the same. The greater the proportion of fixed capital to circulating, the less does value depend exclusively upon quantity of labour, as we have seen by
the examples above given, until we arrive at a case
such as the wine kept to ripen for perhaps many
years, where the whole capital is fixed. Here value
may diverge very widely indeed from quantity of
labour as its regulator. Therefore it is chiefly owing
to fixed capital (one case alone excepted) that quantity of labour ceases to be the sole cause of value;
that is, owing to a capital which does not maintain
labourers; in other words, a portion of riches withdrawn from ministering *immediately* to the wants of
men. Now this temporary sacrifice of a portion of
wealth must be remunerated, otherwise it never
would be made; that is, an additional value must be
given to the product proportioned to the period during which the said portion of wealth has existed in
the form of fixed capital.

The secret of the whole then is this, that a capital
must give the accustomed remuneration to its owner,
whether employed in the maintenance of labour or
not; so that if locked up for years, either in such a
shape as cannot at any time be *directly* serviceable to
man, as machinery for instance, or else in the form of
such a commodity as wine, to improve by keeping,
it will give a product, great part of the value of which
depends not on labour, but on the long continued
sacrifice to which the proprietor has been put in ab-
staining from using so much wealth in employing

labour. For had he so used it, he would by degrees have realized thereon a succession of profits. Therefore, the sacrifice he submits to is measured by the amount of profits which he would have realized on a capital originally equal, and employed for the same length of time in maintaining labourers. But this must be made up to him at last.

Therefore, finally, value depends,

1. On the whole quantity of labour bestowed on any commodity, from first to last.

2. On the length of time during which any portion of the product of that labour has existed as fixed capital; that is, in a form in which, though assisting to raise the future commodity, it does not maintain labourers.

But these are precisely the elements of cost of production, as before pointed out.* Consequently value is regulated by cost of production, the constituent parts of which are now well known.†

There is, however, one exception to the principle, that value depends on cost of production. This is the third case above put, where commodities are compared, the one set raised through the medium of circulating capital, the other by independent labourers. Here the values may not be exactly the same, though cost of production nationally considered, and as previously defined, should in the two instances be iden-

---

* See chapter on Production.

† For a more particular account of Cost, see chapter on Gross Profits.

tical. For, as we have seen, wherever fixed capital is out of the question, labour is the only element of cost of production.

But in all these cases, the reason why value deviates in any degree from quantity of labour is, that capital cannot continue to be employed except it give a profit. Now this profit is necessarily in proportion to the capital, *not* necessarily in proportion to the quantity of labour maintained. And even when it is strictly proportional to that labour, commodities are higher by its whole amount than those raised by independent workmen, who realize wages only, not profits.

Cost of production, then, as above defined, regulates the value of commodities. But in what manner does it act? Immediately or remotely? This question has already been answered in the preceding pages, by showing that it influences value, by leading to an increase or diminution of the supply, according to circumstances; to an increase when the present value is such as to give more than the ordinary remuneration for the sacrifices required in production; to a diminution when the case is reversed. Cost of production, then, is only the remote regulator, or cause of value, the immediate being the proportion between the supply and demand. But what is meant by this last term? What is that sort of demand which influences value? This it is of great importance to determine.

It is evident, that if by this phrase be meant sim-

ply the quantity demanded, then this alone does by
no means regulate value. For, if a vast quantity be
consumed, solely because the price is very low, and
the moment this begins to rise, should the quantity
sought decline, then value cannot maintain itself, and
must instantly sink to its former level. Thus, when
there has been a superabundant crop, of wheat for
instance, the consumption increases perhaps fully in
proportion to the supply, and yet the price does not
rise, nay, is much lower than usual. The reason of
which is, that people consume more, only because
corn has fallen, and were it to rise ever so little,
would content themselves with less. They are willing
to spend as much on bread as formerly, but no more;
so that if they can get a larger quantity for their
money, well and good; if not, they will do with a
smaller. So long as this disposition of mind lasts,
the whole wheat in the country will not exchange for
more of other things, than it did when the crop was
an ordinary or very deficient one. Before the price
can rise, it is necessary that the buyers be both able
and willing to purchase a greater quantity than usual,
even although at an advanced rate. If this determination hold, their eagerness will enable the sellers to
increase the price of their grain. Therefore the intensity of the demand must be taken into account.

That a demand such as will raise commodities, depends in part upon its intensity, has just been shewn.
That it also depends in part on the quantity demanded, is no less certain, for this circumstance greatly

influences the intensity itself. Thus, if it be seen
that a great number of people are desirous to have
some commodity, this very fact has a tendency to increase the sacrifice which the buyers are willing to
make. Therefore, though intensity be the only cause
which at last determines value, yet as this cause is itself greatly modified by the quantity demanded, this
circumstance also must be included in our notion of
that demand which regulates the value of commodities. It is composed, then, of two elements, Extent
and Intensity.*

Here it may be worth while to remark, that when
the cost of production of any commodity rises, it by
no means necessarily follows that the quantity brought
to market must be diminished, in order that the price
may advance. At first, no doubt, this will probably
be the case, since the sellers find the buyers extremely
indisposed to give more than usual. But after the
latter have found that they cannot get it at the same
price as before, then the original quantity may be
brought forward without causing any fall. For the
pertinacity of the sellers who are determined not to
accept of less than what may secure them a fair profit,
will at length overcome the obstinacy of the purchasers. The one have a firm resolution, the others
not. In estimating, therefore, the supply which acts
upon price, we must take into account not merely the
quantity brought to market, but also the degree of

* See Malthus' " Definitions in Political Economy," chap. vi.

eagerness of the sellers to get their produce disposed of. No doubt the former acts upon the latter, but as we have just seen, not always. For the quantity brought forward may be the same, and yet the anxiety to sell, less. So that the elements of the supply correspond to those of the demand; consisting, first, of the quantity supplied; secondly, of the degree of firmness in the resolution of the sellers, not to part with their goods under a certain price. Now, a change in cost of production always modifies the last, namely, the pertinacity of the sellers, and if need be, the first also. By one or both of these means it regulates value.*

* Some writers make a distinction between Real and Relative value, meaning, as it would appear, by the former, cost of production. But what advantage can be derived from applying the same term to the cause, and to the effect, is, to me, I confess, inexplicable. This can serve only to render more confused, a subject already sufficiently intricate. Another and better separation is that of Natural from Market value, signifying by the former its ordinary state as determined by cost of production, by the latter, the actual value of any commodity at any time and place, which, according to the vicissitudes of supply and demand, may vary more or less from the usual level, to which however it constantly tends. Natural and market price are of course correlative to natural and market value.

CHAPTER IV.

ON EXCHANGE; CONTINUED.

In tracing the causes which regulate the exchangeable value of commodities, nothing has been said concerning a rise or fall of wages. But has this no influence upon value?

Wages, as we have seen above, are paid out of circulating capital. Now, after capital of both kinds comes to be used in production, it has been shewn that value is regulated *immediately* by the total value of that employed, whether fixed or circulating. But the higher wages are, the greater must be the amount of circulating capital required in order to raise or fabricate any commodity, and *vice versa*. It might therefore at first appear that its value must rise or fall with a similar variation in wages.

But here we forget that a rise or fall of wages affects the amount of circulating capital required in the production, not of one commodity only, but of all. Now, whatever affects all commodities, and all equally, changes not the relation in which they formerly stood to each other. Were the powers of industry so much increased that the same labour and capital as formerly, could raise or fabricate double, triple the quantity of all sorts of things, the nation would certainly be twice or three times as rich as before, but the value of every object would be unchanged. A given quantity of corn, say a quarter, would command neither more nor less of cloth, hardware, wines, or other luxuries. The same would be the case in regard to value, were the powers of labour and capital universally and equally diminished. As compared with the products of other countries, there would no doubt be a difference, but this needs not here be taken into account; for upon the above suppositions, this difference would be felt alike by all home commodities.

So then, if the rise or fall of wages, by increasing or reducing the amount of circulating capital required, affected equally all branches of industry, the relative values of their results would not be altered. But it does not affect all equally. It is, as we have seen, the total value of both kinds of capital employed, that determines *immediately* the value of the product. But the proportion of these is very different in different cases. Supposing the total value to be the same, a much greater share of this consists, in some instances of fixed, in others of circulating capital. Now, it is evident that those employments in which the proportion of the latter is great, will be much more affected by a rise in wages, than those in which it is small.

Let us suppose two capitals, each worth L.1000, to be vested in different employments, but that in the one case, raw materials, machinery, and other articles of fixed capital, compose one half of the value, the remaining half consisting in necessaries for the maintenance of labour; while in the other instance, these two elements amount to L.800 and L.200 respectively. Now, these capitals being of equal value, so also will be their products, supposing them to be completed in the same time. But let us suppose that a rise of 10 per cent. takes place in wages. In consequence of this, the one industry cannot be carried on to the same extent as formerly, without an expenditure to the amount of L.1050, while the other will require but L.1020. The products, therefore, which before were of the same value, cannot continue so for any length of time, now that the capitals advanced are no longer equivalent, without forming an exception to that equality in profit which tends always to establish itself. That on which the greatest proportion of circulating capital is expended, must therefore rise in value as compared with the other; or, in other words, this latter must fall in reference to the former.

And here, again, we may remark another proof of what I before attempted to establish, that value does not even *ultimately* depend upon quantity of labour alone. For, in this case, the products vary in value without the least alteration in the labour bestowed upon each, but merely on account of a change in the reward of that labour.

But what has been here shown in the instance of two commodities, must be true in respect to any number, that is, with regard to the total mass of the products of industry. A rise of wages will elevate the value of all those where the circulating capital expended bears a great proportion to the fixed, as compared with others in which this ratio is reversed. And of course a fall of wages must lead to an opposite effect. Those produced under similar circumstances will not undergo any alteration in their value as measured the one by the other. Both will have required an addition of circulating capital, and precisely the same addition; therefore, their relation to each other in exchange will remain the same.

Taking, as before, two capitals, each worth L.1000, of which, in both cases, L.600 consist of fixed capital, L.400 of circulating; it is clear, that if a rise of 10 per cent. take place in wages, instead of L.400 being spent in each instance in maintaining labour, L.440 must now be advanced, if the production is to continue on the same scale as formerly. The total capital employed will then in both cases amount to L.1040 instead of L.1000. But as the capitals continue to be of equal value, so also must their products. Consequently the rise in wages alters not the proportion in which they will exchange for each other. These products being wheat and barley, if previous to the augmentation in the reward of labour, one quarter of the former could command two of the latter, it will continue to do so still.

From what has been now said, it follows, that if there were any commodity in the production of which fixed and circulating capital entered for nearly equal

parts, then all those articles in raising or fabricating
which circulating capital was employed in a proportion greater than one-half, would, upon an advance
of wages, rise in value as compared with the first.
Others, on the contrary, whose cost consisted chiefly
of fixed capital, would, upon a similar occurrence, fall
in reference to the same.   If we could suppose money
to be this commodity, then all the products first mentioned would, upon an increase of wages, rise in Price,
and all the latter fall.   For price, as we have seen, is
nothing else than the value of any article measured
by the quantity of money for which it will exchange.
Certainly it does at first appear very strange that a
commodity should fall in price on account of a rise in
wages, but the fact is thus easily explained.

Let us see what are those branches of industry in
which the greatest proportion of fixed capital is employed.   In all countries where manufactures on a
great scale have long been established, and capital has
greatly accumulated, an immense value is vested in
buildings necessary for carrying on extensive works,
in machinery for supplying the place of human exertion, and in raw materials which may be considered
as the basis of the finished product.   Scarcely a year
passes without the invention of some plan for economising labour by the substitution of machinery moved
by inanimate agents.   The proportion of immediate
labour, and consequently of circulating capital, is
therefore constantly diminishing in those employments,
while that of fixed capital receives a corresponding

increase. The products of such manufactures will therefore be those most subject to a fall in price in consequence of a rise of wages. On the other hand, an agricultural capital being composed in great part of necessaries for the maintenance of labourers, the price of raw produce will have a tendency to advance. With regard to cattle, sheep, &c. the case will however be different, for, on a pasture farm, the circulating capital bears but a very small proportion to the fixed,—smaller probably than in any manufacturing employment whatsoever.*

All this no doubt goes upon the supposition of money being a commodity intermediate, in the circumstances attending its production, between the two extremes. Were it imagined to depend more on fixed capital than on circulating, then the price of those articles to which much machinery has been applied, would remain nearly stationary, while agricultural produce would rise still more than on the former hypothesis. Again, were money a commodity requiring a great proportion of immediate labour, and consequently of circulating capital, then the products of the soil would vary but little in price, those of manufactures experiencing a still more considerable depression. In all cases, however, the articles derived from agriculture and manufactures would exchange for each other in a proportion different from before. The former, with the important exception of live

* This is a point of much importance to be attended to.

stock, would command more of the latter than they did previous to the rise of wages.

What has been here proved in regard to the effects of a rise of wages upon the value of commodities, must of course be true conversely in the event of a fall. All those in the production of which fixed capital has entered in a larger proportion than circulating, will rise as compared with others which have sprung up under opposite circumstances. The same argument applies to this case as to the former.

Thus, on the whole, it appears, that a rise or fall in the reward of labour, while it causes no change in the relative value of commodities produced under similar circumstances in regard to the proportion of fixed and circulating capital, does alter the exchangeable relation of those where these circumstances are different. We have seen, moreover, that there would be an alteration in prices; not a general rise or fall thereof, but a rise in some commodities, a fall in others, while a few would undergo no change at all.

It has been also shown, that the means by which a variation in wages has an influence upon value, is by increasing or diminishing the total value of the capital required, to a greater extent in some employments than in others. If it increased or diminished this capital in all cases equally, there would be no alteration whatever in the result.

Thus, the effects of a change in wages upon value, are perfectly consistent with the doctrine laid down in the preceding chapter. They are, as I have pointed out, quite at variance with the ideas of those who consider quantity of labour as its sole regulator.

Before concluding this subject, it may be as well to observe, that the greater durability of the fixed capital has the very same effect as a larger proportion. For the longer it will last without repair, or more strictly, the less the necessary renewal in a given time, the less of course the quantity of labour required to keep it in a proper state. Therefore the less does circulating capital enter as a part of the expences. Consequently, this case is not essentially different from the former.*

To conclude this long investigation. On turning to the preceding chapter, we shall find that it has there been proved, that wherever fixed and circulating capital enter into the production of commodities in proportions different in the cases compared, value always ceases to vary exactly as the quantity of labour, and the more the fixed capital prevails, the greater the deviation from the general principle. Now, what is here shown, fully corroborates the above conclusion, for we see that in the circumstances supposed, a change in the reward of labour causes the same effects as an alteration in its quantity. Therefore, the principle, that value depends upon quantity of labour, is now found to be still farther restricted.

* The whole of this part of the subject in respect to the effects of a rise of wages on value, has been so ably and thoroughly treated by Ricardo, that it is the less necessary to dwell upon it here at great length.

From the whole of this long discussion, the conclusion then is the following. The principle that value is regulated by quantity of labour is limited by these causes:

1. By the use of fixed capital.

2. By the employment of circulating capital also, but in a particular case only, before explained.

3. By a rise or fall of wages, when accompanied with peculiar circumstances, stated in the present chapter.

Now, circulating capital has in reality nothing to do with this last case, for the result would be the same were it supposed not to be employed, but the fixed capital to belong to the labourers themselves. All that is essential is, that in the instances compared, fixed capital should bear a greater proportion to immediate labour in the one case than in the other.

The only circumstance in which circulating capital has any effect on value, is that mentioned in the former chapter, where commodities raised through its means are compared with others produced by labourers working on their own account. The effects of fixed capital are not only more general, but are also far greater, and as we have seen, would be felt even though no rise or fall of wages should take place. For in the instances brought forward in the previous chapter, no variation of this sort was supposed. This last is consequently a really separate cause, distinct from the two former; though, where

fixed capital exists not, or is found in the same proportion, its effects are not perceptible. For, as before observed, what is common to all objects compared, is the same as if common to none. In order
that there may be a difference in the result, there
must also be some variety in the preceding circumstances. Therefore a variation in wages is truly a
third cause, limiting the general principle that value
depends upon quantity of labour.

One remark only remains, and then I conclude.
If value were necessarily in proportion to quantity of
labour, and not, as I have shown, to the value of the
capital employed, no fixed capital, except of the most
simple and indispensable nature, could ever have
been accumulated. That it is accumulated, is the
strongest proof that can be given, that a value is derived therefrom distinct from labour. Let us suppose a manufacturer to spend L.1000 a-year in maintaining workmen. Now, it is clear, that if he, like
many others, choose to substitute machinery for human exertion, it must be from an expectation of at
least equal profit. If he gained 10 per cent. on his
capital before, he will hope to realize, after the
change, as much certainly, if not more. Let it be
imagined that he spend L.500 in purchasing a machine, and employ the remaining L.500 in the support of labourers, as formerly. Now, the amount of
the annual produce necessary to replace his stock,
and afford a profit of at least 10 per cent., must depend upon the durability of the machine. Suppose

that it require repairs to the extent of L.100 a-year. Consequently, L.600 worth of capital, fixed and circulating, is consumed every year, while a value equal to L.400 remains as it was. Therefore, in order that the manufacturer may realize 10 per cent. on the whole, it is essential that the yearly produce be at least equal to L.700, of which L.40 are required for the profit on the L.400 worth of machinery, which continues unchanged. Unless he gain this L.40 in addition to the L.660, which replaces with a suitable remuneration the capital really consumed, it is evident that the speculation must be a losing one.

But as we see that very durable machinery is actually made use of, we may be sure that in general there is no such loss. Therefore, value must be in proportion not merely to the capital truly consumed, but to that also which continues unaltered, in a word, to the total capital employed. And if this be true, it is utterly impossible that it can depend entirely upon quantity of labour, as in the preceding pages has, I trust, been fully proved.

From the above example, one important conclusion may at once be derived, which is, that the introduction of machinery may often be followed by a falling off in the gross produce of industry. While the manufacturer employed L.1000 in maintaining labourers, it was necessary, in order that he might gain a profit of 10 per cent., that the annual return should equal L.1100. But after the establishment of the machine, L.700, as we found, was sufficient for this purpose.

Were we to suppose that profits were doubled in consequence of the change, still the produce would amount to no more than L.800. This is a remark of the very greatest importance, as it shows that the interest of the Master and that of the Labourer may often be quite at variance, since the latter is benefited by the amount of gross produce, while the former looks to profits only ; and that the invention of machinery, which may increase the gains of the one, is, in the first instance at least, generally injurious to the other. But of this more hereafter.*

* See Ricardo on Machinery, " Principles of Political Economy," ch. xxxi.

PART II.

DISTRIBUTION OF WEALTH.

CHAPTER I.

GENERAL IDEA OF DISTRIBUTION.

THE general principles of value and exchange necessary for elucidating the great subject of distribution, being now understood, we may proceed to this division of the science of wealth which forms the proper object of the present essay.

There are two kinds of distribution, of which the one may with propriety be called primary, the other, secondary. Primary distribution is that which takes place between the owners of the different sources of wealth. The first question then is, who are these owners? and the second, and far more complicated, what are the causes which determine the proportion of the whole produce which falls to the share of each of these classes of persons?

After the whole amount has been divided among the owners of the different sources of production, each of these may impart a portion of their wealth to other sets of people who perform towards them various services conducive to their advantage or amusement, but who are not concerned in increasing the riches of a country. Such are the extensive classes of soldiers, sailors, and the civil servants of the state, lawyers, physicians, divines, musicians, players, etc. None of these, otherwise very different sorts of men, take any part in the production of wealth, and therefore can have no title to any portion in the primary distribution. They must depend then for their means of subsistence upon those who do partake in it, that is, they must obtain their wealth out of the stores of others by a secondary distribution.

Our attention must here be directed entirely to Primary distribution which alone properly belongs to political economy.* This, as has been observed, takes place between the owners of the different sources of wealth, of whom none are willing to contribute to the result gratuitously, but desire to have a portion of the product.

* Although Adam Smith in his chapter on wages has treated of the causes which regulate the pay of those who, in the language of political economy, are unproductive labourers, yet this is no reason why they ought to be included in a treatise on this science. For a great deal of the wealth of nations is but remotely connected with the main object of the work. So excellent however is all there said on the present subject, that no one I am sure would wish one line expunged. Mr. Storch has treated of what he calls *biens internes*, that is, *immaterial goods*, but with great propriety, has carefully separated this theory from that of national riches. Had M. Say done the same, his work would have been all the better. I take this opportunity of recommending to the attention of my readers, the Theory of Civilization, being the second part of M. Storch's great work. It is now some years since I perused it, but the impression of its excellence remains very strong. I may here also remark, that what he calls Secondary Distribution, comprises not only all that I include under that term, but, in addition, the whole doctrine of exchange, of which, for reasons stated in the proper place, I have thought fit to form one of the leading divisions of the science.

In the earliest stage of society, there is, as we have seen, but one class of persons engaged in the business of production. Hunting and fishing are the only means of procuring subsistence, and these are pursued by all. And there being but one class, the whole produce must belong to it; consequently there can be no distribution. But as soon as capital is created, and its owners form a distinct order, then society comes to consist of Capitalists and Labourers, each possessing a source of wealth peculiar to itself. Now if these classes co-operate in any employment, each by means of its own particular source of wealth, it is clear that the product must be divided between them. But afterwards, there rises up another set of men, who though they may be, and indeed generally are possessed of some capital, are still not necessarily so, and yet contribute greatly to the progress of industry, while at the same time they form an order different from that of common labourers. These are the heads of establishments, agricultural, manufacturing or commercial. The labour of these men must be allowed to be distinct from that of ordinary workmen, inasmuch as general direction and superintendance differs from manual exertion. Neither are they of necessity capitalists, but may conduct their business by borrowed funds. But be that as it may, they must, independently of the return to capital, receive some reward for their peculiar sort of labour or trouble as we may better call it, as well as for the risks they run. That they do so is evident, other-

wise what advantage could be derived from borrowing? And that capital is constantly borrowed for the
purpose of being employed productively, who can
doubt?

The English language is rather in need of a specific word to express this class of men. The French
call them *entrepreneurs*. For want of a proper term,
I shall beg leave to style them *masters*. The whole
produce then, will be distributed between Labourers,
Capitalists, and Masters, who may be looked upon as
another and a higher order of labourers, whose remuneration however is regulated very differently from
the latter.

In enumerating the sources of wealth, I mentioned
land as one. While the population of a country is
still thin, and good land unappropriated to be had in
abundance, as in the back settlements of America,
nothing of course will be paid for the use of that
which each man is free to occupy and cultivate at
pleasure. But when the whole land of a country becomes private property, or at least the most fertile
and best situated part of it, such of the owners thereof as are unwilling to cultivate their own possessions
are able to let them to others, who agree to pay a
certain portion of the produce, or the value of the
same, for the use of the original powers of the soil.
In addition to the three other classes of persons, a
fourth now comes in for a share in the distribution
of the gross amount. We have Labourers, Masters,
Capitalists, and Landlords, possessed respectively of

the three sources of wealth, Labour, Capital, and Land, the first of these being common to the two former sets of people.

But are there no other sources than these? Wind, running water, steam, inanimate agents as I called them, have formerly been mentioned. But it so happens, that either these are afforded spontaneously by nature in unlimited abundance, or else they are of a quality such as to be incapable of appropriation, because they cannot be fixed, no, not for a moment. So that in either case, no one fortunately can monopolize them for himself, and exact for the use of them a portion of the produce which they help to create. Running waters, indeed, in countries thickly peopled, and where power for moving machinery is much wanted, may not unfrequently be paid for to the owners of the land on their banks, but wind evidently never. Steam also, by which such wonderful results are now brought about, though not a spontaneous gift of nature, can by no means be appropriated, because it cannot even for an instant be fixed or arrested.

But we must remember, that what is true of land, is equally so of the bowels of the earth as of the surface, also of the fishing waters contained within the land, both capable of being appropriated, as well as the soil, and for the use of which, therefore, a part of the produce, or of its value, may be paid to the owner.

Having now pointed out the different classes of persons among whom the total produce of any employment is to be distributed, it remains to trace the causes which regulate the proportion which falls to the share of each. This is one of the most important questions in political economy, and the numerous controversies which have arisen upon it, would lead us to suppose that it must be one of the most complicated. But notwithstanding all that has been said and written on the subject, it may well be doubted whether the theory of distribution has ever yet been thoroughly elucidated. The works of Ricardo have thrown more light upon this branch of political economy, than those of perhaps any other author, but I consider it certain that his views are not altogether correct. And if the ideas of Ricardo are not quite accurate, still less so are those of his followers, who, as is usual with disciples, have on most questions pushed the principles of their master much farther than he had ever done, making no account of those exceptions and limitations which had been pointed out by that eminent writer. No one perhaps has more clearly shewn some of the errors of the Ricardo school than Mr. Torrens, in his very able work on the External Corn Trade. But to discuss all the conflicting opinions which have been delivered on this subject, is not my object, but availing myself of all the lights I can find, to give as far as possible an accurate theory of the distribution of wealth.

The total produce then is to be divided between

the labourer, master, capitalist, and landlord.   That portion of the whole which goes to the share of the last, is known by the name of Rent.   Since in all new countries, however, where plenty of good land still exists unappropriated, rent, as will be shewn afterwards at large, does not exist, it is evident that there must be causes which regulate the distribution of the produce among the other classes previous to any rent being paid.   We may therefore treat of these first, and omit for the present the consideration of landlords as a distinct order in society.   Remain then labourers, masters, and capitalists.   All English writers on political economy with whom I am acquainted, treat of the two latter as forming but one class of men, to whom the last mentioned term is applied.   Now, as has been shewn above, this is by no means correct, as the person who owns the capital, and he who directs the work, may be, and indeed frequently are, different.   Therefore, each must be entitled to a distinct part in the common product.*   What English authors call profit is the total surplus which remains to the capitalist and the master, after replacing the whole capital, fixed and circulating, expended in production. I do not mean to quarrel with this use of the word, but merely to point out distinctly what elements it comprehends.   Whether the master be or be not the owner of the capital, the employment of which he superintends, the total surplus or profit must at all

* By French writers this distinction is always attended to.   The *entrepreneur* and the *capitaliste* are never confounded.

events first come into his hands. If the capital do belong to himself, the whole of this surplus will of course remain with him, if not, a subdivision will take place between the capitalist and master.

But we need not trouble ourselves at present with this subdivision. This will be an after consideration. All we have to do with just now, is that portion of the whole produce which belongs to these two classes of persons whether combined in one or not. We may then, in what more immediately follows, consider them to be united, and designate the individual in whom both characters are found, by the name of Master-capitalist. The word Profit, when used alone, without any qualification, I shall employ in the same sense as English authors do, but instead of saying *profits of capital*, a phrase essentially incorrect, shall adopt the expression, *profits of master-capitalist*, or *gross profits*. Instead then of labourers, masters, and capitalists, the three classes between whom, as was said, the total produce was to be divided, we have to consider at present only labourers and master-capitalists, two being supposed comprehended in one.

CHAPTER II.

ON WAGES.

SINCE labour is an original source of wealth, the only original one which depends upon man, as the labourers form by far the most numerous class of the community, and as, moreover, the variations in their number and condition have a great influence on profits, it seems advisable to commence the subject of Distribution, by an inquiry into the causes which determine the rate of Wages.

The real wages or remuneration of the labourer, consist in the amount of necessaries, of comforts, and luxuries, which his exertions enable him to command. In that early period of society which precedes the accumulation of capital in the hands of a particular class of men, the whole produce of industry, as has been above remarked, belongs exclusively to the labourer. At that period there is in reality no primary distribution, since the sources of wealth are in the hands of but one class of persons. But as soon as there arises another set of men, possessing capital both fixed and circulating, to a sufficient amount, it becomes customary for them to employ labourers, who now no longer work entirely on their own account, but also

on that of their masters. If the labourers lived on
their own funds during the continuance of the business, it is clear that the product would be divided between them and the owners of the fixed capital, according to some previous arrangement. But, if they
had not wherewithal to support themselves during this
period, the capitalist might supply them with food and
other necessaries on condition of their abandoning all
claim to a share in the finished commodity. The
food, &c. must then be equivalent to this share, or if
there be any deduction, it can be that of discount only on the advances. This advance might, it is evident, be made either in the shape of corn, clothing,
furniture, &c. or in money by which these might be
procured. And this is the mode generally adopted
in all countries where industry and wealth have made
much progress. In almost all cases, the labourer
receives his remuneration previous to the completion
of the work, and this advance is usually made in
money.

But as money will command at different times very
different quantities of the necessaries and comforts of
life, from causes which affect either the production
of the precious metals, or that of other commodities,
it follows, that a rise or fall of nominal or money-
wages does not necessarily imply a corresponding
change in the real remuneration of labour. Still, the
quantity of money received by the workman must,
in a great degree, depend upon the rate of his real

wages, the causes regulating which, I now, in the first place, therefore, proceed to explain.

The *immediate* cause which determines the rate of wages, is the proportion existing between the supply of labour and the demand.

But this proportion itself depends, on the one hand, on the productiveness of those branches of industry by which are raised the necessaries of life; on the other, upon the style of living rendered necessary by the nature of the climate, or considered by opinion as necessary to the existence of the labouring population. Consequently, the Productiveness of the above branches of industry, the nature of the Climate, and the state of Opinion, are the ultimate causes which regulate the rate of wages.

In considering the immediate cause, I shall begin by examining the nature of the Demand, and the effects which its variations produce on the reward of labour.

To constitute a demand for labour, as well as for any commodity, it is not sufficient to wish for it; it is necessary to present an equivalent, in the one case, to the workman as a recompense for the sacrifice he makes of his ease; in the other, to the owner of the goods for the abandonment of his right of possession. But the only equivalent which can serve the purpose of the former, consists in the funds necessary for his maintenance. The greater then in any country the amount of funds set apart for the employment of labour, the greater the demand. Now, that portion of the national wealth, either actually engaged, or intended to be engaged in the work of production, is known, as has been before observed, by the name of capital. This is of two kinds however, fixed and circulating, the former consisting in raw materials, implements, machinery, buildings, and various other elements already enumerated; the latter, in the food and other necessaries required by the labourer. But it is evident that demand must depend upon the amount of the latter species of capital alone. However great may be the quantity of all the various objects which make up fixed capital, this cannot have any *immediate* influence upon the number of persons which the other can maintain. The raw materials, implements, machinery, &c., while they are consuming, confer benefit upon no one, as has been already remarked. So far then there is a pure loss or sacrifice of national wealth, submitted to, however, by the capitalist, for the sake of the expected return. To him indeed it is a matter of perfect indifference in what shape his advances are made, whether they be fixed in durable machinery, or employed to feed and clothe a number of persons, provided always his profit be the same. But to the nation, to the labouring class at least, this is far from being an affair of no consequence. For, from the increase of the one species of capital, they derive no immediate benefit, while every augmentation in the other instantly raises the demand for their services.

It appears, then, that the demand for labour in any country is exactly in proportion to the amount of circulating capital existing in the same. The supply remaining unchanged, every increase in these funds, by increasing the competition among the owners thereof, none of whom are willing to leave their stock unemployed, tends to raise the rate of wages. When a decrease takes place in the same, it is among the labourers that the competition becomes greater, each of them fearing to be thrown out of work. The final result of this would be, supposing always the supply to remain fixed, that the whole of the increase or diminution would be added to or deducted from the sum total formerly paid away to the labourers, by means of a corresponding change in the wages given to each. It is unnecessary to dwell longer on this topic, which seems sufficiently evident.

The point upon which I am most anxious to insist is, that although the demand for labour will generally increase as capital augments, still it by no means follows that it will do so in the same proportion. As society advances, a great part of the funds destined to be employed productively, are vested in machinery and other elements of fixed capital. In the early stages of advancement in wealth and industry, this forms comparatively but a small share of the whole national stock. But as the capitals of individuals increase, and the division of labour becomes more perfect, improvements are gradually introduced, the object of which is either to amend the quality of com-

modities, or to raise them at a smaller cost. These
improvements generally consist in the substitution of
machines for manual labour. At every change of
this kind, the fixed capital of the country is increased
at the expence of the circulating. The master-capitalist is now no longer obliged to keep so large a proportion of his funds in the shape of food and other
necessaries. Having employed a number of labourers *once for all* in constructing a machine, the value
of the circulating capital advanced to them during
the work becomes fixed in the result, which, instead
of being consumed in great part by labourers, and
reproduced at short intervals, may, on the contrary,
last for years, with but little reparation. A much
smaller annual produce will now suffice to afford the
master-capitalist his usual profit, which is all he looks
to. Since only a part of his stock is consumed yearly, it is enough if the value of that portion alone be
returned, together with a profit on the whole. The
value of the rest is represented by the machine,
which remains nearly as it was. But as a machine
can neither feed nor clothe any one, it is quite evident, that for a time the funds for the maintenance
of labour are absolutely diminished. It thus appears
that the introduction of machinery tends to lessen
the *gross*, though it may augment the *net* produce.*

---

* See chapter on Value at the end, for a case in proof of this. For
an exact account of what is properly *net* produce, see chapter on Revenue. In order to understand its nature thoroughly, it is necessary
to be previously acquainted with the whole theory of distribution.

The first effect, then, of the above change will be a
falling off in the demand for labour, and a consequent
decline in the rate of wages. And what is here proved
by reasoning from general principles, is confirmed by
the most ample experience in all countries. On such
occasions, the discontent and misery of the operatives have often broken out in acts of the most fearful outrage, principally directed against those dumb
instruments, which they, not without reason, considered as the cause of all their sufferings. By and
by, no doubt, the increased productiveness of industry resulting from the use of machinery, by facilitating the accumulation of circulating capital, will restore its former amount, and call again into employment the disbanded workmen. When this shall
happen, the national capital will, on the whole, have
increased, but the demand for labour, and the reward
thereof, will be the same as before.

This is sufficient to show that capital may augment
without any benefit whatsoever thereby accruing to
the working classes, nay, rather with a temporary
injury from the previous fall in wages. It is not, until, in the progress of industry, favoured by the new
inventions, circulating capital shall have become increased beyond what it formerly was, that a greater
demand for labour will spring up. Demand will then
rise, but not in proportion to the accumulation of
the general capital.

In countries where industry has much advanced,
fixed capital comes gradually to bear a greater and

greater proportion to circulating. Every augmentation, therefore, in the national stock destined for reproduction, comes, in the progress of society, to have
a less and less influence upon the condition of the labourer.

Every addition to fixed capital, is made, as has
above been proved, at the expense of the circulating.
This, I conceive, is a principle of great importance,
and pregnant with deductions. The first consequence
thence drawn, is, that the primary effect at all events
of such a transformation, is to diminish the demand
for labour. But what will be the ultimate result?
It is commonly said that the evil experienced by the
labouring class, is but of a temporary nature; that
though for a time they may suffer by a number of
them being thrown out of employment, yet that
sooner or later their services will again be required;
nay, that owing to the increased facilities for the accumulation of capital, the demand for them will ere
long become greater than ever. But this will depend
very much upon the nature of the occupations in
which the use of fixed capital has been introduced.
The ultimate effects of such a change will be very
different in agriculture for instance, from what they
are likely to be in manufactures. The evils resulting
from the invention of machinery, to the labouring population employed in the latter, will probably be but
temporary, liable to be perpetually renewed however,
as fresh improvements are constantly making for economising labour. The reasons why the evil is in this

case likely to be only for a time, are these. First, those master-capitalists who have introduced the use of the new machinery, being enabled by these means to fabricate a larger quantity of goods in proportion to the expense than formerly, will, until the competition of others has reduced their value, enjoy extraordinary profits. Their capability of saving out of the same, and adding to their capital, will consequently be increased. Part of these savings may be vested in fixed capital, but a portion of them will be made to consist of circulating also, since the former must always require some of the latter to set it a-going. Secondly, as by degrees the value or price of the manufactured goods falls in proportion to the diminished cost of production, each consumer of these commodities will have his power of saving increased, since a smaller share of his revenue will suffice for purchasing as much as he requires for his private use. Hence, a greater facility for accumulating capital, some of which may be supposed to find its way to the manufacturing industry in question. Thus the means of an increased Supply of the fabricated articles, and of employment for an additional number of workmen, are at hand. And, thirdly, there can be no doubt that the fall in the price of these products will cause an extension in the Demand for them.

Thus, it appears by reasoning from general principles, that the introduction of fixed capital into manufacture, in the shape of machinery, though for a time it may throw out of employment a considerable body of persons, will yet probably be followed, after a longer or shorter period, by the re-engagement of the same, or even a much greater number of labourers. And experience amply confirms this truth. Compare the hosts of workmen who now crowd the mills of Manchester and Glasgow, with the scanty population supported by the manufacture of cotton, previous to the invention of Arkwright's spinning jennies!

But, in agriculture the case is widely different. The demand for raw produce cannot increase in that rapid way in which it may for manufactured goods, for the simple reason adduced by Adam Smith, that the capacity of man's stomach is very narrow, but his desires in other respects insatiable. Therefore the labourer thrown out of employment by the invention of rural machines is not at all likely to be again employed in agricultural pursuits. A long time may elapse before an increase of population takes place sufficient to cause a fresh demand for food. But the change of all others most fatal to the country people is the conversion of arable land into pasture. For the quantity of labour that can be employed on a grazing farm is small indeed. Almost all the funds which formerly supported men, are now vested in cattle, sheep, and other elements of fixed capital. And as the number of animals which any tract of grass land can support, is necessarily limited, and consequently the number of persons employed in tending them, there is no chance of any farther demand for agricultural labour. Accordingly, wherever pasture has been substituted for corn, there the rural population has been suddenly and permanently diminished. And as we may easily suppose a change of this sort cannot be brought about without very great suffering, so may it well be doubted whether the ultimate result be one devoutly to be wished. But of this more will be said in future in discussing the Theory of Rent, and the Nature of Revenue, where it will be shown, that the decrease in the *gross* produce of the soil, which in this case is certain, is probably not at all compensated, as in that of improved machinery, by an augmentation even in the *net* result, notwithstanding the rise in the landlord's income. Enough, perhaps, has here, however, been written, to show that of all the evils which in the progress of society befall the labouring class, the change from arable to grazing husbandry, is beyond comparison the greatest.*

Having now explained sufficiently for our present purpose, wherein consists the Demand for labour, and stated the effects which fluctuations in the former produce on the remuneration of the latter, I shall go

---

* From what is said above, I would not for a moment have it supposed, that any thing like an argument is meant to be got up against agricultural machinery. Since it is a law of nature that general good is purchased by partial evil, we must try to alleviate those ills we cannot prevent. That indeed is a singular argument, which, had it been acted up to, would for ever have condemned mankind to the spade and rake. The plough and harrow were in their day the greatest of innovations, and still are the most useful of all machines. But the same objections must formerly have applied to them, as now to more complicated inventions. In like manner, the partizans of the spindle might have risen in arms against the spinning-wheel.

on to consider the other condition of the proportion, namely, the Supply. A more detailed discussion on the effects felt by the working population, from the various modes of investing capital, will be better understood afterwards, when we shall have investigated the subject of Profits.

The supply of labour is made up of two elements; first, the total number of the labouring population; secondly, the number of days in the year, and of hours in the day, during which it is customary to work.

That the supply of labour varies with the number of persons both able and willing to toil for their support, it surely requires no words to prove. Still this is not the only circumstance which constitutes that supply. One country may have fewer working people than another, but if the inhabitants of the former give themselves but little repose during the course of the year or day, the quantity of labour which they bring to market in a given time may be as great as in the latter, the population of which may be supposed more fond of ease, or more desirous of amusement.

If we suppose the demand for labour, and consequently the funds for its support, to remain constant, every variation in the number of workmen, or in the length of time throughout the year or day which they may give to toil, will cause an inverse change in the rate of wages.

If the labouring population increases without any augmentation in the funds just mentioned, it is quite evident that on the whole they must be worse off, since the same quantity of food, clothing, fuel, &c. is to be divided amongst a greater number of persons. There are but two ways in which this evil can fall on the people. The old labourers may continue to receive the same remuneration as formerly, in which case nothing will be left for the new, who must therefore inevitably perish for want, or depend for a precarious subsistence on the charity of their fellows or superiors. Or if all do get employment, and if the funds for the maintenance of labour be distributed pretty equally amongst them, each individual must gain less than formerly; that is, wages must fall. And this is generally the way in which the evil is felt. As population increases, if the circulating capital which supports it remain the same, each workman begins to experience more and more difficulty in getting employment. Masters finding that there is no want of hands, are more hard to deal with. But the labourer is unwilling to accept of a less remuneration for his services. He, therefore, perhaps remains out of work for a period, till want beginning to stare him in the face, and time hanging heavy on his hands, he is fain to submit to those terms which formerly he spurned. If, on the contrary, circulating capital still remaining the same, the number of labourers were to diminish, suppose by emigration, it is clear 'that the effect would be reversed. The same quantity of food and other necessaries would be divided amongst a smaller body of men, and therefore the condition of those left behind, must on the whole be ameliorated. And this benefit would not be confined to a few, but would spread itself over the mass of the population.

Thus, then, it appears, that the condition of the labourers, that is of the great majority of every nation, must in a great degree depend upon the *limitation of their numbers.*

But the supply of labour which serves to determine its reward, depends also in part upon the number of days throughout the year, and of hours during the day, generally devoted to toil. Let us suppose two countries, the population and capital of which are at the present moment the same ; and let us, moreover, imagine, that in the one, men labour from the beginning to the end of the year without any intermission, while, in the other, every seventh day is dedicated to repose. Now, there can I think be little doubt, that the inhabitants of the latter would gain more in proportion to their toil, than those of the former. The rate of wages would consequently be higher in the one case than in the other ; for, by this rate, is meant the proportion which exists between the quantity of labour undergone, (which is made up of two elements, its intensity and duration,) and the reward obtained for the same. To some, indeed, this advantage might at first sight appear much greater than it possibly can be. For, by the supposition, the funds for maintaining labour are at present the same in both countries. But the population is the same.

Therefore it might be rashly concluded that the share
of each labourer in these equal sums might, one with
another, be as great in the one country as in the other;
in this, for instance, where there are but 315 working
days, as in that where there are 365. But such a
deduction would be extravagant in the extreme.
For we must remember that the fewer the days of toil,
the less the work done ; so that if one-seventh be taken
from the labour, the same proportion must be withdrawn from the product. Were we then to suppose
that the master must pay to his men the same sum as
formerly, notwithstanding that they worked so much
less, he would be entirely deprived, not of profit only,
but of a portion of his capital also. Thus, if we imagine a master to employ L.1000 in the support of labour, if profits are at 10 per cent., the annual produce
will be worth L.1100. Now, if in future the men
refuse to toil for more than 315 days in the year, instead of 365 as formerly, it is evident that the product in that time must be reduced by one-seventh,
that is, to L.943. So that if the sum earned by the
labourers were to remain the same, the master would
at the end of the year be L.57 out of pocket, besides the
loss of his profit. This serves to show us that there
is a natural limit to the rise of wages, which can never
be passed, nor even reached, namely, the degree of
productiveness of industry. But of this I shall have
to speak immediately.

All, then, that we can conclude, is, that the limitation in the number of working days has a tendency to raise the rate of wages, though to what extent, is by no means easy to say.

In what has now been said, I have supposed, for the sake of simplicity, the population and capital to be the same in both countries. But this case, it is clear, is by no means a probable one, or at least would be but momentary, for with such a difference in the quantity of labour, and consequently in the work done, it is to the highest degree unlikely that there would not speedily be a difference in the capital. For as the produce of 315 days must be far less than that of 365; the national stock cannot in the two instances be long at a par, except saving become much more common in the former case. Now, it may be said, that this retarded progress of capital will be sufficient to neutralize all advantage which at first might be felt by the people from a limitation in the number of working hours. If they exert themselves less, they will also receive less in proportion, for the funds on which they depend accumulate more slowly. But this is a question which will be examined presently, when we come to consider the ultimate causes regulating wages. For our present purpose, it is enough, if it be shown that a limitation in the quantity of labour, however produced, has a tendency to elevate its reward.

The above principle applies equally to the case in which the customary hours of labour during the day are supposed to be different in number. The ratio between capital and population being the same, ten

hours' work in one country, may be no better rewarded than a shorter period in another, provided the
practice of dedicating these different portions of the
day to exertion, be in the two situations generally
adopted. The cause is the same in the present instance as in the former. The quantity of labour
offered, that is, its supply, is in reality very unequal
in the two countries, although the population be the
same, while the funds for its employment and maintenance, and consequently the demand, is identical.
Therefore labour cannot but be rewarded at a different rate.

If this be so, we cannot regard with too much jealousy any encroachment upon the hours or days of
repose afforded to the working classes. And even
were it otherwise, so great are the advantages, religious, moral, and intellectual, arising from leisure,
that periods of this kind cannot be too highly prized.
The very circumstance of a change from time to time
in our accustomed occupations and trains of thinking,
is of immense importance to the human understand-
ing. And if this be true in all states of society, it is
peculiarly so where division of labour has been carried to a great extent; which, while it contributes to
swell prodigiously the general result, has a strong tendency to cramp individual intelligence. The man,
the most part of whose life is spent in fixing the
twentieth part of a pin, if debarred from periods of
leisure can scarcely escape imbecility. For variety of
occupation, which prevents excellence in any, is never-

theless favourable to general acuteness and dexterity. If the Christian religion had conferred no other temporal benefit on mankind, than the separation of one day in seven for rest, this alone would be sufficient to entitle it to the eternal gratitude of the great mass of the population. The French Convention attempted to confine the day of repose to one in ten ; and had it permanently succeeded, we can hardly conceive any greater injury which it could have inflicted on the people—the people whose especial organ it was supposed to be. In some Catholic countries, the number of holidays may have increased to an extravagant degree. This of course is an abuse of the principle, which, however, seems more agreeable to humanity than the opposite extreme. It is surely more conducive to the happiness of the labouring class, which forms the vast majority of every nation, that they should afford to be idle, or amuse themselves during a considerable portion of the year, than that they should be obliged to toil incessantly even from tender years for twelve or fifteen hours a-day, perhaps in apartments heated to excess, in an atmosphere laden with extraneous matter, and vitiated with noxious effluvia. Those who think that an increase in the mass of national wealth cannot be too highly purchased, are apt to regard with displeasure these periods of recreation, and to consider them as just so much time thrown away. But in the eye of the philosopher, the mode in which riches are distributed, and the degree of labour which it costs the poorer classes to earn their share of them, are matters of at least as much importance as their total amount.

The cupidity of master-capitalists, the necessities of those they employ, and the practice of paying by the piece, have a constant tendency to extend the number of working hours, and thus by augmenting the supply of labour, to lessen its remuneration. And here I must make a remark of considerable weight, but which I do not remember to have seen previously stated, that the increase of fixed capital tends to the above result. For where so great a value is lodged in machinery, buildings, &c. the manufacturer is strongly tempted not to let so much stock lie idle, and therefore will employ no workmen who will not engage to remain for many hours during the day.* Hence also the horrors of night labour practised in some establishments, one set of men arriving as others depart.

As children generally abound in the neighbourhood of manufactories, and as, moreover, they are not free agents, but are obliged to work by parents rendered hard-hearted by indigence and desire of gain, who are glad to make any thing by them, the labour

---

* This may account for a circumstance which I have remarked in cotton mills, that almost all the people are young. The reason of this, as far as I could learn, is, that after middle age they are no longer fit for the work, which is said to be very hard. They are then sent away and replaced. Upon asking what became of these poor people, I could get no satisfactory answer. They did not know. In a late debate in the House of Commons, it was stated by Mr. Brotherston, himself a manufacturer, that some masters would add L. 100 a-week to their gains could they induce their men to work but one hour more a-day.

of these young creatures is often paid at an inconceiv-
ably low rate. The abuse of infant labour is one
which calls loudly for the interference of the legislature. Though the government of any country should
be very shy of intermeddling between the workman
and his employer, for rarely can it do so with advantage, yet in this case there are circumstances which
justify a departure from the general rule. The principal of these is, that a child is not a free agent. He
does not work of his own accord, but is forced to it
by his parents. In almost all instances, it has been
thought that parental affection was a sufficient gua-
rantee for the humane treatment of children. But in
the present case, experience has shown the contrary.
Desire of gain has been found a sufficient motive to
induce fathers and mothers to condemn their infant
offspring to toils which must either destroy them prematurely, or entail, on after years, disease and defor-
mity. Since, then, these natural protectors cease to
perform their duty, it is fit that the task devolve on
the legislative body, who, by forbidding altogether
the employment of children under a certain age, and
by limiting for a few years more the number of hours
during which it shall be lawful to work them, may
hope to correct in some degree this enormous evil.*

* This was written before the late Factory Bill was passed, which,
however, I am afraid is much eluded. The manufacturer is exonerated
by the physician's certificate of their being above the age required,
while the latter is beset by parents anxious to send their children to
labour, and who swear them to be above nine years old. I have myself seen many employed in cotton mills since the passing of the above
act, who were certainly under that age.

The immediate cause which regulates the rate of wages, namely, the proportion between the supply and demand of labour, has now been discussed. I have pointed out wherein consists the demand as well as the supply, and shown that any increase or diminution of the former has a tendency to raise or depress the reward of labour, while similar changes in the latter have exactly an opposite effect. The rate of wages, then, varies directly as the demand, and inversely as the supply.

From this it is evident, that there are but two ways in which the condition of the labouring class can be ameliorated ; either by an augmentation in the funds set apart for their maintenance, or by limiting the numbers among whom they are to be divided. The question then is, which of these expedients is likely to be the most effectual ?   And this brings us to the ultimate causes of the rate of wages.

Here it may be observed *in limine,* that one of these means is evidently much more in our power than the other. To increase the productiveness of industry is far from being always possible ; to restrain the progress of population depends but on the human will.   Nay, all the inventions fallen upon, in order to augment the return to labour, capital, and land, are insufficient to balance one permanent disadvantage, which becomes more sensibly felt as society advances, namely, the necessity of recurring to inferior soils after the better have been fully cultivated.   Therefore it follows immediately, that if in spite of this greater difficulty of obtaining food, population go on as rapidly as before, (supposing this to be possible,) it must of necessity be far more miserable. Consequently, the expediency of some check upon the too quick increase of the human species, in those situations at least where subsistence is procured but scantily, seems at once evident.

But we must remember that although strictly speaking the progress of population may be retarded to any extent, as this depends entirely on the Will, yet that there are bounds fixed by nature to the advantages derived from limitation of numbers. These bounds are determined by the productiveness of industry, of agriculture especially. However restricted the population may be, it is evident that the wages of labour can never exceed the amount of the gross return to all the sources of wealth, nor even come up to the same. For part of the produce must always be set apart to replace fixed capital with a profit, not to mention the profit on circulating capital which may or may not be employed. This observation must be carefully borne in mind in all our investigations on this subject. The same remark may be expressed perhaps more simply thus; that a man's wages for a day or year can never exceed or even equal what he can produce in the same time.

This being premised, I may now go on to consider more particularly the question with which we set out; as to which of the two expedients above stated is likely to be most effectual in permanently improving the condition of the great body of the people. And to this an answer will be easily found, if the truth of the following proposition be first acknowledged, namely, that population has a natural tendency to increase faster than subsistence can be procured, except under very peculiar circumstances, which necessarily are but local and temporary. A mass of evidence sufficient to fill three volumes has been brought forward by Mr. Malthus in proof of this, in a work which will immortalize its author; and which every political economist ought carefully to study.

I shall in the present instance limit myself to a few simple observations, which may perhaps be sufficient to render the matter tolerably clear.

The tendency of population to increase faster than subsistence can be procured in most parts of the habitable globe, is proved by reference to those countries in which food is most easily obtained. Such are regions abounding in tracts of fertile land, much of it as yet uncultivated, but continually being taken in and occupied by colonists from old states, where the arts of industry have long been known, and carried to a high pitch of excellence. In such circumstances are placed the United States of America. Here, then, if any where, population may be supposed to go on unchecked by the difficulty of procuring subsistence. By a reference to this country, we shall be able to acquire a good idea of the rate at which the numbers of mankind have a natural tendency to increase. It appears by the census that the population of the whole of these vast regions has for some time past been in-

creasing so fast as to double itself every twenty-five
years, but that in the newly settled and purely agricultural districts, it has gone on with such rapidity
as to produce the same effect in the incredibly short
period of fifteen years. Even a less time than this
has been stated, but I am anxious rather to keep within
the bounds of truth than to wander beyond them.
Fifteen years then we may consider as the period
during which population would double itself under
the most favourable circumstances. This fact of the
exceedingly rapid rate at which the numbers of mankind have a tendency to increase, is one of immense
importance, but of which, but for the discovery of the
vast and fertile regions of America, we might, perhaps, have been for ever ignorant. The rate of augmentation in the old world is so very different, that
no one could ever have supposed it possible that in
any circumstances it could be so rapid as experience
has proved it to be. In the countries of Europe, if
population double itself in fifty years, it is thought a
great deal. In most of them the rate of increase is
far less than this, in others, as in some parts of Switzerland, it is probably stationary, and in a few, as Tur-
key for instance, it is likely that the number of inhabitants has rather a tendency to decline. But the
physical constitution of man is not different in the old
world from what it is in the new, in fact, they are
originally but one people. The passions are not less
vehement in the former than in the latter, and desire
of offspring is probably the same in both. There is,

therefore, every reason to suppose, that the population of the one *has a tendency* to increase as fast as that of the other. If it does not actually so increase, it must be from the operation of some cause which counteracts that tendency.

It cannot be the nature of the climate, for the air of Europe is at least as favourable to human life as that of America. The only cause of sufficient importance to explain so general an effect, is the difficulty of obtaining subsistence for the support of a family. In all old countries the best and most advantageously situated lands have for a long time been under cultivation, and therefore, as a demand arises for more food, recourse must be had to those less fertile or more remote, which give not the same return. The difficulty of raising subsistence, and consequently, of maintaining a family, is therefore greater and greater as the country becomes more thickly peopled.

It appears then from the example of the back settlements of America, that population, as depending upon the moral propensities and physical frame of man, has a tendency to increase at such a rate as to double itself every fifteen years. But in the old countries of Europe, even in those in which improvements in industry have made the greatest progress, it is thought very remarkable if fifty years be the period of doubling, while very few come near to this. It appears, moreover, that the only cause at all adequate to account for this difference, is the increasing difficulty of raising and procuring additional supplies of food as society advances. Therefore, as it is this difficulty which checks the progress of population, it follows that the latter has a tendency to multiply faster than the means of subsistence can be procured any where but in newly settled and fertile districts. How much the tendency of the one to increase exceeds that of the other, is proved by the very slow rate at which population augments in old countries, as compared with its rapid progress in more favourable situations.

But perhaps it may be said, though it be true that in the present state of all old countries, subsistence is procured with difficulty, yet that improvements in agriculture may hereafter be made which may enable its products to keep pace with the natural progress of population. Such a supposition, however, is extravagant in the extreme. The use of machinery and division of labour which perform such wonders in manufactures, can be introduced but in a very limited degree into rural employments. The necessity of having recourse to inferior soils as population advances, after all the best have been cultivated, is a disadvantage to which the greatest discoveries in the modes of tillage and the rotation of crops form but a very feeble counterpoise. This is proved by the fact, that countries having plenty of fertile territory, but in which the processes of culture are rude in the extreme, can still raise corn far cheaper than nations the most advanced in the career of art and industry. The wheat of Poland and southern Russia, so backward

in every improvement, can be grown at less than half
the cost of that of England. To suppose then that
discoveries may hereafter be made which shall increase the return to agricultural labour and capital to
such an extent as to enable the means of subsistence
to keep pace with the natural progress of population,
is a pure hypothesis, at variance with all past experience, and therefore in the highest degree improbable. Can any one really imagine that by any expedient food could be raised in Europe in such abundance as to allow the numbers of its inhabitants to
double themselves every fifteen years? But such are
the lengths to which those must be prepared to go,
who advocate the possibility of increasing the means
of support so as to keep pace with the unchecked
career of population.

If this be true, the question above put as to the
most effectual plan for ameliorating the condition of
the labouring class, admits of a ready solution. If
the power of population be so much greater than that
of raising subsistence, it follows that we may increase
the latter to any extent we are able, without at all
permanently improving the circumstances of the great
mass of the people. The only difference would be,
that after a certain period of prosperity had elapsed,
their numbers would be augmented. They would be
as poor as ever, and more of them.

This is the first consequence of the great principle
above laid down and proved. The next is, that po-

pulation *must* be checked in some way or other to a certain extent. That it *is* so, is proved also by the experience we have of all old countries, in which the inhabitants increase so slowly as compared with those of states newly settled, in which it is permitted to run its natural course. The only questions then which can now be made, are, first, as to the best mode of restraining it, and, secondly, as to the extent?

There are but two ways in which the increase of mankind can be checked. If population be allowed to go on to the utmost extent which the means of subsistence even in the most favourable years will permit, numbers of persons, on the first occurrence of scarcity, being left partially or entirely destitute of support, must either die of absolute starvation, or of diseases brought on by unwholesome and insufficient nourishment. This is what has been called the Positive Check, and presents to our view the most appalling misery, death attended by every circumstance that can affright humanity.

The other mode in which population can be restrained is, by limiting the number of births. Between these two expedients we have to choose, for there is none which does not come under one or other of these heads. Will you have a labouring class always poor and often wretched, or one at all times removed from the extreme vicissitudes of fortune? Do you prefer a population, great part of which is continually being swept off prematurely, among whom want and dirt are for ever giving rise to, or propagating disease, to a race healthy and robust, comfortable in themselves, and harmless to others? Such is the question.

Much of the prejudice which has existed on this subject must have abated, had it been considered that it is impossible for population to run its natural course in old countries, that it must be checked somehow or other, and, therefore, that the only doubt can be as to the means by which this may best be brought about. Will you have the Positive or the Preventive check? Do you think it most expedient that the numbers of mankind should be brought within the limits of subsistence by the invincible operation of want, or by the exercise of that reason and self-control which distinguish man from the rest of the creation? The question once fairly put, it seems impossible but that much of the disfavour with which this doctrine has been hitherto regarded, must be overcome. And here a very important observation presents itself, which is, that it by no means follows that a country in which the preventive check prevails, shall, in the long run, support a smaller population than one in which the positive predominates. In the latter, the numbers may increase more rapidly for a time, till arrested by want and disease; but in the former, though longer of arriving at the same point, they will nevertheless reach, and probably even surpass it. For the principal cause of the misery felt in those countries where births are extremely numerous, is the permanent existence of a great mass of population too young to be able to earn their subsistence. This is the grand source of poverty to individuals as well as to the nation. Children under a certain age consume, and largely too, where they can, in proportion to their size, without giving any return. An infant brought up to the age of nine or ten, and then carried off by disease, is, so far as wealth is concerned, a pure loss to his parents, and to the country at large. His whole subsistence for so many years is entirely thrown away. And since, where the positive check prevails, this effect is constantly taking place on a great scale, we may thence judge how much the national riches must suffer from such a cause. This helps to explain the wretchedness of Ireland and other such districts. Wages are low, and they are to be shared among numbers of unproductive beings, many of whom never become any thing else. But in states where the preventive check prevails, and where, consequently, if there be fewer births, deaths are also less frequent, a smaller proportion of the whole population is of tender years, more arrive at the age of maturity, and live longer as productive labourers. No wonder, therefore, if the people be better off. Now a body of inhabitants of this description will evidently raise more wealth than even a much larger one composed in great part of infants; therefore, the means of a future advance in population will be greater in the former case. Whereas, a people, who by their im-

providence bring into the world a greater number
of human beings than they can possibly rear up in
health, by this conduct, not only render themselves
for ever miserably poor, but after a certain time,
even arrest the future increase of mankind, by stop-
ping the main source of riches, the Labour of an
adult and vigorous race. *

On the whole then, it appears that it by no means
follows, that the population of a country where the
preventive check prevails over the positive, shall, on
the long run, be less; but that its progress, though
for a time slower, will be more lasting, till ultimately it outstrip the other.† Its nature also would be
very different in the two cases, in the former, comprising a much larger proportion of adults than in
the latter.

And this seems the proper place to take notice of an
objection to the Malthusian doctrine which I remember
to have somewhere heard. It is this. A man, it is said,
can always produce more than he can consume, and
therefore by diminishing the number of labourers,
the nation is a loser. Now, this objection embraces
an assumption and an inference. Let us for a moment grant the former. But because an able-bodied
man always raises more than his consumption, does

---

* By the last census, it appears that the population of Ireland has
increased less rapidly than heretofore. As there is no reason to attribute this to any improvement in the habits of the people, the fact helps
to corroborate the above conclusion.

† " Chi va piano, va lontano," says the Italian proverb.

it therefore follow that helpless infants can? One
grand argument in favour of restraining the progress
of population by means of the preventive check, is
precisely that we may substitute an adult and healthy
race for those disabled by childhood or disease. And
we have just seen, that where that restraint prevails,
the former description of people bears always a greater
proportion to the latter than where the positive is
chiefly felt. The case in which grown up men without young families emigrate to distant parts, is one in
which the smallest benefit, if any, may be supposed
to accrue to the nation they quit. That the riches
of the country will thereby be lessened, supposing
they could get full employment at home, there can
be no doubt, for by the supposition they carry away
arms able and willing to work. But still the labourers left behind may be benefited by their absence, by
obtaining a larger share in the produce of industry.
So that a diminution in the amount of national wealth
may be more than compensated by a distribution
thereof more favourable to the lower orders. The
only difficulty in this case is, that as it is supposed
that if the emigrants had remained at home they
would have produced more than they consumed, it
follows, that so far the capital of the country must
increase more slowly from their absence, and consequently, on that account, the demand for labour would
also be less brisk. But it seems probable that the
labourers would gain more than they could lose by
the departure of their fellows. For the decrease in

the supply of labour is immediate and certain, while
the falling off in the rate of increase of capital is
more distant and eventual. All the excess of a
workman's production over his consumption is not
necessarily saved by his employer, and added to
stock, much of it may be spent without any return.
And when profits fall in consequence of a rise in
wages, masters are induced to be more economical, so
as to make up for the difference. For these reasons, it
seems likely that even in the case above put, the
poorer class of people would gain by the emigration
of their equals. But this in reality is not the question at issue, for men do not come into the world
ready made with all their powers about them. A
long and helpless infancy must precede. Now, there
can be no question that the greater the proportion of
children in any state, the poorer both individuals and
the nation will be. Therefore, any system which
tends to diminish that proportion must be advantageous to both. In short, what avails it to the labourer that he produce more than he consume, if,
from the number of his class he come in but for a
small share of the whole, and have to divide that
pittance with a wife and half-score of children?

But is the assumption on which the objection is
founded so certain? Can even the adult and healthy labourer always produce more than he consumes? Truly
glad should I be if the case were so. But we must
remember that a man's arms alone are of no avail, he
must have something to work on as well as to work

with. So long as land of tolerable quality remains unappropriated, every one, no doubt, may generally find more than his subsistence, for a little seed, a hoe and spade, are the only elements of fixed capital absolutely necessary. But after the whole territory has become private property, this grand resource no longer exists, and in order to gain a livelihood by a mechanical trade, more stock in the shape of new materials and implements, is essential. If then a man neither possesses these, nor is able to borrow them, nothing remains but to let his services to others. But why should it be supposed as certain that the amount of these and other elements of fixed capital possessed by the nation at large, must necessarily be sufficient fully to employ all the members of the same? Theory shews no reason for this, and experience I fear amply proves the contrary.

In regard to the *extent* to which it may be advisable to carry the preventive check on population, it is impossible to give any general rule, for it must vary with the different circumstances of every country. In some few situations scarcely any check seems required, no inconvenience being felt from the most uncontrolled rate of increase. But such districts are every day diminishing, as the earth becomes more and more cultivated and peopled. Even in the United States of America, it is in the back settlements only that the power of population is developed in all its extent. The rate of augmentation, though still rapid, is by no means equally so on this side of the

Alleganies.   Already, it would seem, the positive
check has begun in some degree to operate, in these
older states, since the poor and destitute are not quite
unknown.   If then the preventive check has become
necessary even on the banks of the Delaware and
Susquehana, in countries which have been settled for
about two centuries only, and still far from being
thoroughly cultivated, how much more must it be
required in France or England, peopled in a degree
for ages, and whose soil has for the most part been
long under tillage!   In New York and Pennsylvania,
no vast manufacturing population exists liable to be
thrown out of employment by a thousand accidents,
from the important changes of war and peace, down
to the ever varying caprice of fashion.   But even there
some degree of prudence is already necessary to prevent the too rapid increase of inhabitants.   If in
England it shall not be exercised to a greater extent
than at present, those evils which have hitherto been
too often experienced, will, as manufactures and commerce increase, become more and more appalling.
At every change of trade, on every improvement of
machinery, on every occurrence of scarcity, the numbers thrown out of employment and reduced to extreme indigence will become greater and greater;
whose united misery must be always regarded not
only in itself as a great public calamity, but also in
its consequences dangerous to free government, to the
general right of property, and even to the very existence of civilized society.

And here I must recur to a topic already hinted at, which is, that let population be arrested in its progress as much as it may, still the rise of wages thence derived is limited by the productiveness of industry. In other words, that a man can never receive more for the labour of a day or year than with the aid of all the other sources of wealth, he can produce in the same time. Nay, as has been already observed, his pay must be less than this, for a portion of the gross produce always goes to replace fixed capital with its profit. Now in very many countries of Europe, the possible rise of wages is perhaps less than might be imagined.

Let us suppose that Gross Profits are in England ten per cent., which is perhaps not below the truth. Suppose also a master to employ two thousand pounds in any branch of production, one-half being vested in fixed capital, the rest, consisting of food, &c. for the maintenance of fifty labourers at twenty pounds each. Then at the above rate of profit, the product, if completed in the year, will be worth two thousand two hundred pounds. Were we now to imagine that wages rose from twenty to twenty-two pounds a man, the profits of the master would be reduced to one-half, that is to five per cent.,* below which we can scarcely suppose them to fall. So immense a reduction in the income of the employer, would therefore make but a very small addi-

---

* They would, in fact, be rather less than five per cent.

tion to the pay of each labourer. But it may be said, the rise of wages would be followed by a corresponding augmentation in the price of the produce. But in discussing the subject of Value, I have shewn this to be impossible.

This example may serve to shew us, that the possible advance of wages is in most parts of Europe very limited, the reason of which is, that as it becomes more and more difficult to raise subsistence, the income of the labourers forms gradually a larger and larger proportion of the whole produce, supposing their real reward to remain the same. Consequently, the remainder, out of which alone any augmentation can take place, becomes smaller and smaller. But this will be shewn at large under the head of Profits. No doubt it will make an immense difference to the workman, whether he have to support himself alone, or, in addition, a crowd of helpless children. From smaller families then, and consequently a diminution in the number of mouths to be fed by wages, much more than by a rise in the rate of these, is future relief to be expected to the labouring classes. And if savings be made during youth and health, their condition may be rendered pretty comfortable.

In most countries of Europe, a single man of sound constitution finds in general no great difficulty in supporting himself. I say in general, for in manufacturing districts revulsions are apt to occur, which for a time throw numbers out of work. It is when children multiply and sickness comes on, that the galling yoke of poverty is felt.

But we must remember, though in many parts of Europe wages probably cannot rise very much, yet there is nothing to hinder their falling, if not prevented by the prudence of the people. The low price of labour in Ireland, as compared with the neighbouring island, is a sufficient proof of this. Were the habits of the peasantry here to become the same as in Munster, there can be no reason why the result should not also be the same.

These remarks may prepare us for the more definite solution of a question already touched upon, namely, what rise of wages may be expected from the emigration of able-bodied labourers, or what comes to the same thing, from a limitation in the number of working hours. In those countries where this kind of income already swallows up a large proportion of the gross produce, it would be vain to suppose that by any emigration it could possibly be greatly elevated. The degree of productiveness of industry does not admit of such a rise. For the same reason, no abridgement in the time generally devoted to toil, could, under the same circumstances, have much effect. But if by this diminution in the supply of labour, a fall in wages be prevented, the benefit to the great body of the population will still be very considerable. And it is probable that this would be the amount of the advantage. Indeed it is evident, that if the emigrants leave their country because they cannot be fully employed, their absence must be a wholesome relief to the mother state, and to the poorer classes especially, who will be relieved from so much injurious competition. In districts where wages are very low, it is clear that emigration might produce greater effects, for in that case there would be more room for a rise. But if not accompanied by a greater prevalence of the preventive check, the benefit would be but temporary.

In the early progress of states, when none but land of the first fertility need be 'cultivated, so great is the excess of a man's production over his necessary consumption during the time, that it is probable his fellow-labourers may gain more by the addition made through his exertions to the national capital, than they lose from his competition. But in old countries the case is reversed. The gross produce is then so much diminished from the necessity of having recourse to inferior soils, that the subsistence of the men employed engrosses so large a proportion as to leave but little over. Therefore each individual can contribute but in a trifling degree to the augmentation of the common stock of the society. Consequently, in such circumstances, the labourers lose more by the competition of their fellow, than they gain from the addition made by him to the national capital. Hence his absence must be to them a benefit. And this seems the true solution of that difficulty formerly stated.

But we must remark, that the very cause which

renders emigration an advantage to those left behind, namely, the reduced return to agricultural industry, also limits the extent of the good. This cause prevents wages from greatly rising, so that emigration can serve chiefly to hinder them from falling.

The operation of the different checks to population, depends, in different countries, on particular circumstances in their physical situation, or moral condition, which it is now necessary to explain.

I have before said, that the proportion between the supply and the demand of labour, which is the proximate cause of the rate of wages, is itself regulated on the one hand, by the productiveness of those branches of industry by which are raised the necessaries of life; on the other, by the style of living rendered necessary by the nature of the climate, or considered by opinion as necessary to the existence of the labourer. That, therefore, the Productiveness of Industry in the above branches, the nature of the Climate, and the state of Opinion, are the ultimate causes which determine the rate of Wages. The first of these being already considered, the two latter alone remain to be examined.

It is quite evident, that the most indispensable wants of men vary much according to the climate under which they live. Without extending our regards beyond the boundaries of Europe, how different, for instance, are the necessities of the inhabitants of Southern Italy, and those of England—of the poor man exposed to the cold and fogs of London, and the half-naked Lazzar-

oni who bask in all the luxury of the unclouded sun
of Naples! The one must have a house to shelter
him from the inclemencies of the weather—fire during a great part of the year, warm clothes, and, comparatively speaking, a generous diet, composed in
part of animal food and fermented liquors. The
other, during a considerable portion of the twelve
months, scarcely requires an habitation at all, much
less can he stand in need of fuel, except for a few
weeks perhaps in the middle of winter; he demands
but a garment of the scantiest description, a little
ice in summer, and Macaroni. So great a difference
in the indispensable wants of man, cannot but have
a powerful influence on the amount of population.
Were it possible for the labouring class to become as
numerous in England, in proportion to the capital of
the country, as in the kingdom of Naples, it is certain that it could be only for a moment. The means
of support which suffice for maintaining life in the latter situation, would not do in the former. Many
therefore would be swept off from the want of proper nourishment, from cold, and the various maladies
to which these give rise. Thus would the population
be thinned till it became reduced to such a number
as the circulating capital of the country could maintain, according to the more expensive style of living
rendered indispensable by the nature of the climate.
If, then, the preventive check did not operate with
greater force under this less genial atmosphere, without doubt the positive would act in its stead. By

one mode or other the effect must be brought about.* The proportion, then, which the number of the labouring population bears to the capital which supports them, may be permanently greater, and the rate of wages lower in certain countries than in others, for this simple reason, that less is required to support life in fine climates than in inclement ones. The utmost limit to which population can proceed, consistently with the actual state of national wealth, is determined, it thus appears, by physical causes, which are not the same in all parts of the world.

But how far it may fall short of this impassible line, must depend upon moral circumstances—upon the opinion entertained by the labouring class of what is necessary for them. The higher their ideas in this respect, the more limited is the population likely to become. If a man restrict his wishes to a mud cabin, and a few potatoes, when he thinks he can secure these, there is nothing to prevent him from marrying, and having a dozen of children! But if he desire a neat white-washed cottage, decent clothes for himself and family, a comfortable meal of meat and vegetables, and the blazing hearth to

* Since writing the above, I perceive by the public papers, that the population of the kingdom of Naples has increased very rapidly for the last twenty years, having augmented by no less than one-sixth—a progress certainly much more rapid than that of most European countries. It now amounts to upwards of six millions, a number very great if we consider the limited extent of territory, its mountainous nature, and the small degree of industry among its inhabitants. The twenty years reach from 1815 to 1835. During this period also, an epidemic took place, which carried off, it is said, 150,000 persons in addition to the usual mortality.

diffuse cheerfulness around, he will be likely to pause a little before reducing himself to such a condition as must render it impossible for him to command these comforts. To raise the ideas of the labouring class as to what is necessary to their well-being, is, then, of all things, the most important. It is the only way by which the preventive check may be made to take the place of the positive—the only expedient by which the numbers of mankind may be brought within the limits of the means of subsistence, by a diminution of births, instead of an increase of deaths, preceded by every form of misery.

There are two kinds of philosophy applicable to common life. The object of the one is to destroy our wants, and limit our desires; that of the other to enlarge the sphere of these, and at the same time, to point out the means by which they may be satisfied. The one preaches Content, the other Activity. The former deals perpetually in reflections on the vanity of human wishes, the difficulty of attainment, the pain of disappointment, and the unsatisfactory nature of all human enjoyments, even when the object of our desires has fallen within our grasp. It recommends Contemplation, and derives its chief pleasure from looking down with self-complacency and pity upon the crowds below, employed in running the race where fame, wealth, or power, is the goal.*

* " Sed nihil dulcius est, bene quam munita tenere
Edita doctrina sapientum, templa serena.
Despicere unde queas alios, passimque videre
Errare, atque viam palanteis quærere vitæ,

It exclaims with the poet,

> O miseras hominum menteis ! O pectora cæca !
> Qualibus in tenebris vitæ, quantisque periclis
> Degitur hoc ævi quodcunque est ! Nonne videre est
> Nil aliud sibi naturam latrare, nisi ut, quoi
> Corpore sejunctus dolor absit, mente fruatur
> Jocundo sensu, cura semota metuque ?
>
> *Lucretius*, Lib. ii.

The latter species of philosophy, on the other hand, by presenting new objects to our view, stimulates our desires and urges to exertion. It dwells on the pleasure, which always attends activity, even when the pursuit may finally be in vain, the constant languor which accompanies the want of interesting employment, and the barbarism and poverty which never fail to follow in the train of habitual indolence.

Though I am far from denying that the reflections peculiar to the former system may occasionally have their utility in reconciling the mind to an unavoidable lot by the destruction of those desires which cannot be satisfied, and therefore torment to no purpose ;* yet is it certain, that had such principles been generally acted upon to the full extent, the

---

> Certare ingenio, contendere nobilitate,
> Nocteis atque dies niti præstante labore,
> Ad summas emergere opes, rerumque potiri."
>
> *Lucretius,* Lib. ii.

* The punishment which Dante inflicts upon those who occupy the outer circle of hell, is to live in desire without hope.

> " Di tanto offesi
> Che senza speme vivemo in disio."
>
> *Dell' Inferno, Canto* iv.

world could never have risen from rudeness to civilization. No improvement can take place without exertion, and no exertions would be made if desires were extinct. The system, pushed to its last consequences, may be defined as one, the object of which is to deter from the pursuit of every good from fear of evil. But if activity has pains, neither is indolence exempt from them, the very feeling of ennui being from its permanence one of the most intolerable of all; while its enjoyments, on the other hand, are much more limited. The saying of Dr. Johnson, in respect to matrimony, applies exactly to these opposite systems. " Marriage," says he, " has many pains, but celibacy has no pleasures." Allowance of course must be made for the latitude of an epigrammatic remark.

To the labouring class in particular, about whom we are now engaged, the prevalence of the system of *content*, as it may be called, would be most fatal. The fewer their wants, the lower their standard of comfort, the less will be the prevalence of the preventive check on population, the more consequently will this press on the means of subsistence, even in plentiful years, and go beyond them in times of scarcity.

There must always be inconveniences attending the exclusive use of one sort of aliment by the great mass of the nation, as there is much more probability of a dearth in one species of grain or other article of nourishment than in several. But when it is the very cheapest sort of food which is raised, the evil must be felt in a tenfold degree, for in this case it will be impossible for the labouring class to purchase a sufficiency of any other, whether of home or foreign growth; their wages being proportioned to their ordinary style of living. Whereas, had they been accustomed to a higher quality of food, on a failure in this crop, the usual remuneration for their labour would have enabled them to procure some inferior kind of sustenance, which, in other years had served to support dogs, horses, &c., or to minister in some way to the luxuries of the rich. Or a supply of provisions of one sort or another, might be obtained for them from foreign countries. Wheat, on the contrary, it is well known has often been exported from Ireland in large quantities, while the peasantry were dying of hunger from a failure in the potato crop, a fact assuredly most painful to humanity, but under the circumstances perfectly unavoidable. The corn-merchants might, no doubt, have made the starving people a present of their grain, but the latter were unhappily quite unable to purchase it.

The truth of the above principles is proved experimentally by a reference to the various nations of the earth. In those where, in ordinary years, the inhabitants are accustomed to live well, where they are not confined to one species of food, and that too of the lowest quality, dearths are rare, and famines almost, if not, quite unknown. In opposite circumstances, these scourges of the human race commit ravages quite appalling.

In England, for instance, where the labouring class subsist upon wheaten bread, meat, potatoes, &c., famine, properly so called, has long been unheard of. The same is true of France, though not perhaps to a like extent. If any remarkable dearth has occurred in that country during the last fifty years, this is to be attributed to the violence and want of security which attended certain epochs of the Revolution, rather than to any other cause. The labourers subsist there in great measure upon bread of wheat, or rye, in some parts on a mixture of these, but consume less meat than in England. Compare the state of these nations with that of Ireland or India, and how amazing is the difference! In Ireland, where potatoes form the sole sustenance of a great part of the population, famines, we know, are of frequent occurrence with typhus fever in their train. In the east, thousands, tens of thousands are said to perish on a failure of the rice crop. In the latter regions, every thing contributes to restrict the wants, limit the desires, and deaden the exertions of the inhabitants; climate, religion, and the continual insecurity to which property has been exposed during the perpetual changes from one despotism to another which have taken place in that part of the world. Rice, the cheapest of all aliments, forms the sole support of countless myriads.*

* There is but one kind of plant which is said to give even a greater return than rice. This is the banana, of the larger sort, cultivated in Mexico.

It is not, therefore, wonderful, that the desolations of famine should be experienced in the east to an extent far far beyond what is known in any district of Europe. The idea of thousands of our fellow-creatures dying of want, must appal the stoutest heart. Such, however, are the tremendous consequences of the desires of a people being limited to what is just sufficient to support life.

Having now traced the causes, both immediate and remote, which determine the real reward of labour, it only remains to say a few words on Money-wages.

Money-wages evidently depend upon two circumstances, first, upon the causes which fix the rate of real wages; secondly, on the money-value or price of the various necessaries consumed by the working population. The former being supposed to remain the same, it is clear that the quantity of money given to the labourer must be greater or less, according as the price of provisions, &c. rises or falls. For, were it otherwise, his real reward would vary, which is contrary to the supposition.

Notwithstanding, it often happens, that labour falls in dear years, rises in cheap. But the reason of this is, that in unfavourable seasons, a decline in the demand for it frequently occurs, and at the same time an increase in the supply, while in plentiful times the very reverse sometimes takes place. Therefore, money-wages fall or rise in consequence of this change, in spite of the high price of necessaries which tends to produce an opposite effect. This has been so well explained by Adam Smith in his chapter on Wages, that it is unnecessary to say a word more about it here.

But though these occasional fluctuations in the price of provisions and other articles of primary necessity may not immediately cause corresponding changes in the money rate of wages, yet it is certain, that no permanent alteration can take place in the one, without being followed sooner or later by a similar modification in the other. The first effect of any change is often very different from the ultimate. No error is more common, however, than a confounding of the two, since few are capable of looking beyond primary consequences obvious to all, to final but distant ones, which can be traced only by the light of philosophy.*

Before quitting this subject, I must allude to an opinion on the rate of wages adopted by various authors of eminence, but which nevertheless appears to me quite erroneous. It is, that there is a natural or necessary price of labour, in the same manner as of commodities. Mr. Ricardo says, " Labour, like all other things which are purchased and sold, and which may be increased or diminished in quantity, has its natural and its market price. The natural price of labour is that price which is necessary to enable the labourers, one with another, to subsist and to perpetuate their race, without either increase or diminu-

* See more on Money-wages, in chapter on Gross Profits.

tion."* He afterwards observes, "However much the market price of labour may deviate from its natural price, it has, like commodities, a tendency to conform to it." M. Storch, in his very valuable and comprehensive " *Cours d'Economie Politique*," supposes in like manner that labour has its " *Prix necessaire*," which it cannot fall below for any length of time. All above this he calls the " *Salaire superflu.*"

This idea appears to me to have no foundation in fact. There is an essential difference between labour and commodities. If any of these last fall below that price which is necessary to replace with a profit the cost of production, should a diminution in the quantity not be sufficient to raise it, the commodity will very soon cease entirely to be brought to market. But with labour the case is otherwise. To establish a perfect analogy between the two, we must be prepared to contend, that if the labourer cannot gain what is called the natural rate of wages, according to the definition above given, he will speedily desist altogether from working. But this is so far from true, that there is scarcely any pittance, however small, which will not induce him to toil, *provided he can get no more*. He will not sit down quietly and starve. What though his reward be not sufficient to support a family? It may still keep off from himself the pangs of hunger and the certainty of immediate destruction. He will therefore toil and toil on so

---

* Principles of Political Economy, chap. v.

long as his strength permits, however small his remuneration may be.

This state of things, moreover, may last for a long
time. Do we not know that there are countries in
which population has gone on declining for ages?
In Spain, for instance, this is said to have been the
case; and in Asia Minor, Syria, and Northern Africa,
the number of inhabitants has without doubt greatly
decreased since the fall of the Roman Empire. How
could this be, had wages in those countries been generally sufficient not only to sustain the labourer himself, but also to enable him to perpetuate his race
without diminution. It is vain, therefore, to say with
M. Storch, that labour has a *necessary price*, which
it cannot fall below for any length of time. Fortunate indeed would it be for humanity were this
always the case.

It is, I think, of some importance that our ideas
should be set right on this point. If we are per-
suaded that wages can never for any long period fall
below what is necessary for the support, not only of
the labourer himself, but also of his family, our sympathies will cease to be so warmly engaged in behalf
of the most numerous part of the population, we shall
consequently be less active in devising expedients
for improving their condition, and less alive to every
symptom of a declining state of society. Let us then
not forget, that the agony of a dying nation is not
over in a day.

It is singular enough, that what is called the na-

tural price of labour, should be of all the most uncommon. In very few countries, probably, has population ever for any great period been exactly stationary. In general it is either decreasing or advancing. That the numbers of men in any nation
may go on augmenting for a very long time, there
can be no doubt. The population of England has
been gradually progressing for centuries. During all
this period, then, the rate of wages has been higher
than that which is looked upon as natural or necessary. Finally, let us conclude, that the idea of Natural Price, correct in respect to commodities, is, as
regards labour, purely imaginary.*

In some respects, no doubt, there is a great analogy between the causes which regulate the prices of
labour and of commodities. That of the former, as
well as of the latter, depends immediately at least
on the proportion between the supply and demand.
Again, there are certain commodities, of which the
supply not being susceptible of increase at pleasure,
may therefore rise in value to any amount, according
to the demand, which will depend for its intensity
upon two circumstances; *first*, the excellence, or
supposed excellence of the product; *secondly*, its
scarcity. Such are particular sorts of wines, precious
stones, &c. So likewise there are kinds of labour of

---

* Mr. Ricardo himself allows a little further on, that " Notwithstanding the tendency of wages to conform to their natural rate, their
market rate may, in an improving society, for an indefinite period, be
constantly above it."

which the reward appears extravagantly great as
compared with that of others. Such is the labour of
first-rate painters and statuaries, of accomplished
actors, musicians, and singers. The high prices paid
for the services of these persons is owing to causes
similar to those which determine the excessive value
of tokay or rubies, namely, the scarcity of such eminent talents, which very few are capable of acquiring, and the great beauty or vigour of their per-
formances.

Here, however, the analogy ends. By far the
greater number of commodities have a fixed price
determined by their cost of production, above or below which they can seldom remain for any length of
time. None, at all events, can long fall below it.
But it is not so with labour. There is no determined
rate at which its remuneration finally settles; but
the reward may for ages be very different in different
regions, according to circumstances, which have now
been explained. While it enables the countryman
who tills the ground on the banks of the Ohio, to
support in health and comfort a numerous offspring,
a handful of rice may be the portion of him who toils
from morning to night on those of the Kian-Ku.

CHAPTER III.

ON GROSS PROFITS.

HAVING now traced the causes which determine what
portion of the whole produce of industry shall go to
the Labourer, it remains to be seen what are the circumstances which regulate the share of the Master-
capitalist. It has been above observed, that where
rent is out of the question, there are but three classes
of persons who can have any pretensions to a part in
the gross return, labourers, capitalists, and masters.
Reasons, moreover, have been given, why, in the present investigation, the attributes of these last two
classes, should, in the first instance at least, be considered as united in one and the same individual. It
has also been mentioned, that I use the word Profit
taken generally, in the sense in which it is commonly
employed by English writers on political economy.

Gross Profit then is the entire surplus which remains to the master-capitalist after paying the wages
of labour, and replacing the fixed capital consumed.
In the case where rent exists, this also must be deducted before the amount of profit can be known.
But what is meant by replacing fixed capital? In
what manner is a comparison to be instituted between

the product and the stock expended upon it? The
latter may consist of a great variety of articles,
all of them perhaps different in kind from the former;
how then can we determine whether the one be
greater or less than the other, or in what proportion?
In a cotton manufactory for instance, the advances of
the master-capitalist, independently of wages, consist
of raw material, machinery, and buildings. What
comparison can be made between these and the finished commodity calico? This relation can take place
only between objects similar. In agriculture the one
has more analogy to the other, since a great part of
the advances for seed, horses' food, &c. consists of
corn or other articles of raw produce, which also make
up the return. But even here, machines, implements,
manure, and other things are employed which do not
in the least correspond with the nature of those commodities which they help to raise. There must then
be some other way of comparing produce with expenditure, at least in individual instances. With regard
to a whole nation, however, the case is different. It
is evident that all the various elements of the stock
expended must be reproduced in some employment or
another, otherwise the industry of the country could
not go on as formerly. The raw material of manufactures, the implements used in them, as also in
agriculture, the extensive machinery engaged in the
former, the buildings necessary for fabricating or
storing the produce, must all be parts of the total
return of a country, as well as of the advances of all

its master-capitalists. Therefore, the quantity of the former may be compared with that of the latter, each article being supposed placed as it were beside that of a similar kind.

This being premised, we may proceed to inquire in the first place, what determines the total profit of all the master-capitalists of a nation?

It will not be difficult to prove that it must depend upon two causes.

First, Upon the Quantity of the Gross Return as compared with the Quantity of all things expended upon it, in other words, on the degree of Productiveness of Industry.

Secondly, Upon the share in this gross return which falls to the Labourers, that is, on the rate of Wages.

I shall, for the sake of simplicity, suppose that this share, instead of being advanced to the workmen, does not accrue to them until the completion of the product. This can make no change in the real nature of the case. The advances of the master-capitalist will on this supposition consist of those objects only of which fixed capital is composed.

Now, the amount of fixed capital engaged throughout the nation generally, and the quantity of labour applied in conjunction with it, being given, the greater the quantity of all things raised, the greater is the productiveness of labour and capital. And the greater the productiveness, the larger must be the total amount to be divided between master-capitalists and labourers. Now, if the reward of the latter be supposed to remain the same, it is quite evident that every increase in the productiveness of industry generally, must cause a corresponding augmentation in the quantity of that part of the national return which falls to the share of the whole body of master-capitalists. Consequently, the more will remain to them, after replacing the quantity of all things expended as fixed capital, which, by the supposition, undergoes no change. That is, their profits will rise with every increase in the productive powers of labour and stock. If so, the data remaining unchanged, they must fall with every diminution of those powers.

Therefore, it is proved that this productiveness is *one* cause at least, which regulates the amount of national profits.

If we now imagine that the return to labour and capital remains constant, what are the causes which in this case can occasion a rise or fall in profits? On this supposition, the whole quantity produced being given, the amount of profit must depend entirely upon the mode in which the sum total is divided between those entitled to a share in it, that is, the master-capitalists and labourers. The more that goes to one, the less can there be for the other; the higher the portion of the latter, the smaller must be that of the former. But on which side is found the active cause which determines the proportion in which the produce is divided? Clearly on that of the labourers, by the increase or diminution of whose numbers the rate of wages is determined. Therefore, it is correct to say that the share of the gross return which falls to the master-capitalist, will vary inversely as that of the labourer, that it will rise as wages fall, and fall as wages rise. But the larger the portion of the former, the greater will be the surplus which remains to him, after replacing the whole of his advances; that is, the higher will be the rate of profit. Therefore, on the supposition that the productiveness of industry remains the same, profit will rise or fall according as the labourer's share in the gross produce diminishes or increases, in other words, in proportion as wages fall or rise.

But it was before proved that if wages continue unchanged, profit will vary directly in proportion to the increased or diminished productiveness of capital and labour. Therefore, it is evident that profit varies directly as productiveness and inversely as the amount of wages. These then are the two causes which regulate the rate of national profit.

Before commencing this investigation, I supposed, for the sake of simplicity, that the reward of labour or wages were not paid until the completion of the commodity. It is now necessary to remark, that this is the only way in which we can form a proper idea in regard to the expense to which the nation at large is put, in the work of production. We must not confound the waste of raw materials, implements, machinery, building, &c. in short, all the elements of fixed capital with the consumption of the labourers. The first alone, as already observed, is a pure ex-

pense, cost or sacrifice, in itself benefiting no one, forming the revenue of no one.   Independent of its results,
it is a pure loss.   Not so with the circulating capital
which supports the labourers, that is, the great majority of every state.   Each individual master-capitalist
no doubt, reckons the amount which he pays away in
wages as a part of his expenses, but nationally considered it is not so.   As well might the consumption of
the master or capitalist, whether united in the same
person or not, be counted as an element of cost of
production.   They must live, and so must the labourer,
otherwise no work can be done, but still what they
spend on themselves has no more right to be estimated
in the expense of producing, in the one case, than in
the other.   Wages, then, as well as profits, are to be
considered each of them as really a portion of the
finished product, totally distinct in a national point of
view, from the cost of raising it.   This cost, so far as
objects constituting wealth are concerned, consists,
as I have said, of all those materials of which fixed
capital is made up, and of those only.

But, besides this, labour itself, not what is paid for
it, ought to be reckoned as another element of cost of
production.   Labour is essential to production, every
portion of it therefore is highly useful; but, as in the
case of fixed capital, from its result only, being in itself a pain, or at least a sacrifice of ease which no one
would submit to but from the prospect of remuneration.   The more of it expended in one employment,
the less can there be for another, and therefore if ap-

plied to unprofitable undertakings, there is not only to the individuals a loss of ease without requital, but the nation suffers from the waste of the principal source of wealth. From all this, it will, I think, appear, that I am perfectly correct in classing Labour along with Fixed capital as the two elements of cost of production in a national point of view.*

I am the more anxious to show that the reward of labour ought not to be considered as an element of cost, on account of the consequences which have been drawn from an opposite supposition. Starting from the principle that it is good to diminish the expenses of production as much as possible, and then assuming wages to form one part of these, it has been concluded that the lower the rate at which labour is paid, the better for the nation. Now, the object of Political Economy being to show, not only how the greatest amount of wealth may be obtained, but also how it may be distributed most advantageously among the different classes of society, that must be allowed to be a strange system which would give as little as possible to by far the most numerous body of all, the labourers. This, it is evident, would be a distribution of riches the most adverse of all to the general happiness, nor, as appears from what has been said above, does

---

* See chapter on Production. See also "Wealth of Nations," book i. chap. 5. This is also quite agreeable to common notions and the ordinary use of language; for we constantly hear people say, such a thing has *cost* me much labour or much trouble.

it by any means necessarily follow, that the total amount of these would thereby be increased.

The only effect of this state of things would be, that a portion of the national wealth which otherwise would have been divided among a great number of labourers, must now go to swell the profits of the much smaller body, the master-capitalists. There would be a change in the distribution of riches less favourable to the general happiness, but no alteration in the gross amount. But as the class of master-manufacturers, and others, from their wealth and power, are much more readily attended to in their clamours, than that of labourers, they have generally succeeded in making it believed, that whatever raises their profit must be a national benefit. If this rise be owing to an improvement in the productive powers of labour and capital, they are in the right; but if to be attributed to a fall of wages, they indeed obtain an advantage, but not so the nation, nay, rather it is injured in its most numerous class.

It may indeed be said, although it be granted that in the case of a rise in profits occasioned by a fall in wages, there is merely a change in the distribution of wealth, and none in the actual amount; yet, since masters and capitalists are likely to *save* more than the labourers, therefore such an arrangement as places a larger share of the whole produce in the hands of the former, will have a greater tendency to favour the accumulation of capital, and the future increase of national riches. I shall not now consider how far this may be correct; but, for the present, even granting it to be true, I hesitate not to say, that such an acceleration in the progress of wealth would be dearly purchased, by abridging the comforts, or even luxuries of the great body of the labouring population.

Having now traced the causes which regulate the rate of national profit, as arising from all the various branches of industry, it remains to be seen whether the same principles apply to individual cases, after the division of employments has become established.*

It was remarked above, since the various elements of the capital advanced in any particular occupation are, some, if not all, of a different sort from the product, that consequently they cannot be compared together in *kind*, so as to determine the proportion in which the one exceeds the other. For the same reason, no part of the result can be set aside so as completely to *replace* in the strictest sense of the word, the various objects consumed in the course of the work. Some, no doubt, may be replaced *in kind*, but not all. By far the greater number must be obtained by ex-

---

* It does not seem necessary to discuss at large the principles which regulate the profits of individuals *previous* to the division of employments. For, as on this supposition, each master-capitalist raises all those articles which he may require for a future production, this case becomes exactly the same as that of the nation at large. He and his labourers form of themselves a little community, or nation as it were, independent of all others. In an economical sense they do in truth constitute a nation.

change, a certain portion of the product being necessary for this purpose.

Hence each individual master-capitalist comes to
look much more to the exchangeable value of his
product than to its quantity. The various objects
which once constituted the capital now expended by
him, being themselves possessed of value in exchange,
cannot be replaced without sacrificing for that end a
certain part of the finished commodity. Therefore,
the more the value of the product exceeds the value
of the capital advanced, the greater will be his profit.
Thus, then, will he estimate it, by comparing value
with value, not quantity with quantity. This is the
first difference to be remarked in the mode of reckoning profits between nations and individuals. The
second is, that, since the master-capitalist always
makes an advance of wages to the labourers, instead
of paying them out of the finished commodity, he
considers this as well as the fixed capital consumed,
a part of his expenses, though, we have seen, nationally speaking, it is not an element of cost. Hence
his rate of profit will depend upon the excess in the
value of his product over and above the value of the
capital advanced, both fixed and circulating.

Let us attend to this distinction. Cost of production, as we have seen, when considered in a national
or general point of view, which is the one proper to
political economy, includes two elements, labour and
fixed capital. But, we now find that it is understood
in a different sense by each individual master-capita-

list. The whole value of the capital advanced by him, whether fixed or circulating, constitutes his private expense. I had already pointed out this distinction, the importance of which here becomes manifest. We shall have occasion again to apply it when treating of Revenue. These things being premised, I may proceed to inquire how the profits of individuals are regulated.

And be it well observed *in limine*, that the question of Profit is essentially one of *Proportion*. However great the whole return to industry may be, if the share of it which goes to replace, either directly or by means of exchange, the fixed and circulating capital advanced remain the same, the proportion which the rest bears to this share must also be the same, whether we compare the quantity of the latter part with the quantity of the former, or the value of the one with the value of the other. In either way of estimating profit, its *rate* must be unaltered. Its absolute amount, or the value of that amount, may be doubled, tripled, but if the expenditure or its value be also increased in the same ratio, the *rate* of profit is the same. Profit, therefore, must rise or fall exactly as the proportion of the gross produce, or of its value, required to replace necessary advances, falls or rises. But these necessary advances consist of two parts, first, of circulating capital or labourers maintenance; secondly, of fixed capital. Therefore, the rate of profit must depend immediately upon two circumstances; first, the proportion of the whole pro-

duce which goes to the labourers; secondly, the proportion which must be set apart for replacing, either
in kind or by exchange, the fixed capital. What
then determines the proportion which the labourer
receives? To that inquiry we now proceed.

We have seen that, after the division of employments, the master-capitalist regards much more the
value of his product than its quantity. Still, there
are some employments in which the quantity of the
return, independently of its value, will have a material effect upon the rate of profit, not in those occupations only, but in all. Such are the branches of
industry by which are raised and fabricated those articles of primary necessity wherein the wages of labour chiefly consist. I shall now proceed to prove
this.

Let us suppose that the productiveness of agricultural labour and capital is diminished. The quantity
then of all the elements of fixed capital, such as seed,
implements, &c., remaining the same, as also the
quantity of labour employed, the return is no longer
so abundant as formerly. But though no longer so
abundant, the produce will nevertheless soon rise to
a value as great as before, since the expenses attending its production are as considerable. The smaller
quantity then, will have as high an exchangeable
value as the larger previously possessed. Now, let
us suppose that the entire produce is divided into two
portions, the one destined to replace what has been
paid away to the labourers, the other to restore the

fixed capital consumed, and afford a profit on the whole. By the supposition, real wages, the real amount of necessaries and comforts enjoyed by the labourer, undergo no alteration. These wages, we may conceive, to be paid by the farmer in corn and other articles of agricultural produce. This amount of corn, &c., may be imagined to be divided into two parts, the one is consumed by the labourer in kind for his subsistence, the other is exchanged by him for those manufactured articles of which he may stand in need. Now, it is clear, that if real wages remain the same, there can be no alteration in the quantity of the former of those parts. For, if this quantity were diminished, the labourer would be fed less liberally than before, that is, his real wages would fall, which is contrary to the supposition. The quantity, then, of this part remains the same. As for the other part into which his wages are divided, this no doubt will be diminished in quantity, just in proportion as the produce has risen in value, that is, in proportion to the falling off in the total return to the labour and capital applied. As he does not consume this part of his wages in kind, but exchanges it for other things, it is its value alone in which he is concerned. If it will command as much of manufactured articles as before, he will be as well off as formerly. But the quantity of the gross produce necessary to secure to him a value as great as he previously enjoyed, though absolutely less, must still bear as great a proportion to the whole as before, since value has risen only in the same ratio as quantity has diminished. As for the part of wages which is consumed as food without being exchanged, this we have found, continues to be absolutely as great a quantity as formerly, notwithstanding the diminished productiveness of agricultural industry. Therefore the whole return being less, this part must form a greater proportion of the whole than it did previously. And as the other part of wages which is exchanged for manufactured goods, bears the same proportion as before to the whole, therefore the quantity required altogether for wages, must constitute a greater share of the gross produce. Consequently, the portion which remains for replacing fixed capital and for profit, must be a smaller share of the whole than formerly. Therefore the value also of this share must bear a smaller proportion to the value of the whole, for in the case of similar commodities, value of course varies as quantity. Whatever a quarter of corn may be worth, the value of two or three quarters must always be double or triple that of one.

The value then of that portion of the gross return which goes to replace the fixed capital expended, and to afford a profit on the total advances, forms a less proportion of the value of the whole, in consequence of agricultural industry becoming less productive. But no alteration has taken place in the fixed capital. The quantity of seed, the number of implements, &c. are supposed to remain the same, and there is no possible reason to imagine that the value of any of these has declined. Therefore, out of that portion of the total return which is left for replacing fixed capital, and for profit, an amount of produce must be set aside for the former purpose, possessing a value as great at least as before. But the value of this entire portion bears now a smaller ratio than it did to the value of the whole. Consequently, after separating from it a value equal to that of the fixed capital expended which continues the same, the value of the remainder which constitutes profit, must bear a proportion less than formerly to the value of the gross return. Thus, we see that the value of that part of the product which composes profit, as compared with the value of all the rest, is less than it was previous to the falling off in the return to agricultural industry. That is, the rate of profit has fallen in consequence of diminished productiveness.

We here see also in what manner an increased difficulty of raising raw produce operates so as to cause a fall in profits. Though the return to fixed capital and labour be less than before, yet as the value of the product rises in proportion to the falling off in the quantity, it might at first sight appear that the profit of the farmer would remain the same. That it does not, is owing to the circumstance of a greater proportion of the whole produce falling to the share of the labourer, which greater proportion is necessary to secure to him the same reward as formerly.

But though real wages remain the same, yet as

the labourer receives a greater proportion of the gross amount, he must obtain a greater value. Wages, therefore, will seem to rise, they will rise as estimated in any commodity other than raw produce, in money for instance. Money-wages then will advance, but only so as to compensate the augmentation in the price of those necessaries which they are intended to purchase. Therefore the condition of the labourer cannot be improved on that account.

But it is not the profit of the farmer alone which is diminished in consequence of an increased difficulty in raising raw produce. That of all other master-capitalists suffers to a similar extent. Let us take the case of the manufacturer. No change being supposed to occur in the productiveness of labour and capital in his branch of industry, the quantity of the return to these will undergo no alteration. Neither will the power of exchanging, possessed by this quantity, differ from what it was, with one important exception, namely, the capacity of purchasing raw produce which has risen in value in consequence of the diminished productiveness of agricultural industry. Therefore, to procure the same amount of corn, &c. a greater quantity of manufactured goods must now be given. Whatever, then, may have been the portion of the finished commodity which formerly sufficed for purchasing subsistence for the manufacturing labourers, it is evident that a larger share must now go for that purpose, supposing real wages to remain the same. As for that part of the product

which went to supply the other wants of the workman either directly or by means of exchange, as neither the quantity of the whole return fabricated, nor
its value, except as estimated in raw produce, has undergone any alteration, so neither can the above part
be in any way different from what it was. But that
part which goes to procure food for the labourer is
increased, therefore, on the whole, his share in the
gross amount is greater than before. Therefore the
share which remains for the master must be less.
Consequently, the *value* also of his share must bear a
smaller proportion to the whole value than formerly.
Therefore, after replacing the fixed capital, for which
purpose there will be required a portion as great
certainly as before, whether of the entire quantity or
of the total value, since neither of these have changed,
what is left for profit estimated either in quantity or
value, will bear a smaller ratio to the whole than it
did previous to the increased difficulty of raising raw
produce.

Thus then it appears that the above cause reduces
the rate of profit not in agriculture only, but in manufactures. The same must be the case in commerce,
in every employment, in short, in which human labour
is engaged.

In a similar manner it may be shown that an *increased* productiveness of agricultural industry causes
a rise of profit not in that occupation only, but in all.
To prove the one, is in fact to prove the other.

But it is not an increased or diminished productiveness of agricultural industry alone which influences the rate of profit. The same is true of that which is employed in manufacturing those articles which either nature or custom has rendered necessary to the labourer. A falling off in the return to the labour and and fixed capital so engaged, has precisely a similar effect upon profit, to that resulting from a diminution in raw produce. The only difference is, that the farmer and manufacturer now change places, as it were, in our argument. The effect, moreover, is less considerable, since by far the greater part of wages generally consists of food.

The fixed capital of the master, that is, the amount of raw material, the machines and buildings remaining the same, as also the quantity of labour employed, the produce, of coarse cloth for instance, is supposed to be no longer so abundant. But as this decreases, value rises in proportion, since the expenses have undergone no change. The value of the whole then remains the same as before. But the quantity of cloth required to dress the labourers, if real wages do not vary, must be absolutely as great as formerly. Therefore, just as was shown in the case of agricultural produce, it necessarily comes to pass that a greater proportion of the whole return falls to their share. Consequently, a smaller proportion must remain to the master-capitalist for replacing fixed capital and for profit. And since it requires at all events as great a part of the whole as before for the former purpose, a less must necessarily be left for the latter.

Now, this increased difficulty of fabricating coarse cloth will operate upon the profits of the farmer and others, exactly in the same way as a falling off in the productiveness of agricultural industry acts, as we have seen, upon those of the manufacturer, and in truth, of every description of master-capitalist. Though both the quantity of the return to every other occupation remain the same, as well as its value, except as estimated in those coarse goods, the value of which is supposed to have risen on account of the greater difficulty attending their production, yet this exception is sufficient to render it necessary that a greater share of the total produce of every industrious employment should go to the labourers, in order that they may command the same quantity of necessaries as formerly. Therefore a less share is left for replacing fixed capital and for profit.

Thus we see that a falling off in the powers of the manufacturing labour and capital employed upon those coarse goods which the labourer requires, causes the very same effect upon the general rate of profit as a diminished productiveness in agriculture. The *degree* of that effect may be very different, but its nature is similar. And of course an increase in the above powers must lead to an opposite result, just as in the other case.

Seldom, if ever, after manufactures have fairly been

established in any country, do we hear of a decline in the quantity of the return to the labour and capital employed upon them; but on the contrary, we are frequently told of a great increase. In agriculture the case is reversed, raw produce in the progress of society being raised with more and more difficulty, on account of the necessity of having recourse to poorer soils after all the better have been fully cultivated. Hence profit is acted upon continually by two opposite causes, the one tending to raise, the other to depress it.

To the argument above stated, but two objections, I conceive, can be opposed.

Taking the case of the farmer, it may be said, that, when the return to the labour and capital which he sets in motion is diminished, there are two ways by which he may maintain his profit at its former rate. He may either raise the value of his produce in a ratio higher than the diminution of the quantity, so as to compensate his being obliged to give the labourers a greater proportion of the whole amount, (in other words, on account of the increased money-wages which he pays); or he may throw the loss upon the workmen by reducing their real wages.

Now, as to the first supposition, be it remarked that I have shewn that the falling off in the return to agricultural industry would affect not the farmer only, but likewise all other master-capitalists. Every one of them in whatever occupation he might be engaged, would be obliged to give a greater proportion of his produce in payment of labour. Now, whatever loss affects all masters simultaneously, none can escape from by change of employment.

In vain would the farmer desert his land, and turn his capital to something else; wherever he went he would meet the same evil. Consequently, there could not on this account be any tendency to desert the cultivation of the soil, and therefore no rise in the price of its produce from this cause.

The argument here made use of is in fact identical with that formerly employed to shew that the value of commodities is not affected by a rise or fall of real wages. The same holds true of money-wages, which, as now shewn, are regulated by the productiveness of the labour and capital employed in raising and fabricating commodities of the first necessity. For no alteration is supposed in real wages, nor in the circumstances connected with the production of money, both of which influence the quantity of the precious metals received by the labourer.

A variation in money-wages proceeding from the above cause affects all master-capitalists simultaneously, just as a fluctuation in real wages does. Consequently the effect upon value must be the same in both cases.

Now, it was formerly proved, that although a rise or fall in real wages could not cause a general rise or fall in the value of commodities, yet that it effected some alteration in the relative values of different objects, raising some and depressing others. We

found that an augmentation in real wages would
have the effect of elevating the value of those articles,
the quantity of labour employed upon which is great
as compared with the fixed capital; supposing this
value to be estimated in other commodities, in the
production of which the proportion of these two
sources of wealth is reversed. It was shewn that the
value of agricultural produce for instance would rise
as measured by many manufactured articles. The
same will happen upon an increase in money-wages
caused by a decrease in the powers of industry. It
is quite evident that the farmer who employs so
many labourers, must suffer much more by such an
augmentation than the master-manufacturer, great
part of whose outlay consists in machinery, raw material, and other elements of fixed capital. If, therefore, the produce of the former did not rise as compared with that of the latter, the profits of the cultivator would be reduced in a greater proportion than
those of others. But this cannot be, so long as the
transference of capital from one employment to another remains free and unimpeded. Consequently,
the value of agricultural produce will rise as estimated by the quantity it will command of those articles,
the fabrication of which mainly depends on fixed
capital.

As measured by these commodities then, the augmentation in the value of corn consequent on diminished productiveness, will be greater than merely in
proportion to the falling off in the quantity. Through

this rise the farmer will be able to supply the wants of his labourers for clothes, &c., by means of a somewhat smaller share of the total return than formerly went for this purpose, and thus will maintain his profit on a level with that of others.

In this way, and to this extent only, can a variation in money-wages, (that is, in the proportion of the gross produce received by the labourer,) affect the value of commodities. It can neither raise nor depress them generally, but only change the ratio between them, elevating some as compared with others, which it lowers in a corresponding degree.

In truth, the very notion of a general rise or fall in the value of commodities seems to involve an absurdity. For, were all things to rise or fall, the proportion in which they would exchange for one another would be exactly the same as if they remained stationary. This has been already observed. It is only in reference to the cause of value, cost of production, that the idea can be conceived at all, but if this rise or fall universally, there may be less of every thing raised, but any fixed quantity of one commodity will still command or exchange for the same quantity of another. Each object will still have the same power of purchasing as before, if the expences attending its production, though absolutely greater, be still relatively the same; so that both the *effect*, exchangeable power or value, properly so called, and the *cause*, cost of raising, may, when different articles are compared, still in all cases bear to each

other the same ratio. And value is essentially a relative quality. If the circumstances attending the
production of money alone did not vary, then indeed
all other commodities might rise or fall in Price. But
this would be a matter in itself of no consequence
whatever, at least so far as profit is concerned.
Though the master-capitalist might sell his produce
for a greater sum of money than before, yet as he
would be obliged to give more for every article, both
of fixed and circulating capital, his profit would, after
all, be exactly the same.

The other objection urged against the conclusion
we lately arrived at is, that upon a falling off in the
productiveness of agricultural industry, as well as of
that employed in fabricating coarse goods, the master-capitalist will reduce the rate at which he formerly paid his labourers, and by this deduction from
real wages, profit may be kept up to the same level
as before. But the rate of wages is regulated by
causes peculiar to itself, depending, immediately at
least, upon the proportion between the supply of labour and the demand. These conditions remaining
the same, no alteration in the real reward of labour
will ensue upon a change in the gross return to it and
fixed capital. If diminished productiveness cause a
decline in the demand for workmen, then, no doubt,
a part at least of the loss will fall upon them. But
this is only a conditional and remote effect of the
above cause, not a necessary and immediate one.
Should the decrease in productiveness be considerable

and permanent, then, no doubt, real wages must also suffer, otherwise the whole of profit would be swallowed up, which, for any length of time, is of course impossible. And this is what really occurs in all countries as the return to agricultural industry progressively declines, in consequence of inferior soils being forced into cultivation, to supply the increasing wants of the people. Wages and profits are both affected, but in what proportion the loss may fall on each must depend on the prudent or improvident habits of the labouring part of the community. At all events, there can be no reason to suppose that the whole injury is sustained by this the most numerous body.

An argument similar to the above applies to the supposition, that an increase of real wages would result from an improved productiveness of agricultural or manufacturing industry. The one case is just the converse of the other. If the whole benefit of this increase be not felt by the master, at least a part of it will.

These objections then being removed, the conclusion we arrived at remains unshaken, that an increased or diminished return to the labour and fixed capital employed in producing those commodities of primary necessity, which chiefly make up the wages of labour, causes a rise or fall in the rate of profit. And we have seen that this effect is brought about by an alteration in the proportion of the gross produce which falls to the share of the labourer, this proportion being lowered in the one case, in the other raised.

We have thus found, that *one* cause, at all events, of an alteration in the proportion of the gross return which becomes the share of the labourers, and hence in the rate of profit, is an improvement or decline in the productive powers of industry. But is this the only cause? Certainly not. A rise or fall in real wages will have exactly the same effect in increasing or diminishing the proportion of the whole return, or of its value, necessary to replace the advances made to the labourers.

The degree of productiveness of industry is now supposed to remain unchanged, but a general rise to take place in real wages, that is, in the amount of necessaries and comforts received by the workman. Now, the total return to a similar application of labour and fixed capital remaining the same in any branch of employment, if the value be also constant, it is evident, upon a rise of wages, that a greater proportion of the whole, or of its value, must be set apart for maintaining labour, and consequently, that a less will remain for replacing fixed capital and for profit. And what occurs in this particular department of industry will take place in all. If the value of commodities remain unchanged, each master-capitalist will be obliged to separate for wages a greater share of his produce, or of the value of the same. A smaller, therefore, will be left over. But the same proportion of the whole as formerly, will be required for restoring, either directly or by exchange, the fixed capital consumed in any employment, if the value of things has not altered. Consequently, a smaller part of the gross return or of its value will remain for profit.

But it may be said, every thing will rise in value. In treating the subject of value, as well as in the remarks just made upon a rise of money-wages, I have, I think, sufficiently proved the absurdity of this supposition. I have shewn, that whatever affects all occupations, and all equally, has no more influence upon value than if it did not exist. That the idea of a general rise in the value of all things, involves, in fact, a contradiction, and that a general rise of prices could not cause the least alteration in profits one way or another. That a certain change, however, would ensue in the value of commodities, some rising, as compared with others, which decline in a corresponding degree. I also explained, that this arose from the increase of wages being felt more severely in some occupations than in others, in those, namely, in which the quantity of labour immediately applied is great, and the value of fixed capital small. Finally, that this change, in the relations of commodities to one another, by no means exempted the master-capitalists from suffering in their profits, nor even at all diminished their total loss, but only served to distribute it more equally among the different orders composing that body.

Therefore, it may be considered as proved, that a

general rise of real wages increases the proportion of the gross produce, or of its value, which goes to the share of the labourers, and causes a corresponding fall in the rate of profit.

At the commencement of this inquiry, I remarked, that the circumstances which immediately determine the rate of profit, are, first, the proportion of the whole produce received by the labourers; secondly, the proportion which must be set apart for replacing fixed capital. It was observed, that whatever the absolute quantity of the return might be, if these proportions continued unaltered, the rate of profit could not be affected.

Now, we have seen, that the proportion belonging to the labourers depends upon two causes,—

First, the Productiveness of the Labour and Fixed Capital employed in raising articles of primary necessity—the elements, in fact, of real wages.

Secondly, the Rate of the real reward of Labour. It remains to be known what are the causes which regulate the proportion of the gross produce, or of its value, necessary for replacing fixed capital.

To me it seems certain, that an increased facility of raising the various objects which enter into the composition of fixed capital, tends, by diminishing this proportion, to raise the rate of profit, just as in the former case of an augmented return of the elements of circulating capital, which serves to maintain labour.

Let us suppose a society divided into two distinct

classes of producers, agriculturists and manufacturers, the former employed in raising not merely corn
or other sorts of food, but also raw materials, such
as flax, hemp, wool, wood,—every thing in short necessary to make up their own fixed capital, as well
as that of the latter. Now let us imagine, that in
consequence of improvements in the processes of cultivation, the return to the agricultural labour and
capital is doubled. No change is supposed to take
place in the quantity of manufactured goods. This
being the case, though the value of any fixed portion
of agricultural produce will fall very much as compared with fabricated articles, yet as this fall will be
simply in proportion to the increase in the total return to farming industry, the total value of the former, as measured by the latter, will be the same as
before. In regard to manufactured goods, the quantity of which has not changed, as each portion of
them will command a greater amount of raw produce
than formerly, so likewise will the whole. The value,
then, of the farmer's gross return, as measured by
wrought goods, will be the same as previously, while
that of the manufacturer's entire product, as estimated in corn, &c. will be greater. And I think it
will appear evident, that without supposing any dis-
placing of capital, the profits of both will be increased.

First as to the farmer. A very great part of those
various elements necessary for production, which I
have included under the general term of fixed capi-

tal, can be supplied by the cultivator, out of the produce of his own farm. This is the case with the seed he commits to the ground, the food of his labouring horses, and of cattle, whether labouring or not, also the materials of his implements, in part at least.. Now, be the amount of the gross return small or great, the quantity of it required for replacing what has been consumed in these different forms, can undergo no alteration whatsoever. This quantity must be considered as constant, so long as production is carried on on the same scale. Consequently, the larger the total return, the less must be the proportion of the whole which the farmer must set aside for the above purposes.

I have said, that the quantity set aside for replacing fixed capital must be considered as constant. For, in estimating increased productiveness, we may either suppose the labour and fixed capital to remain the same, and the return to be augmented, or those elements of cost to be diminished, and the result to continue unaltered. And having adopted the former mode of reckoning, that fixed capital should be invariable, is, of course, a part of the preliminary conditions of the question.

But to return to the case I have above supposed. We found that the value of the gross produce of the agriculturist, as compared with manufactured articles, remained the same. But now we see, that a smaller proportion of this sum total, and consequently of its value, is required for restoring the various elements of fixed capital with which the farmer can supply himself. Therefore, *on this account*, a greater must be left for profit.

I have here made no allusion to an alteration in the rate of profit, resulting from a change in the proportion of the whole, which may go to the labourers, in consequence of the increased productiveness of agricultural industry. It is sufficient to remark, that from the principles above laid down, it follows, that this cause would not act contrary to the one we are now considering, but in the same direction.

But to proceed. How is the manufacturer affected? His return continues the same in *quantity*; but its *value*, as estimated in agricultural products, is, as we have found, increased. Consequently, a smaller proportion of it will suffice, for procuring from the farmer, by exchange, those various elements of fixed capital with which the latter can supply him, such as the raw material of manufactures, and other articles necessary for implements, machinery, and buildings. Therefore, *on this account* again, a greater proportion must be left for profit.

Thus we see, that profit would rise in both occupations, and that without any transference of labour or capital from the one to the other. The augmentation of the farmer's profit would be owing to the increase in the *quantity* of his produce, its *total* value remaining the same; while the manufacturer would be benefited by the greater power of purchasing possessed by his.

Exactly in a similar manner it may be shewn, that a greater difficulty in raising the various objects which enter into the composition of fixed capital, by increasing the proportion of the gross produce necessary for replacing it, tends to lower the rate of profit.

I shall now proceed to show, that an increased or diminished productiveness of the industry employed in raising commodities which do *not* enter into the composition of fixed capital, can have no influence on the rate of profit, except by affecting the proportion of the gross amount which goes to maintain labour.

Taking the case above stated, let us now however suppose, that instead of the products of the farmer, those of the manufacturer are doubled, by improvements in machinery and in the division of labour, the cost, of course, still remaining the same. However great for a time the profits of some masters may be, still it is certain, that ultimately the value of wrought goods must fall in the same proportion as the quantity has increased, so that the value of the sum total, as measured in agricultural products, will be the same as before. Therefore the proportion of the gross return necessary for purchasing from the farmer the various elements of capital expended, whether fixed or circulating, will be unchanged. Therefore no effect will be produced on the rate of profit in this way. No doubt the manufacturer will be able to clothe his workmen by means of a smaller proportion of the entire return, as has been shewn above, and thus his profit will be raised. But in no other manner will it be influenced.

Again, in consequence of the great increase in the return to manufacturing industry, the corn, &c. of the farmer will command a much greater quantity of wrought goods than formerly. The value, then, of his gross produce, as measured in fabricated articles, will rise. But the value of the food of labourers, of that of horses and cattle, of seed, &c. all which are advanced by himself, rises exactly in the same ratio as the result; this last being in fact composed of these very elements. If then these made up his whole expenditure, profit would bear the same proportion to it as before, both being increased in value, and in the same degree. But they do not constitute his whole expenses. The labourers must be clothed as well as fed; and this clothing the farmer will obtain, by the sacrifice of a smaller proportion of his produce, as has already been shown at full. Therefore in this way, but in this way only, would his profit be affected, as was that of the manufacturer.

Thus it appears, that however great may be the increased return of those commodities which do *not* enter into the composition of Fixed Capital, it is by changing the proportion which goes to Wages, and by this alone, that the improved productiveness influences the rate of profit in any occupation. If, then, there be any articles which help to make up neither fixed capital nor circulating, it follows that profit can in no way be affected by any alteration in the facilities for raising these. Such are luxuries of all kinds. Though the proof of this might already appear sufficient, yet at the risk of being tedious, I shall still proceed to illustrate this case more at length.

Let us suppose a society composed on the one part of farmers employed in raising corn and other necessaries; on the other, of a class of Agriculturists, whose sole occupation is to cultivate the vine. Let us now imagine, that by means of improved methods of planting, dressing, pruning, &c. the quantity of grapes, and hence of wine, grown and made at the same expence, is increased twofold. But the value of the liquor will soon fall in proportion to the augmentation in its quantity. On the other hand, the value of the corn-farmer's produce will rise as compared with wine. But the value of his expenditure rises also as estimated in this beverage, precisely in the same ratio; for wine forms no part of his advances, neither of the fixed capital, nor of that required to maintain labour. Therefore the proportion between the value of Reproduction and that of Expenditure, always estimated in wine, will remain constant. Of course the corn farmer will be benefited by the increased quantity of wine, for his profit will go much farther in the purchase of it; but still the rate of that profit will not be changed; for his capital, were he to employ it in that manner, would also procure him a proportionally greater stock of that liquor.

It is evident also, that the profit of the vine grower continues the same. Though his produce has increased in quantity twofold, yet its value as measured by the corn of the farmer has diminished in the same ratio. The *total* value, then, of his gross product, remains the same.. Consequently, the same proportion of it will be required for purchasing from the farmer the elements of fixed capital he may stand in need of, such as vine stakes, &c., as well as for procuring subsistence for his labourers; since wine is supposed to form no part of that subsistence. Therefore the same proportion must be left over for profit; whether we compare quantity with quantity, or value with value. No doubt the vine grower will be benefited; for as the surplus is greater in absolute quantity, he will be able to consume more of his own liquor than formerly, without encroaching upon that share of it which he has been in the habit of exchanging for other things.

Thus it is, then, with luxuries of all descriptions. Master capitalists gain by the abundance, because their profits will command a greater quantity for their private consumption; but the rate of this profit is in no degree affected either by their plenty or scarcity.

If, in any country, wine be considered as a necessary part of the labourer's maintenance, then, indeed, a rise or fall in the productiveness of the labour and capital employed in raising the vine, would affect profit in the same way, though by no means to the same extent, as an increased or diminished facility attending the growth of corn.

I have now traced the causes which regulate the rate of profit in individual cases, after the division of employments has become established. These causes we have found to be,

1. The Productiveness of the Industry engaged in raising those articles of primary necessity which are required by the Labourer for Food, Clothing, &c.

2. The Productiveness of the Industry employed in raising those objects which enter into the composition of Fixed Capital.

3. The rate of Real Wages.

A variation in the *first* and *third* of these causes, acts upon profit by altering the proportion of the gross produce which goes to the labourer : a change in the *second* affects the same, by modifying the proportion necessary for replacing, either directly or by means of exchange, the fixed capital consumed in production ; for, as was shewn in the commencement, profit is essentially a question of proportion.

In discussing the subject of National profits, we had already seen that productiveness of industry in general, as well as the rate of real wages, were the causes on which these profits depend. And it was remarked, that the case of individuals previous to the division of employments, was similar to that of a nation at large. But now, in investigating the causes which regulate the profits of individuals after the division of employments, we have found that in some particular branches of industry, an increased or diminished productiveness has an influence upon these, while in others it has none. For it has been shewn, that a greater facility of producing luxuries has no effect upon the rate of profit. The master is benefited as a consumer, like any one else, but that is all. By an improved productiveness of other things, he gains doubly, both as a consumer, and as a master-capitalist. Therefore the conclusion we have now arrived at, while it fully confirms that previously drawn in treating of national profits, at the same time points out more explicitly to what limitations it is liable, by shewing that it is not, strictly speaking, every branch of industry, the degree of productiveness of which is of importance in the present question. And we have seen that the reason why a change in the productiveness of industry in certain branches affects profit, is this; that a quantity absolutely as great, of all objects composing fixed capital, is required, and one nearly as great of all those of which real wages are made up, whether the supply of the various articles therein comprised, be scanty or abundant. It is on account of the sameness in the absolute quantity of these two parts, that any increase or diminution of productiveness affects profit. If the two former be constant, of course the last must fluctuate. If exactly the same quantity always went for wages, then the whole loss or gain would fall to the master. But as real wages may rise or fall in some degree, the injury or benefit is thus often shared between him and the labourer. And thus we are naturally led to the other cause of a variation in profits, namely, a rise or fall in real wages.*

Having now traced the causes which determine the rate of profit, we shall be able to answer some questions which have arisen, and to refute some erroneous views which have been taken of this subject. It has been asked whether wages and profits can rise or fall together, or if they can both be higher or lower in one country than in another.

By attending to the principles above laid down, it will not be difficult to answer this.

Let us suppose a country newly settled, in which both capital and population are scanty in proportion to the extent of territory. In these circumstances, none but lands of the highest fertility, or those most advantageously situated in the neighbourhood of the sea, or a navigable river, will be occupied and cultivated. The return to the labour and capital employed in agriculture will consequently be very great. But as hands are scarce, wages will be high. Does

---

* Mr. Ricardo saw very well, that the question of profit was entirely one of proportion ; but unfortunately, he seems always to consider the whole produce as divided between wages and profits, forgetting the part necessary for replacing fixed capital. Hence he was led to conclude, that profits could be affected only by a rise or fall of wages ; by which he always means not Real but Money Wages. This theory is evidently incomplete, since profit, as we see, may vary from other causes. And even so far the fact is not properly stated, at least the ultimate cause of the variation in money wages, and hence in profits, is not pointed out, namely, a change in the productiveness of industry.

it therefore follow that profits will be low? By no means. Since the gross produce is so abundant, the true reward of the labourer, his command of the necessaries and comforts of life, though absolutely great, may still constitute but a small proportion of the whole, smaller even than in countries where real wages are lower. Consequently, a larger share of the total amount will be left for his employer. Thus, profits as well as wages may be higher than those of a country in opposite circumstances.

But the same productiveness of industry which serves to pay the labourers largely by means of a small proportion of the gross return, renders also a smaller share necessary for replacing the other expenses of the cultivator. The quantity of seed, of food for horses and cattle, remaining the same; the greater the produce, the less proportion of it, of course, will be required for those necessary outlays. Therefore, *on this account* also, profits will be high, whatever may be the rate of wages.

The conclusions thus arrived at by reasoning from general principles, are fully confirmed by experience. The United States of America is a country such as above described. Population and capital are both scanty as compared with the vast extent of its territory. Accordingly, it is very certain that both wages and profits are higher in that part of the world than in England.

As to the first, we are told by Adam Smith, that in his time common labourers in the State of New York earned three shillings and sixpence currency a-day, equal to two shillings sterling ; and superior workmen, such as ship-carpenters, no less than six shillings and sixpence.   Moreover, the price of provisions, as he observes, is every where in North America much lower than in England : " If the money price of labour, therefore, be higher than it is any where in the mother country, its real price, the real command of the necessaries and conveniences of life which it conveys to the labourer, must be higher in a still greater proportion."*

Notwithstanding this, profits, as is generally allowed, are also higher in North America than in the British dominions.   Two circumstances in particular serve to prove this.   The first is, the higher rate of interest in that country ; though, as shall be shown hereafter, this alone is not a sufficient evidence of a high rate of profit.   The other circumstance is more conclusive, I mean the very rapid accumulation of capital.   It seems impossible that this could go on increasing as it does in the United States, unless the profit on its employment were very great.

Thus, it appears that both wages and profits may be higher in one country than in another ; or than in the same country at a more advanced period of its progress in wealth and population.   Of course, there-

---

* In the present year (1836,) the workmen at the harbour of New York, not content with their wages of a dollar and a quarter a-day, equal at least to five shillings and three pence, demanded a dollar and a half, and rebelled in consequence.

fore, both may fall as the circumstances of society change.

It is also clear that a diminished productiveness of industry may either affect profits only, real wages remaining as high as ever; or if accompanied by a decline in the demand for labour, that the loss may fall partly on the one, partly on the other. Thus, wages and profits may sink either together or not. Now, we have seen that in the progress of society both eventually suffer.

This idea, that wages and profits could not rise or fall together, and consequently that they could never both be higher in one country than in another, seems to have arisen from the peculiar sense always attached by Mr. Ricardo to the former term. When he says that wages vary, he does not mean that the real reward of the labourers is different, but simply, that they obtain a greater or less proportion of the whole produce. Now, we have seen that profits are influenced not merely by the proportion which goes for wages, but also by that necessary for replacing fixed capital. So that even in Mr. Ricardo's sense of the above term, profits may rise or fall independently of any fall or rise in wages. But, in truth, the signification alluded to is not only unwarranted by the ordinary use of language, but is of no advantage whatsoever. When we say that wages advance or decline, every one naturally supposes that the condition of the labourer is changed for the better or worse. If this is not meant, what possible information do we obtain

as to the welfare of the great body of the people?
But, as above observed, if the gross return be small,
a larger proportion of the whole may give the labourer
a less command of necessaries, than in other countries
where industry is more productive. So that in the
language of Mr. Ricardo, wages would be *higher* in the
former country than in the latter, while to common
apprehension, as well as in the scientific discourses of
all other writers, they would in reality be *lower*.
Now, though we may give a more strict definition to
words in ordinary use, it is not allowable completely
to change their signification. Were this permitted,
we should have a second confusion of tongues without
the presumptuous attempt to build another Babel.*

Rate of wages, then, does *not* mean, either in this
treatise, or in common or scientific language, the proportion of the gross produce which goes to the labourer. But some relation is no doubt implied. A comparison is always instituted between the quantity of labour undergone and the reward obtained for the same.
In this alone is the workman interested. Quantity of
labour is compounded partly of its intensity, partly of
its duration. These remaining constant, real wages

* From these and some other similar observations, I would not be
supposed to undervalue the merits of Ricardo, still less to deny my
deep obligations to that eminent writer. But the greater the reputation of any author, the more necessary it becomes not to allow his
faults to pass unnoticed. The above error has thrown much confusion over the whole theory of distribution.

No over-sight is more common in philosophy than by changing the
meaning of a word to arrive at conclusions which wear the air of no-
velty, while nothing is really new, but the altered signification of a term.

vary with every increase or diminution in the amount of necessaries and comforts which such exertions enable him to command.

Rate of profit, on the other hand, always means the proportion which that part of the gross produce bears to all the rest. In this alone is the master-capitalist concerned.

I must now allude to an opinion on the subject of profits, which is supported by high authority, that of Adam Smith, as well as of other eminent writers on political economy. This opinion may be best stated in the words of the author of the " Wealth of Nations." He says, " The increase of stock which raises wages tends to lower profit. When the stocks of many rich merchants are turned into the same trade, their mutual competition tends to lower its profit, and when there is a like increase of stock in all the different trades carried on in the same society, the same competition must produce the same effect in them all." Book I. ch. iv.

Plausible as this statement may at first appear, it is, I hesitate not to say, fundamentally erroneous. If in any particular employment indeed, profits should happen to rise above those obtained in other occupations, it may readily be granted, that under a system of liberty, capital and labour would naturally be directed to the more fortunate branch of industry, till the accumulation of its products, by lowering their value, should have reduced these profits to the ordinary level.

But it is a very different thing to say, that by the

competition of master-capitalists, this ordinary level
itself is lowered.   I shall proceed to shew that this
cannot be.

Suppose a nation divided into two distinct classes
of men, the one employed in agriculture, the other in
manufactures.   Let us also imagine that capital has
been accumulating very rapidly, and that its owners
are anxious to vest it in some profitable occupation.
Part of this superabundant stock then, we may well
conceive, will be absorbed by agriculture, part by
manufactures.   In consequence of the great competition among farmers anxious to dispose of their produce, we will for a moment imagine that its value
falls and their profits in proportion.   But by the supposition, the very same events are taking place at
the same time in manufacturing industry.   According
to the theory which we are now considering, the value of wrought goods is also believed to decline from
a similar cause, and in consequence thereof, the profits of the master-capitalist.   Agricultural produce
then falls as compared with manufactured articles,
and at the same time, the latter fall as compared
with the former.   But this is an evident contradiction, for it is nothing else than saying that the value
of agricultural produce, at the same moment, both
rises and falls as estimated by the quantity of manufactured goods for which it will exchange.   Therefore, the premises which lead to so absurd a conclusion cannot but be false.

Could we suppose it possible that the Price of

every commodity, both raw and fabricated, should fall in consequence of the competition among the producers, yet this could not in any way affect profit. Each master-capitalist would sell his produce for less money, but on the other hand, every article of his expenses, whether belonging to fixed capital or to circulating, would cost him a proportionally smaller sum. Thus his real condition would be just the same.

Adam Smith has brought forward in support of his opinion several instances of rich countries in which capital had greatly accumulated, and where, as he observes, profits are lower than in poorer states. Thus, he says, " Holland is richer for its extent than England, and England than France or Scotland." " Profits, accordingly," he remarks, " are no where so low as in the first, and they are lower also in the second than in the two last." We may grant the fact, but object to his explanation. He does not omit to notice, that in those countries where profits are the lowest, wages are the highest. This helps us to the true account of the matter.

Owing to the diminished return to agricultural industry, resulting from the necessity of having recourse to inferior soils; or what comes to the same thing, on account of the great expense of bringing food from a distance, money-wages are always high in thickly peopled countries, which are also those where, in proportion to their extent, the greatest amount of capital is found. In other words, in such situations, a large share of the gross produce belongs to the labourer. But it is not the accumulation of stock which causes the fall of profit, but the diminished productiveness of the industry employed in raising the necessaries of life. This increases money-wages, and at the same time lowers profit in a corresponding degree.

There is another error closely connected with the preceding; to which last, indeed, the one we are now about to consider may be supposed to have given origin. Such is the notion, that profit necessarily depends for its existence upon sale or exchange. Thus an author,* who has written one of the best and most comprehensive treatises on Political Economy, while he allows, that the master or *entrepreneur* pays the landlord's rent and the wages of labour out of the gross produce of industry, nevertheless supposes that he is dependent for his profit on the sale of his commodity. Profit, he says, is paid by the consumer. Is there then none in that state of society which exists previous to the introduction of barter or exchange, and the division of employments? If a master-capitalist raised all the different articles of which he might stand in need, whether for his private use or for the continuance of his business, and if, after replacing directly out of his produce every object consumed during the work, there should remain a surplus over, would not this be profit? The introduction of exchange does not alter the real na-

* M. Storch.

ture of the case. Instead of applying himself to the production of half a dozen commodities or more, he now restricts himself to one. His surplus, then, will be represented by a certain quantity of this one object, instead of many various ones. If he choose to retain it in his own hands, it will constitute his profit ; if he exchange it for other things, it will appear in a new form; that is all the difference.

The idea of profits being paid by the consumers, is, assuredly, very absurd. Who are the consumers? They must be either landlords, capitalists, masters, labourers, or else people who receive a salary from one or more of these for some service or other. Do master-capitalists, in different occupations, pay each other their profits? According to this idea, each man is supposed to be working for his neighbour, not for himself. Is it then the labourers who pay them? In vain, it would seem, the workman conceives, that when he has got his wages, they are all for himself. No ; he must give back a part of them at least, to make up the profit of his master. So is it with the landlord. When he receives his rent from the farmer, he naturally supposes that it is all his own, and that he may do what he likes with it : by no means; a portion of it must be returned to his tenant. It is not easy to imagine any thing more ridiculous than this notion. The truth is, that competition so settles the value of all things, that, generally speaking, no man can gain at the expense of another in fair trading. All no doubt gain by the facility of exchanging

their respective products, which facility allows each
to restrict himself to one occupation; an order of
things which has been proved by experience to be
the most favourable to an increase in the quantity of
every commodity. But inasmuch as *all* are bettered,
it cannot be at the expense of *any*. In the ordinary
state of things, when one man barters the produce of
his industry for that of his neighbour, or exchanges
it for money, the value he gives away is fully equal
to that which he receives. For would any one for a
continuance agree to accept of less? This observation alone is quite sufficient to prove, that profit, in
the usual condition of the market, is not made by exchanging. Had it not existed before, neither could
it after that transaction.

In treating of the Sources of Wealth, we found
that it depends for its existence on a co-operation of
the powers of nature with those of art, of the inanimate world and brute creation, with man. From
what was then said, it follows that the degree of
productiveness of industry must depend upon two
things; first, the natural fertility of the surface of
the earth, or of its bowels, whence are derived metals
and minerals of all kinds, as also of the waters from
which fish can be procured; secondly, on the degree
of skill with which labour is applied in conjunction
with capital and with inanimate agents, wind, water,
and steam.

Now, what chiefly distinguishes agriculture not
only from manufactures, but also from commerce, is,

that it is comparatively much more dependent upon nature, less upon art. A small degree of superiority in soil may be sufficient to counterbalance a considerable advantage from the improved machines and processes used in cultivation. Poland and Southern Russia, with their rude instruments and imperfect rotation of crops, can still raise corn much cheaper than England, which is supposed to have carried agricultural skill farther than any nation in the world, except perhaps Belgium. Still, these improvements, so far as they go, tend not only to render corn more plentiful and cheap, but also to raise the rate of profit.

Manufactures, on the other hand, and commerce, are mainly dependent on human skill. In the infancy of nations, corn and other raw produce, may, to say the least, be quite as cheap as in more advanced periods, and of a quality equally good; but in the early states of society, fabricated articles are uniformly both dear and bad. Nothing is manufactured but objects of the coarsest kind, and at a price extravagantly high, as compared with what it becomes in the progress of industry.*

Commerce, for a long time, is no more advanced than manufactures. All goods of much bulk transported from one place to another, are, in rude ages, exceedingly enhanced in price. It is long before the means of conveyance become greatly improved. Ca-

---

* Even in North America, a country which has had the benefit of European art and knowledge, wrought goods are still very dear. A coat of good cloth costs in the United States from L.8 to L.10.

nals there are none, and roads for perhaps half the
year are impassible except on horseback.   To this
day, in many parts of Spain, a mountainous country,
there is no other way by which corn can be transported
from one province to another, but on the backs of
mules.   There may consequently be a glut in Anda-
lusia, while the inhabitants of Navarre are dying of
hunger.   The nature of the country no doubt opposes great obstacles to easy communication, but by
human skill these might be greatly surmounted.
Russia, on the other hand, though a country still in
a very barbarous state, possesses facilities of intercourse unknown to more polished nations.   These
are natural facilities however, which it required no
great ingenuity to take advantage of.   During many
months, the flat plains of that vast region lie deeply
buried in snow.   Over these wastes, where not a hill
appears, sledges laden with merchandize glide along
with inconceivable rapidity.*   In such a climate, canals and rail-roads would alike be useless for half the
year, but instead of them, the highways of nature are
open to all.   In general, however, much skill, labour,
and capital, are necessary in order to improve the
means of communication.   Countries long peopled
and civilized, in which both agriculture and manufactures have made considerable progress, may be still
very deficient in this respect.   For more than two
centuries, France has fabricated silks, which have

* See Storch " Cours d'Economie Politique."

helped to supply all the markets of Europe, its soil is generally cultivated, its Capital is a principal seat of the arts and sciences, of luxury and refinement, whence issue daily a hundred newspapers; yet, till of late, there was not in the whole kingdom more than a canal or two, fully terminated and kept in tolerable repair, and by far the greater number of roads still are during half the year in a deplorable state.*

There are two principal causes which tend to keep commerce behind both agriculture and manufactures. The first is, that the advances of funds necessary for improving the means of intercourse within a country are much greater than ameliorations in other branches of industry require. The second is, that the benefit is not so immediately felt by those who undertake the expense. The capital required for making a canal, rail-road, or even a common highway of any extent, is very great as compared with what may suffice for constructing a saw-mill, thrashing machine, &c., or for setting up a stocking-frame or power-loom. Again, though the tolls may in the long run amply restore all the advances with a fair profit, yet, before the intercourse has increased enough for this purpose, the original projectors may be ruined. Nothing is more common than to hear people say in reference to some scheme of this sort, that it will be highly useful to the public, but a bad speculation for individuals.

---

* Since the Revolution of July, however, the work of canals has been pushed with great activity.

For these reasons, works of this description have, in most countries, for a long period been undertaken by government alone. It is not until a state has made great advances, not in wealth only, but also in knowledge, that the part of government comes in this instance to be taken by associations of private persons. But at whatever period, and in whatever way, improvements in commercial intercourse are introduced, they tend like those in agriculture and manufactures, not only to increase the mass of commodities, but also to raise the rate of profit.*

From the fact above stated, that agriculture depends much more upon nature, and less upon art than manufactures and commerce, it follows that the former has rather a tendency to decline in productiveness as society advances and population augments, while the others constantly progress. As the numbers of the people increase, new lands must continually be taken into cultivation to supply the extended wants of the inhabitants. But as we may well suppose that at first the most fertile were preferred to those less favoured, so after a time, the former being already occupied and fully turned to account, recourse must be had to the latter. Therefore the return to agricultural industry must on this account have a

---

* A new road exactly corresponds to a new machine. By the old machine, goods might no doubt be fabricated, but more slowly and fewer of them. So, by the old roads, merchandize might continue to be transported, but these being either less direct or more difficult to pass along, a smaller quantity only could be sent at a time, and it would be longer on the way.

tendency to diminish. This tendency may no doubt be somewhat counteracted by improvements in farming, but still to a certain extent only. The effect will be modified, not prevented, as is proved by experience. Countries thinly peopled, possessing no ingenious machines for sowing, reaping, or thrashing grain, and knowing little of the benefits derived from a due rotation of crops, can still raise corn at a cheaper rate than nations the most civilized and improved. Of this, Poland and England have already been brought forward as instances. The reason of the fact can only be that the circumstance of not being obliged to cultivate any but fertile land, is an advantage possessed by the former, more than sufficient to counterbalance all the skill of the latter.

Profit, then, will *on this account* have a constant tendency to fall in the progress of wealth and population.

But, on the other hand, the products of manufacturing and commercial industry as steadily increase in quantity as they improve in quality. The rise in the raw material, which they derive from agriculture, retards them, no doubt, a little in their course, but the vast discoveries in machinery, and the prodigious facilities for intercourse afforded by numerous canals and rail-roads far far outstrip this obstacle to their progress, and leave us lost in amazement as well at their present state as at the prospect of their future advancement. Now, these improvements must greatly tend not only to increase the mass of commodities, and diminish their price, but also to raise the rate of profit.

Thus we more clearly see the truth of that statement formerly made, that in the progress of society, profit is acted upon in two different ways. The increased difficulty of raising raw produce has a tendency to lower its rate, while the improvements in manufacturing and commercial industry have just the opposite effect.

There is still another consequence to be drawn from the fact, that agriculture depends more upon nature than manufactures and commerce, which is, that the wealth built upon the former, reposes upon a much more secure basis, than that founded on the two latter. Nature is universally more permanent than Art. If the pyramids of Egypt have as yet escaped the common decay which awaits the works of man, it is only because they were so constructed as to condemn them to utter inutility. Parnassus still raises its double peak in air, though the Muses have long ceased to wander through its holy recesses. The fountain source of inspiration still tinkles on the ear, while the temples of the God strew with their mighty fragments the hills and plains of Greece.

" Art, Glory, Freedom fail, but Nature still is fair."

Manufactures and commerce are not exempt from

the usual lot of humanity. They are attached to no one soil, peculiar to no climate, but can fly on rapid wings, from the rock of Tyre and the lagoons of Venice to the Thames or Mersey, from the Mersey to the Hudson or Potowmack. Nor are foreign wars or internal revolutions alone fatal to their progress. The competition of other nations is fully as much to be dreaded. What country can pretend to say, this is the seat of art and industry, here shall they dwell unrivalled? Whatever advantages are due to man, all may hope to share, nor can the secrets of human skill be monopolized for ever.

Agricultural prosperity, on the other hand, is less subject to the caprice of fortune.

While Carthage is but a name, and the palaces of Venice are tumbling into its sleepy canals, while a stately cathedral and cemetery alone attest the former grandeur of Pisa, while grass grows in the streets of Bruges, and even Holland begins to decline; the plains of Lombardy, in spite of the double scourge of war and despotism, have not ceased to be the richest district in Europe. A happy climate, a soil naturally fertile, an inexhaustible supply of water from the Alps, these are sources of wealth, which not all the rage of man has been able to destroy. In manufactures also, it is only so far as nature presents peculiar advantages, that we can expect a lasting superiority. Abundant mines of coal, copious streams of water, are gifts on which we may with much more confidence rely, than on any improvements in the division of labour or the construction of machinery. Should England long continue to supply half the world with its merchandize, this commercial empire will chiefly be owing to those subterranean treasures, which, we may hope, will prove inexhaustible.

CHAPTER IV.

ON THE NET PROFITS OF CAPITAL.

IN commencing the inquiry into the subject of Profits, I mentioned that I took this term, as is usual with English writers, to signify the entire surplus which remains to the master-capitalist after replacing all the capital, fixed and circulating, expended in production. At the same time, I observed, that this whole surplus was not always the property of one individual, for that one person might be the owner of the capital, another might take upon himself the trouble and risk of employing it; and thus that profits really comprehended two very different species of income, one being a compensation for the use of capital, the other for the trouble and risk incurred, and the skill exerted in the business of direction and superintendance. Gross-profits then may be properly divided into two parts, the net-profits of Capital, and the profits of Enterprize. It remains for us to determine what are the causes which regulate the proportion in which gross-profits are divided between the two.* When the same person who directs the employment of capital is also the owner of it, there is no way by which we can determine how much of his profits he receives simply as capitalist, and how much belongs to him in the capacity of head of an establishment or master. Our conclusions on this subject then must be drawn from an observation of what takes place when the capitalist and master are different individuals.

Were capital never borrowed but by those who intended to invest it in some advantageous employment, it is evident that the proportion in which gross profits should be divided, would entirely depend upon the competition between capitalists and masters, between those who were anxious to derive an income from their funds without the trouble of personal superintendance, and others who were willing to charge themselves with this office. In this case, the share of each would solely depend upon the amount of capital offered to be lent on the one hand, and on the number of persons able and desirous to employ it on the other, they being at the same time supposed capable of presenting good security for the regular payment of the interest, and the final reimbursement of the capital. But in the actual state of things, the latter class of men are prevented from

* The phrase *net profits of capital* may appear almost a tautology, but since the term *profits of capital*, which is perhaps more correct, has been constantly used by English writers to signify *gross profits*, it cannot be employed on the present occasion. Net-profits of capital, when estimated and paid in money, are called Interest.

making so good a bargain with the capitalists as they
otherwise might; by the competition of another set
of people who are anxious to borrow, but do not intend vesting the funds so procured in any productive
employment. These are they whose expences have
gone beyond their income, and who must therefore
have recourse to loans to meet the demands made
upon them. In most wealthy communities, no in-
considerable amount of funds is required for this
purpose, particularly when we consider that government stands in this character when it raises loans
from its subjects. These loans are had recourse to,
because the ordinary revenues of the state are insufficient for the wants of the treasury, either from a
falling off in the receipts, or from an increase in the
expenditure, and the sums raised in this way are generally at least, if not invariably, spent unproductively, that is, without a return in any material shape.
In the same light we must regard foreign governments who send their agents to raise loans in any
country.

From all these sources, then, from private individuals who have spent beyond their income, from the
government of the country, and also from foreign
governments, may arise a demand for the funds of
capitalists, no part of which is destined to a productive employment. But besides this class of borrowers, there is also another who, like the former,
are anxious to obtain loans, without intending to vest
the sums thus procured in any profitable branch of

industry, but differ from it in other particulars.
These are persons who have been unsuccessful in
trade, whose speculations have failed, and who therefore are threatened with bankruptcy and ruin, if they
cannot find means of meeting the demands of their
creditors at a stated period. These, of all others,
are under the most urgent necessity of borrowing, in
order to maintain their credit, on which success in
business mainly depends. Neither, it is evident, are
these borrowed funds employed by them productively,
or intended to be so, but are to be paid away to others
in lieu of value previously received. However different this class of persons may be from those who,
being engaged in no occupation, live beyond their
income, still in this they both agree, that they constitute a body of men anxious to borrow, and yet
distinct from those who apply to capitalists, in order
to obtain the funds which they do not themselves
possess, but by means of which alone their talents
and industry can be turned to account. Now, the
skill and industry of the heads of establishments who
trade on borrowed funds are less well paid than
otherwise they would be, owing to the competition
of the two other classes of persons above described.
For it is evident, that what is paid for the use of capital, or interest, as commonly called when estimated
in money, must depend upon the proportion between
the borrowers of every description on the one hand,
and the number of persons having capital to lend on
the other. To a capitalist it is of no consequence

how his funds are employed, provided the security be good, and the rate of interest at least as high as is usual at the time. This is all he looks to. He will be quite as willing to lend on the mortgage of land, or of the public revenues, to supply the unproductive consumption of the landlord or of government, as to furnish the merchant and manufacturer with the means of extending their business, supposing no difference in the security or in the annual interest.

It is then by the competition between all the borrowers having good security to offer, and all the capitalists of having funds to lend, that the Rate of Interest must be determined, which I consider as nothing else than the Net Profits of Capital estimated in Money. Whatever remains to the master of any establishment, agricultural, manufacturing, or commercial who puts in motion borrowed capital, after paying these profits or interest to the owners of the stock, constitutes the profits of enterprise, the remuneration of the skill exerted and the trouble and risk which necessarily accompany all productive occupations. The profits of enterprise then depend upon the profits of capital, which we must measure by the interest paid on good security. I say good security, for where that is not the case, there is no limit to the amount paid for the use of capital; it will depend entirely on the risk which the lender runs of losing both principal and income. And of course, such exorbitant interest cannot be paid out of the profits of any productive employment, nor could the capital

have been borrowed with this view, since it is sometimes so high as to exceed the Gross Profits made in
any branch of industry.   Thus we know that sixty
per cent. was formerly often paid for money in Ben-
gal, and perhaps still is occasionally.   Such an interest as this could never be paid out of the profits derived from the employment of the capital borrowed;
it must then be defrayed out of income arising from
other independent sources of riches, and therefore is
not a *primary* revenue but a *secondary* one, according
to the signification I affixed to those terms in commencing the enquiry into the distribution of wealth.
The same is the case with all the interest paid for capital borrowed without a view to profitable employment, even when the security is good, and the rate
therefore moderate.   Since it is not employed productively, of course the sums paid annually for it must
be derived not from itself, but from other sources
of income, whether land, labour, or some other capital.

Were capital never borrowed with any other view
but that of productive employment, I should consider
the remuneration paid for it as a perfectly fair measure of the Net Profits of capital, in which case the
remaining portion of Gross Profits would also represent accurately the Profits of Enterprise.   But as interest must in some degree be raised by the number
of persons who borrow for unproductive consumption,
it follows that it is not so exact a criterion of what
ought properly to be looked upon as the net profits of
capital, as it otherwise would be.   By means of these

unproductive borrowers the net profits of capital may with justice be considered as raised above their natural level, while those of enterprise are of course depressed to a corresponding degree. However, in practice, the rate of interest may safely be taken as the best measure of the rate of net profits on capital, in fact, it is the only one we have.*

In order, then, to determine what regulates the rate of the net profits of capital, we must find out on what the rate of interest depends. But this, as before observed, varies according as the proportion changes between all the borrowers having good security to offer, and all the persons having capital to lend. It is this proportion, together with the intensity of

---

* We must always however bear in mind, as above observed, that it is only in countries where good governments are established, and security consequently prevails, that the ordinary rate of interest can be taken as a measure of the rate of net profits of capital; for in nations less happily circumstanced, interest is so high, from the want of certainty of re-payment, that capital can never be borrowed with a view to productive employment, and therefore the rate of the former can constitute no criterion of the net profits of the latter. And although we should not suppose interest to be so excessive as to preclude all borrowing with a view to advantageous investment, yet wherever compensation for risk constitutes a very important part of the annual payments, I cannot look upon interest as representing truly the net profits of capital. It is only where the risk is reduced to little or nothing, or at least is not reckoned, that the criterion is just. In England, for instance, at the present day, we cannot, I think, consider compensation for risk as at all entering into the interest received from funds lent on what would be called good security; for though there is always some risk in lending, so also is there in keeping at home in one's own hands; the one therefore balances the other. Nay more, we know that people constantly put money into their banker's hands merely for safety, for they do so place their funds even when no interest is expected.

the competition between these two classes of people, which determines the ordinary rate of interest. But both the proportion between the numbers of borrowers and lenders, and the intensity of the competition will much depend upon a particular circumstance, namely, how much may reasonably be expected to be made by the use of capital in conjunction with the skill and industry of the master, that is, on the amount of gross profits supposed likely to be realized. Where much can be made by the employment of capital, much we may easily suppose will be given for its loan. For, the prospect of these large profits will bring a greater number of borrowers into the market, and the same cause will make them consent more readily to pay a high interest. Therefore, high gross profits are one cause of high interest. And if capital were never borrowed for any purpose but that of productive employment, the rate of interest might, it would seem, afford a very good criterion whereby to judge whether gross profits were high or low. But since we have found that there are other classes of persons who borrow with no such view, and who, therefore, in their bargains care not how much may be made by capital, and as these are often of great importance, comprising the government of the country as well as of other states, it follows that the rate of interest cannot be taken as a sure index of that of gross profits. We must then content ourselves with stating high or low gross profits to be one cause of high or low interest.

One proof how much interest is affected by the demands of what we call unproductive borrowers is derived from the fact, that during the whole of the last century, as well as the portion already elapsed of the present, the rate of interest on good security has been higher in time of war than in time of peace, owing, no doubt, principally, if not entirely, to the demands of government for loans.*

In this case, then, interest varied independently of gross profits, for we can have no reason to suppose these to have been uniformly higher in war than in peace. But were we even to suppose, that capital was never borrowed with any view but to productive employment, I think it very possible that interest might vary without any change in the rate of gross profits. For, as a nation advances in the career of wealth, a class of men springs up and increases more and more, who by the labours of their ancestors find themselves in the possession of funds sufficiently ample to afford a handsome maintenance from the interest alone. Very many also who during youth and middle age were actively engaged in business, retire in their latter days to live quietly on the interest of the sums they have themselves accumulated.

---

* See Tooke, " Considerations on the State of the Currency," where this subject is very ably treated. From this it would follow, that war is advantageous to capitalists, but injurious to masters. It increases interest at the expense of profits of enterprise.

This class, as well as the former, has a tendency to increase with the increasing riches of the country, for those who begin with a tolerable stock are likely to make an independence sooner than they who commence with little. Thus it comes to pass, that in old and rich countries, the amount of national capital belonging to those who are unwilling to take the trouble of employing it themselves, bears a larger proportion to the whole productive stock of the society, than in newly settled and poorer districts. How much more numerous in proportion to the population is the class of *rentiers*, as the French call them, in England, than in America, where almost every body is employed in some business or other! As the class of *rentiers* increases, so also does that of lenders of capital, for they are one and the same. Therefore, from this cause interest must have a tendency to fall in old countries which have made great progress in wealth, independently of all considerations of what nature may be the borrowers, productive or unproductive, or whether gross profits be high or low. For whatever purposes capital be borrowed, the above cause might create a fall in interest when profits were stationary or even increasing.*

* There can be no doubt that the establishment of savings banks now so common in England, and which are daily spreading in France, by affording to the labouring class a secure investment for their surplus earnings, must swell very considerably the amount of capital not actually employed by its owners, and must, therefore, tend to lower the rate of interest.

Should I refer in proof of the above statement, to the rate of interest in old and rich countries where good governments are established, and consequently where security may be had in money transactions, as, for instance to England, and especially Holland, where long ago, two per cent. was the common rate,* the fact might be allowed, but its explanation doubted. It might be said that the low reward to capital borrowed, in such countries, is owing to the low gross profits which can be made by its employment. And I do not mean to say that this is not one cause of the decline of interest as nations become richer, for we formerly found in investigating the subject of gross profits that these do actually fall as countries increase in wealth and population. All I say is, that this is not the *only* cause; the increase of the class of lenders, which arises out of the augmented riches of the nation, is another and very influential one.

It may not be considered here out of place to remark, that from this notion that interest always varied with the rate of gross profits, have arisen very erroneous ideas with respect to the causes on which a rise or fall of these last depends. One source of these errors has already been mentioned in the preceding chapter, but this seems to have been another. Since it was observed that interest generally fell as a country advanced in wealth, and since it was

---

* Adam Smith says, that in his time the government of Holland borrowed at two per cent., and private persons of good credit at **three.** Book i. chap. x.

supposed that this fall was owing to a previous decline in gross profits, the conclusion was thence
drawn, that the accumulation of capital tended directly to depress their rate, by increasing the competition among those who employed stock productively.
" The increase of stock," says Adam Smith, " which
raises wages, tends to lower profit. When the stocks
of many rich merchants are turned into the same
trade, their mutual competition naturally tends to
lower its profit; and when there is a like increase
of stock in all the different trades carried on in the
same society, the same competition must produce the
same effect in them all."*

As I have attempted to refute this notion, when
discussing the subject of Gross Profits, it is unnecessary to dwell upon it now. I bring it forward at present, solely for the purpose of showing a second source
whence this erroneous opinion may have had its origin. That the rate of interest falls in a country as
capital accumulates, and the class of lenders increases,
is very certain, but I have shown above, that this by
no means proves a fall in the gross profits of master-
capitalists. A false analogy was drawn from the condition of a lender to that of a producer, whereas their
positions are quite different, and since it was observed
that the rate of interest fell with the increased competition of capitalists having funds to lend, it was
supposed that the gross profits of producers must do

* This has been quoted before, but it seemed necessary to repeat it
here.

so too; overlooking the grand truth that profits owe
their existence to a law of the material world, whereby the beneficence of nature when aided and directed
by the labour and skill of man, gives so ample a return to national industry as to leave a surplus of
products over and above what is absolutely necessary
for replacing in kind the fixed capital consumed, and
for perpetuating the race of labourers employed.   If
the whole produce were just sufficient for these purposes, no permanent deduction under the name of
profit could be made from the share of the labourers,
without leading to their continual decrease and final
extinction.   Therefore, in such a case, profit could
not permanently exist.   But let the gross produce
be ever so little more than is strictly essential for
the above purposes, and the separation of a distinct
revenue from the general mass, under the appellation of profit, and belonging to another class of men,
becomes possible.   In fact, however, the total produce is generally sufficient to allow the labourers
much more than is absolutely necessary for their
present support and future perpetuation of the race,
and to give a profit besides.   Now this profit consists, in the case of a nation, of many commodities,
in that of an individual, of perhaps only one, and is,
an effect of the beneficence of nature, aided and directed by art.   To understand the theory of profits,
it is above all things necessary to be thoroughly convinced of the truth of this fundamental principle.
So long as we suppose that gross profits, whether of

nations or individuals, owe their existence to the competition between master-capitalists, we are far indeed from a right comprehension of the subject. For a refutation of this error I need only refer to what has been formerly said on this point.

Competition may equalize profits among the different orders of master-capitalists, by changing the value of commodities, but cannot *create* the commodities themselves in which profit consists. Also, the competition between capitalist and master may determine in what proportion gross profits shall be divided between them, supposing that something to be divided already exists. The only competition which can affect the general rate of gross profits, is that between master-capitalists and labourers, though the very existence of the former as a distinct class is dependent on the productiveness of industry.*

This, then, is the summary of the doctrine of the net profits of capital. The rate of these must depend, partly upon the rate of gross profits, (for where the whole is greater or less, so also is likely to be each

---

* We must always remember, however, that it is in certain occupations only, that the productiveness of industry influences the rate of profit. Whether luxuries, fine goods, &c. be raised with ease or difficulty, is, in that respect, of no consequence; for by a rise in price, a small quantity of delicacies may give quite as much profit as a larger at a lower rate. Profit, as we have seen, is affected by the quantity of the return to those branches of industry alone, employed in producing the necessaries of the labourer, and the various elements of fixed capital. So that the most ordinary sorts of agriculture, manufactures of coarse goods, of implements, and machinery, and the commerce which transports their products, are the true sources of this revenue in all occupations. See Chapter on Gross Profits.

division of the whole,) partly on the proportion in which these are separated into profits of capital and those of enterprise. This proportion again depends upon the competition between the lenders of capital and all the borrowers having good security to offer; which competition is influenced, though by no means entirely regulated, by the rate of gross profit expected to be realized. And the reason why competition is not exclusively regulated by this cause, is, because on the one hand many *borrow* without any view to productive employment; and, on the other, because the proportion of the whole national capital to be *lent*, varies with the riches of the country independently of any change in gross profits. Were it not for these circumstances, the profits of capital would bear to those of enterprise, a more constant ratio than they now do.

CHAPTER V.

ON THE PROFITS OF ENTERPRISE.

HAVING now treated of Profits in the Gross, and also of the Net Profits of Capital, to complete this branch of our subject, it only remains for us to investigate the peculiar nature and causes of the Profits of Enterprize.* And it is perhaps the more necessary to dwell a little upon these, since, in general, they have not been separated by English authors from the whole profit derived from capital and industry combined. The same oversight, however, has not been made by the French economist, Say, or the Russian, Storch. By them the *Profits de l'Entrepreneur* are carefully distinguished from the *Profits des Capitaux*. And in truth, such a separation is not a matter of philosophical accuracy merely, but really enters into the view of all persons at the head of productive establishments. They consider nothing as their gain or profit, but what they make over and above the current interest of money, and very justly; for supposing them possessed of capital, they have no occasion to put themselves to any trouble, to give up their leisure, to exert their intellectual faculties, and to

---

* The phrase Profits of the Master might also be used, but Profits of Enterprise is both more concise, and less liable to be misunderstood.

incur the risk of failure, in order to enjoy an income equal to this interest. And if the capital does not belong to those who employ it, the interest upon it is always reckoned by them as a part of their expences; so that in both cases, what remains over and above the interest of money, or in other words, the net profits of capital, is alone considered by them as the proper gain derived from their industry, and the only compensation for the risk and trouble to which they are put. It is therefore quite essential to consider this surplus by itself.

And here, in commencing, I must remark the compound nature of this kind of revenue. It is not, like the income of the labourer, derived from labour alone. Indeed, whatever of toil there may be in the occupation of a master, is rather that of the head than of the hand; for though many chiefs of establishments do themselves put their hands to the work, yet in doing so they cease for the time to be masters, and become operatives. Neither is the amount of profit or gain at all in proportion to the quantity of toil or skill employed, as in the case of the labourer; for though undoubtedly an assiduous and intelligent master will have the advantage over an inferior in these respects, and the sum of his gains will so far be more considerable, yet this can make but small amends for a deficiency of capital. A man of ordinary talents and prudence, with a large capital, will always obtain a greater amount of profit than the most able and active individual whose funds are comparatively small. The profits of enterprise, then, are for the most part, proportioned to the capital employed; and it is in this way they are always calculated, as well as profits in the gross, and the net profits of stock. Still they are not so entirely dependant upon the amount of capital, but that considerable scope is left for the exercise of individual talents and assiduity, which are pretty sure to meet their reward. Thus, though by no superiority of knowledge, intellect, or activity, can a person who employs capital to the value of L.5000, realize as great an amount of profit as another with L.10,000, except it be in the case of some remarkable speculation indeed, which lies entirely out of all calculation, and is so rare as not to be worth dwelling on; yet a very able master, who thoroughly understands his trade, may perhaps make as much with L.5000, as another with L.6000 or even L.7000. Thus, the profits of enterprise constitute a revenue of a two-fold nature, depending principally on the amount of capital, and varying with it, but at the same time liable to rise or fall within certain limits, according to the intellectual and moral qualifications of those who put it in motion. They may, then, in all propriety be considered partly as the natural reward of these mental qualifications, partly as a revenue derived from the power of commanding the use of capital for a certain time; whereas the net profits of capital are properly the income drawn from the *possession* of capital.

As, however, the mental qualities above referred to are incapable of measurement, the profits of enterprise are always estimated solely in regard to the proportion they bear to the capital employed.

So much it seemed necessary to say with respect to the *nature* of the branch of revenue now under consideration. A right notion on this point will be of essential service to us when we come to treat of the differences in gross profits in different occupations. But we must first trace the causes which determine the general rate of the profits of enterprise.

Having already discussed the subject of profits in the gross, as well as that of the net return to capital, the present question cannot detain us long. The rate of the profits of enterprise must evidently depend, as do those of capital, partly on the rate of gross profits, partly on the proportion in which these last are shared between capitalists and masters. The greater the whole which remains to be divided, after replacing all the outlay required by the work, the greater is each part thereof likely to be. This is so evident as not to require being dwelt upon.

So far, therefore, the causes which determine the rate of the profits of enterprise are the same which regulate the rate of gross profits, which have been already considered. But what settles the proportion in which these last are divided? Now in treating of the profits of capital, this question has been already answered. We have seen, that it depends upon the ratio which all the lenders have to all the borrowers having good security to offer, and on the intensity of the competition between them. This determines the ordinary rate of interest, which measures the net profits of capital; and therefore it must also fix the portion which goes to constitute the profits of enterprise. Whatever remains after deducting the former, must, of course, make up the latter.

It appears by this exposition, that the causes which determine the proportion above mentioned, affect directly the profits of capital, and through them act upon those of enterprise, so that the latter are subservient to the former. Here, however, it may be said, and, in fact, it has been so laid down by Say, that the profits of the master, or *entrepreneur*, as the French call him, are determined by the ratio which exists between the quantity of his peculiar sort of labour demanded on the one hand, and the quantity offered on the other; on which supposition it would follow, that the causes which settle the proportion in which gross profits are divided,* act directly upon the profits of enterprise rather than on those of capital. This is exactly the reverse of the view I have taken of the case, and appears to me quite erroneous.

That the rate of interest, or of the net profits of

* Le prix de leur travail (that of *entrepreneurs*), est réglé par le rapport qui se trouve entre *la quantité demandée* de ce genre de travail d'une part; et la quantité qui en est mise en circulation, *la quantité offerte* d'autre part. Liv. ii. ch. 7.

capital, is determined by the proportion between the quantity of capital offered to be lent, and the quantity demanded by those having good security to offer, is so plain a proposition, as not to seem to admit of gainsaying, nor is it denied by Say himself, to whose views I have just now alluded. But that the profits of enterprise are regulated by a competition such as that above mentioned, is a statement I do not well understand. For who demands the labour of a master? No one that I know of. If any one, it must be the person having capital to lend. But he does not look out for people to employ his funds, but simply for those on whom he can rely for the punctual payment of the interest. To him it is quite immaterial whether he lend to masters of productive establishments, to landed proprietors on mortgage, or to government, provided the security and rate be the same. The labour, then, of masters, cannot be said to be demanded.

Again, when masters come into the market to borrow, they do not set forth their talents in business, their industry and activity, but produce their securities, whether personal or landed. Therefore their labour is not offered. There is, consequently, no analogy between their case and that of an ordinary labourer, who expects to be paid in proportion to the skill and habits of assiduity which he is supposed to possess. Thus we see that the labour, if we so call it, of a master, is neither demanded nor offered; from the very nature of his position he always works for himself, and if the whole profits of his calling do not belong to himself exclusively, it is not because he has lent his services to any one else, who gives him an allowance, but because he has borrowed funds for the use of which he must pay. The deduction, then, from his profits, must depend solely upon the amount of the compensation he has bargained to make, that is, on the rate of interest agreed upon. Thus we again arrive at our former conclusion, that the profits of enterprise depend upon the net profits of capital, not the *latter upon the former*.

Were there any class of labourers who might be compared with the masters of establishments, it would be the foremen or overseers hired to superintend the works of an extensive concern. Their labour is not of a manual kind, but chiefly, if not solely, that of direction, belonging more to the head than to the hands, and requiring special knowledge, activity of mind and probity, rather than bodily dexterity. But this very case will serve to shew us how different is the position of the master from that of any labourer, even of the highest order.

A foreman receives a fixed salary from his employer, which does not depend upon the vicissitudes of trade, which does not rise as profits rise, or fall as they fall. Besides, the salary of any person of this description, in an extensive concern, where alone he is wanted, though large as compared with the pay of common labourers, is quite insignificant when placed beside the profits of the master. The causes which determine its amount are precisely similar to those which regulate the ordinary wages of labour, the proportion between the supply thereof and the demand, though the high qualifications necessary in this line, always keep the supply so short as to insure to the services of overseers a handsome reward.

The factors or agents employed by merchants to carry on their business in foreign ports, to buy and sell for them, and, in short, to perform all the transactions of commerce, approach more nearly to the condition of masters, for whatever mental qualities are necessary in the one are equally so in the other. But still, these persons are but servants after all, receiving a stated salary either fixed or varying with the profits which they may realize for their employer, according as has been agreed upon, but, at all events, bearing but a feeble proportion to those profits. Neither do they run any risk of losing capital; a diminution in their income, supposing them to be paid in the last mentioned manner, is the worst they have to fear.

What essentially constitutes the character of master, is the possession of all the qualifications necessary for carrying on any business, in conjunction with a power of commanding capital, whether his own or not. The peculiar advantages attending this state are, that whatever profits he may make by his industry, over and above interest, all belong to himself; the disadvantages, that he is constantly liable to lose, not only his income but the capital also, for more or less of uncertainty attends all productive occupations. It is the risk and trouble to be incurred, the variety of talents and knowledge required for carrying on any business, which, together with the necessity for presenting good security, always limit the number of persons who create an effective demand for capital to be employed productively.

From these causes, the interest on borrowed funds is kept down, so as after paying it still to leave a large surplus for the especial profits of the master. As we have formerly observed, this surplus would be even greater were it not for the unproductive borrowers, government and others, who by their competition, tend to keep up the rate of interest. In countries where security is good, however, it is probable that in ordinary circumstances, interest does not swallow up more than the half of gross profits, so that the other half at least constitutes the share of the master.

I consider it of no little importance to attend to the circumstances above stated, as essentially characterising the head of an establishment, and which act as causes limiting the number of persons who create a demand for capital borrowed for productive purposes; because it is thus only that we can explain why the master without any capital of his own, without land of his own, and without manual labour, should still gain so large a share of the annual revenue of the country. The position of master requires, in the first place, the union of several moral and intellectual qualities, activity, prudence, knowledge, the fruit often of long experience and practice in a subordinate capacity of at least some one branch of industry; acquaintance with the best markets for buying and selling, an aptness to detect cheating and trickery, as well as to discover sincerity and open dealing, and therefore, a practical insight into human nature. Those who enter upon business without the possession of these qualities, and others of the same kind which may well be imagined, sooner or later become bankrupt, and therefore can no longer create a demand for capital to carry on their trade. In the second place, though the master does not labour with his hands, yet his head must be constantly at work, his time and pains must be given principally to the management of the concern, which, without his superintendence, would soon go to ruin; and he must frequently be liable to mental anxiety. Therefore his species of industry is by far the most valuable of all, partly because it is most difficult to excel in, partly because the whole success of the establishment depends upon it, and consequently the welfare of the labourers employed, as well as the interests of the capitalists who may have lent their funds, or of the proprietor who has given the use of his land. So that upon the prosperity of the master's affairs, depend not only his own fortune, but that of all the other owners of the sources of production. No wonder, then, that this trouble and responsibility are so highly paid.

In the third place, a certain degree of risk attends all productive employments, although conducted with great prudence and ability. Disasters which no foresight could anticipate, frequently overtake the best managed enterprises, and bring along with them a loss not merely of fortune, but even of honour. For among the class of masters, bankruptcy, however unmerited, is always attended with some disgrace. There are many instances of persons having committed suicide upon a failure in business, which act has been in great measure attributed to their not being able to endure the degradation to which they supposed themselves fallen. These instances, I believe, are found chiefly among great merchants.

Lastly; in order to obtain the use of capital not possessed by himself, the master must present good security, which circumstance alone, would keep out of competition with him the great majority of mankind.

Now, all these circumstances restrict greatly the number of persons able and willing to borrow capital in order to vest it in some productive employment, and, therefore, as before observed, enable masters to retain out of gross profits, a large proportion for the profits of enterprise.

But there is another character in which we must regard the master, and a most important one. He is the general distributor of the national revenue; the person who undertakes to pay to all the owners of the different sources of wealth, their share in the annual return—to the labourers, the wages of their labour—to the capitalist, the interest of his funds—to the proprietor, the rent of his land. The incomes of all these classes pass through the hands of the master, before they are finally received by those who have a right to spend them. Thus we see that he acts a most important part in the economy of society.

In reference to their interests, indeed, all those who concur in the business of production, may be divided into two classes. On the one hand are masters, on the other, labourers, capitalists, and landlords, combined. The interests of these two grand classes are diametrically opposed to each other. It is the master who *hires* labour, capital, and land, and of course tries to get the use of them on as low terms as possible; while the owners of these sources of wealth do their best to *let* them as high as they can.

It is sufficient at present to have merely touched upon this classification, for on summing up the theory of distribution, I shall return to the subject.

CHAPTER VI.

ON THE RATE OF GROSS PROFITS IN DIFFERENT EMPLOYMENTS.

HAVING now traced the general causes which regulate the ordinary rate of gross profits, as well as those which especially determine the rates of the profits of capital, and those of enterprise, it only remains for us to turn our attention to the causes of the differences in the gross profits gained in different occupations.

In discussing the subject of profits in the gross, I alluded to the notion entertained by many, but which I attempted to show is a fundamental error, that profits owe their existence and their ordinary level to competition between the producers; and at the same time, as well as in investigating the theory of interest, I mentioned what I conceived to be the principal sources of this fallacy. But though competition can produce nothing, and therefore cannot give origin to profits, or determine whether the productive powers of any country shall on the whole meet with a scanty or an abundant return; yet it

constantly tends to establish an approximation to
equality between the profits gained in different occupations.   And this it does, not by altering the return in quantity to any given amount of labour and
capital, which is quite beyond its power, but by
changing the value of that quantity.

Competition, then, so regulates the value of commodities, that the gross profits derived from the employment of equal capitals shall constantly tend to
an equality.   The manner in which competition produces this effect, is by inducing a greater number of
master-capitalists to engage in those employments
which for the time happen to give a larger profit
than others ; or, what comes to the same thing, by
encouraging those already occupied therein, to borrow more largely, for the sake of extending their
transactions.   In one or both of these ways, a greater
quantity of the commodity in question is brought to
market, and the price is brought down till the profit
on its production is reduced to a level with that gained in other trades.   Where profit in any business
happens to fall below that usual in other branches
of industry, a process exactly the reverse restores
it by degrees to the ordinary rate.   This is so evident, and so generally allowed, that I do not think
it worth while saying a word more about it.   But
what I wish to remark, is, that this tendency to a
common level may be checked more or less by causes
peculiar to certain branches of trade, so that profits
shall be higher or lower in some than in others.   And

here I do not allude to causes which create a temporary glut or scarcity of one or more commodities, and which are necessarily but of short continuance, nor to artificial monopolies as a source of high profits; but to causes more permanent and inherent in the nature of different occupations. These causes are of two sorts; they are either intimately connected with the peculiar character of certain branches of industry, or they depend simply on the scale on which they are carried on—the very same employment giving very different rates of profit, according as it is exercised in a great way or in a small.

The following causes may be placed under the former head.

First. It appears that the greatest profits must be gained in those occupations in which the most *risk* is run. For it is only the expectation of such unusual gains which induces any one to incur that risk, and the knowledge or fear of this uncertainty narrows competition in such branches. The former circumstance affords a motive to embark in hazardous undertakings; the latter gives the power of realizing therein unusual profits.

Thus, great fortunes are occasionally made by new adventures, as by shipments to countries hitherto little visited by the commercial world. Also, speculations in which the returns are long in coming in—in which years perhaps must elapse before the profits can be secured, give higher gains than those in which the returns can be more speedily calculated upon.

And this partly from the cause above stated—the greater *risk* which accompanies these long-winded transactions, partly from the field of competition being still more narrowed from the comparatively small number of persons possessing funds sufficiently great to enable them to afford the outlay required, and to wait so long for their money. Thus, great fortunes are more suddenly made by merchants engaged in foreign commerce, than by those employed in the home trade.

But, because those employments in which the risk is greatest give higher profits to a few, than others in which there is more certainty, yet it does not follow, taking all the persons engaged in them, that the gains on the whole are greater in the more adventurous than in the more safe branches of industry. For, if a few make fortunes more rapidly, a greater number fail of securing any thing at all, lose even their capital, and become bankrupt. This occurs more frequently at least, than in the more known and common avocations. Indeed, taking into consideration the natural hopefulness of man, his tendency to believe himself born under a lucky star, how much the example of the bad success of others is thrown away upon him, and how great is the effect of a few brilliant instances of a contrary fortune, there can be little doubt that more persons are enticed to enter upon these hazardous speculations, than the proportion of prizes to blanks would justify.

Bacon classes among the *Idola Tribus* (those sources

of delusion inherent in the very essence of the human mind, at all times, and in all states of civilization,) the tendency to be more struck by affirmative than by negative instances, so that one case of the former may often outweigh a hundred perhaps of the latter ; and, assuredly, the example of all lotteries, of which the lottery of trade is one, bears ample witness to the truth of this remark.

It is probable, then, I think, that the most hazardous employments of capital are precisely those in which, upon the whole, the least profit is gained, the losses of some more than counterbalancing the great winnings of others. Smuggling is to those who succeed, the most lucrative of all occupations ; but for one that makes a fortune, twenty are ruined.

Under this head comes another cause of the great profits gained in certain occupations, one to which I have already alluded, but may now state more particularly, namely, the great command of capital required in certain departments, which must limit the competition therein to a few. There are certain products which are said to be best made in a large quantity, the quality depending greatly upon this circumstance. Porter, we are told, is of this nature. In consequence of this opinion, be it well or ill-founded, the making of London Porter has for a long time been confined to a few very wealthy individuals, who have therefore been able to combine and keep up the price of this liquor, so as to enable them to realize great profits. Now, however, by the importation of Irish porter, these great brewers are threatened with a breaking up of their monopoly; for people begin to find that a beverage of this description, cheaper, and but little inferior to that of London, can be made in the capital of the sister island.

I have already stated the cause now under our consideration, as influencing the profits of those merchants who send shipments to distant parts, whence the returns are long in coming in.

Another case in point is, that of army contractors; the great fortunes sometimes made by whom, are, owing to the limited number of persons able to undertake so great a speculation, which circumstance enables them to drive a very advantageous bargain with government.

The princely incomes formerly enjoyed by the farmers-general of the public revenue under the old régime in France, depended upon the same principle. And there is this difference between the cause of high profits now under review, and that before mentioned, that in the present case the profits realized are really greater than in most other occupations which do not require so great a command of capital: whereas in the instance of risk, high profits are more apparent than real, for the extraordinary gains of a few are counterbalanced by the losses of many.

We come now to consider a second class of causes which have a very material influence upon the rate of profits in different occupations, raising it in some, depressing it in others, and thus giving rise to very considerable variations from a common level. These causes are connected, not with the peculiar character of any branch of industry, but simply with the scale on which it is carried on, and the value of capital invested. But in order thoroughly to understand this branch of the subject, we must revert to what has above been stated with respect to the nature of the profits of enterprise. And here we shall find fresh reasons for the utility, nay, the necessity of the distinction between these profits and those of capital, which I have adopted from French writers on Political Economy.

We found that the profits of enterprise represent that portion of gross profits which serves in part as the reward of the talents, skill, and trouble exercised and undergone by the master of an establishment, in part is a compensation for the risk he incurs in entering upon the business of production. Whatever remains to the master, over and above this reward and compensation, we also found must be regarded as an income arising out of the power of commanding capital, quite distinct from the revenue derived from its possession. Therefore, the profits of enterprise may, with propriety, be considered as made up of three parts; one being the salary of the labour or trouble of the master, another an insurance for risk, and the remainder we may call his surplus gains. The first of these ought to vary with the degree of trouble to which the master is put; the second will of course be proportioned to the amount of capital employed.

Now, since of two occupations, of which the one takes in twice or three times as much capital as the other, the former may not require much more trouble or superintendence than the latter; it follows that that part of the profits of enterprise which we call salary, ought to be nearly the same sum in both. As for the insurance of risk, it may be considered as constant; for where the chances of failure are alike, it bears always the same proportion to the capital employed. Therefore, the larger the capital vested in any business, the smaller must be the proportion of the profits of enterprise which goes for the master's salary and insurance together, and, consequently, the greater must be his surplus gains, not only absolutely, but relatively to the capital engaged.

This will be rendered very clear by an example. We may suppose two manufacturers having command of capital to the amount of L.10,000 and L.5000 respectively, and engaged in two branches of production, the difference between which lies chiefly in the cost of the raw material, the number of labourers being the same in both. I put this instance for the sake of simplicity, for here the trouble of the two masters must be nearly identical. To establish the principle we have in view is sufficient; the modifications in the degree of superintendence required may afterwards be imagined as creating some little variety in the result, though of course it must always be ex-

ceedingly difficult, if not impossible, to determine with
accuracy the quantity of labour which any head of an
establishment is called upon to perform. In the cases
I now put, the trouble may well be supposed the
same in both.

If we suppose the rate of gross profits to be 10 per
cent. the following will be the accounts of the two manufacturers.*

The first with L.10,000 capital.

Gross profits at 10 per cent.	.	L.1000
Deduct interest at 5 per cent.	.	500
Remains for profits of enterprize	.	500
Deduct salary, suppose	100	
Deduct insurance at 2 per cent.	200—300	
Remains for surplus gains	.	L.200

The second has L.5000 capital.

Gross profits at 10 per cent.	.	L.500
Deduct interest at 5 per cent.	.	250
Remains for profit of enterprize	.	250
Deduct salary	100	
Deduct insurance at 2 per cent.	100—200	
Remains for surplus gains	.	L.50

Thus, we see that the surplus gains of the master
who employs a capital of L.10,000, amount to L.200,

---

* The idea of this illustration is taken from Storch, Cours d'Economie Politique, liv. iii. ch. 13, from whom have been derived various
other hints developed in the present chapter. See also Wealth of Nations, book i. ch. x.

while those of the other with L.5000, are L.50. But 200 bears a much larger proportion to 10,000, than 50 to 5000. Consequently, the surplus gains of the manufacturer with the larger stock are not only absolutely greater, but bear a greater ratio also to his capital. And we likewise see the reason of this: it is because the salary remains the same whether the concern be a great or a small one.

Thus the principle is clearly established, that the surplus gains of the master in any department of industry, increase in a greater proportion than the capital employed ; for the larger that capital, the less important is that part of the profits of enterprize which constitutes the reward of his individual labour or trouble. So that when the concern is very extensive, this reward forms but a very insignificant fraction of the whole.

This is a principle which we shall find to be pregnant with important deductions. And though we should suppose the head of a great establishment to bestow on his occupation more time and pains than the master of a more humble one, yet this could but slightly modify the principle ; for the degree of labour which any person can give in the way of direction and superintendence is necessarily limited by the capacities of an individual, whereas, comparatively speaking, there are no bounds to the capital which may be vested in certain occupations when a market sufficiently extensive is at hand. Besides, the qualities required for conducting a great business, are nearly,

if not quite, the same, as are necessary for a small one,
and certainly are not of so much more rare a nature
as to secure for them a far higher rate of remuneration than in the latter case.   The great master is not
like the great actor or singer, whose services are often immensely paid by reason of the scarcity of first-
rate talents in their departments.   Therefore, what
we have called surplus gains must be considered as
quite distinct from the salary of the skill and trouble
of the master, which, as compared with the infinite
power of progression of the former, may be looked
upon as constant.   These surplus gains do truly represent, as before observed, the revenue derived from
the power of commanding the use of capital, whether
belonging to the person himself or borrowed from
others, and are quite separate from the net profits of
capital which can be enjoyed only by the owner
thereof.   And whereas these net profits vary exactly
as the amount of capital, we have on the contrary
shewn of surplus gains, that the larger the capital,
the greater the proportion they bear to the stock employed.   It remains for us to investigate some of the
consequences of this principle.

But, in the first place, we must take notice of a
particular case, in order to show that it is excluded
from the subject now before us ; and that is, when the
master of some little establishment performs at the
same time the work of a common labourer.   In this
case it is evident, that what he gains cannot all be
classed under the head of profits, though in common

language these may be confounded with the wages of ordinary labour, which in reality form a part of his earnings, he being both master and operative in one. Since, therefore, a part of his income consists of wages, and the rest only of profits, though all be usually so denominated, it follows that his *surplus gains* must bear a smaller proportion to the whole that goes under the name of profits, than where wages are reckoned separately. This is quite evident.

But the case of a petty master who does not labour with his own hands, is on this account essentially different from the last, and his income all consists of profits in the proper and restricted sense of the word. Now, we have shown that the larger the scale on which business is carried on, the more does the proportion decrease, which that part serving to remunerate his talents and trouble, bears to the whole. Thus, in the example given above, we have seen that supposing a capital of L.5000, the salary might be represented by L.100, and the insurance and surplus gains together, by L.150; the former being to the latter in the proportion of 2 : 3; but when the capital was L.10,000, the salary being still L.100, and the surplus gains and insurance equal to L.400, the first bore a ratio to the last of only 1 : 4. Were the capital increased to L.20,000, the proportion would be reduced to 1 : 9, and so on; the more considerable the capital, the smaller the per-centage on it which serves to pay the salary of the master.

One very important consequence which follows immediately from this principle is, that the larger the scale on which any business is conducted, the lower the price at which the master can afford to sell his products; for the less the per centage on the value of the goods sold which suffices to give an ample compensation for his talents, time, and trouble, the more latitude will be left for letting down the rate at which he may be willing to dispose of them, without at all encroaching upon his salary or even approaching it. Thus the wholesale merchant can sell cheaper than the retail, and other things being equal, the retail dealer in a great city, where there is an extensive market which admits of the employment of a large capital, can afford to trade on lower terms than the petty shop-keeper in a country village. I say, other things being equal; for there are other causes which tend the contrary way, and may render goods dearer in a city than a provincial situation—such as the necessity of bringing certain objects from a distance, particularly the bulky articles of agricultural produce ; and the high rent of shops in a metropolis.*

Notwithstanding the last cause, most goods, as observed by Adam Smith, not subject to much augmen-

---

* The high rent of shops does not, like that of dwelling houses, depend so much upon their being placed in a fashionable situation, as upon their lying in a populous district of the city, where the number of customers must necessarily be great. Thus, the rents of the ground-floors of houses in the great street St. Denis, at Paris, inhabited chiefly by the working classes, are higher than in the quarter of the Chaussée d'Antin, the abode of the wealthy, though the rents of all the stories above the street are greater in the latter than in the former situation.

tation in price, from cost of inland carriage, are in reality cheaper in the capital than in the provinces, as manufactured stuffs, groceries, and all objects imported from foreign countries.

Edinburgh is far from a small town, yet even there most manufactured goods are dearer than in London.

For the same reason, all articles sold by retail when demanded in very small quantities at a time, are disposed of at a higher price. It costs as much trouble to weigh an ounce of tea as a pound, a pound of sugar as a loaf of twelve or fifteen. Therefore, the poor who live from hand to mouth pay dearer for every thing than the rich.

Besides, the high rent of shops in a metropolis is probably quite balanced by the greater custom, so that prices are not raised on that account. Supposing the size of the shop to remain the same, the greater the quantity of goods sold, the less per centage need be charged on each article, in order to pay the rent which does not vary. Probably in no part of any capital in Europe are rents so high as in the Palais Royal at Paris.* Considering this, the low price there of some objects of consumption is really quite extraordinary. Within its precincts are many eating-houses in which a dinner, consisting of several dishes and wine, served in a handsome apartment with plate

---

* We may form some idea of these enormous rents, from the fact that a seller of roasted chesnuts pays for a mere stand sufficient for himself and a pan of charcoal, at the rate of forty pounds a year during the season.

and linen, can be had for the very moderate sum of
twenty-pence.   Nothing but the very great numbers
who dine in these places daily can account for so low
a price.   The secret of this, as of similar facts, is, that
there are many expenses which do not increase at all
in the same proportion as the quantity sold.   Of these,
the labour of the master, as we have seen, is one, and
rent of ware-rooms is another.   One shopkeeper may
have twice as much custom as his neighbour, and yet
the space occupied by each may be the same.   Thus,
there are in the Palais Royal other eating-houses
quite as spacious as those above alluded to, but in
which, being much more expensive, the company is
never nearly so numerous.   Plenty of elbow room is
a comfort which must be paid by the consumer of the
viands.   Another expense which does not increase in
proportion to the sale, is that of servants, of cooks
for instance in a well frequented tavern.   In those
cheap eating-houses just noticed, the immensity of
the concern admits of a better subdivision of labour,
so that fewer hands suffice.   Also, it seems likely that
the waste must be proportionally much less, for the
numbers who dine in a cheap place are more nearly
the same every day, than in a dear one, where caprice
and fashion prevail.

Thus it appears, that the fact on which I have
lately dwelt, that almost the same trouble is required on the part of the petty trader as of the great,
is only one instance of the general principle, that
there are many expenses which do not augment

in the same proportion as the quantity sold. It is on this account that an extensive market tends to lower price. Do we not constantly hear those well acquainted with London and Paris say, that no where can a single man live cheaper, provided he know how to set about it?

This very cause now under consideration helps us to explain a circumstance generally allowed, and stated by Adam Smith in particular, namely, the lower rate of profit in a great city. This fact, allowing it to be one, may strike us at first as rather singular. One cause however of this readily presents itself, namely, the high rate of wages in a capital. In Paris for instance, the wages of house servants are much greater than in the provinces. A good woman servant gets in that city sixteen pounds a year, while at Versailles, but a dozen miles off, only twelve are commonly given. In remote parts, the difference is still more considerable. Though Edinburgh be called the capital of Scotland, Glasgow is both a larger and a more increasing town. Accordingly, the wages of domestic servants are higher in the latter than in the former. And if this kind of labour is better paid, the same, we may suppose, must hold good of other sorts.

This cause explains, in part at least, the lower rate of profit in great cities. But that mentioned in the present chapter must also be taken into account. The gross profits of retailers are higher in remote and thinly peopled districts, because in such situations the reward of a peculiar kind of labour forms a larger proportion of that revenue, which thus is greatly swelled. In all places, the salary of enterprise con-stitutes a part of Gross Profits; but the narrower the market, this part is the more considerable.

I shall now bring forward an example which will prove satisfactorily, how much the price at which a master can afford to sell his goods, must depend upon the scale on which his business is carried on.

A capital of L.300 is a large one for a shopkeeper, say a grocer, in a country situation, and there are many localities in which it would not be easy to find employment in that line for so considerable a stock. Now, a village grocer in order to make up for the smallness of the market, generally sells a great variety of miscellaneous articles, such as there commonly is a demand for in the neighbourhood. He must there-fore possess knowledge, extending to a considerable number of commodities, in regard to their prices, qualities, and the best places for obtaining them, and this knowledge must be even more general than is required by the far wealthier city shop-keeper, where the extent of the market permits of a greater subdi-vision of trades. Nor are there any qualifications necessary to the latter which are not likewise so to the former. The acquirements of reading, writing, and a facility in accounts, are indispensable to both, as are a power of calculation and foresight, habits of business, industry, and a character for honest dealing.

In fact, of the two, more knowledge and shrewdness are required in the country tradesman, for as I have said, he usually sells a greater variety of articles, and as the demand for each is more uncertain, his business can be less reduced to a routine, and he must be more frequently put to his wits for a change of stock to meet the fluctuating wants of his customers. So that we may well suppose him entitled to as high a reward for his talents and trouble as his brother shop-keeper of the city.   L.60 a-year must be allowed to be a very moderate allowance for the possession of such various acquirements; indeed, it is less than the wages of a butler, who besides L.50 or L.60 a-year is fed into the bargain.   But not to overstrain the argument, I am willing to put it at the lowest.   Now, supposing interest at five per cent. in order that the country tradesman with his capital of L.300 may gain for himself a salary of L.60, it is necessary that during the course of the year he sell goods to the amount of his stock with a Gross Profit upon them of twenty-five per cent.   And on this supposition, be it remarked, there remains for profits of enterprise, after deducting those of capital at five per cent. a salary only, and that a very modest one; for insurance against risk, and for surplus gains, nothing, absolutely nothing.

Now, let us take the case of the grocer in the city, in whose business a capital of L.3000 may easily be employed.   If, during the year, he sell goods to that amount at only ten per cent. gross profit, there will

remain to him, after deducting the interest on his capital at five per cent. as before, L.150 for the profits
of enterprise, thus leaving L.90 over and above his
salary which we suppose to be L.60 as in the former
case.   So that charging on his merchandize ten per
cent. he has L.90 for a premium against loss and
for surplus gains; whereas, the country shop-keeper
though making twenty-five per cent. on his stock, gains
his salary and nothing more. It is impossible, I think,
to prove in a more satisfactory manner, that the large
dealer can afford to sell much cheaper than the small,
and this because it requires so much lower a per centage on the value sold, to pay the salary of the master, where the total value is great than where it is
comparatively trifling.

But the above example will serve to prove something more.   It shows the advantage of selling a
large quantity at a lower price and rate of gross
profit, rather than a small quantity at a higher price;
for the city grocer in charging only ten per cent. had
surplus gains to a considerable amount, greater than
even his whole salary, while the village grocer, with his
gross profit of twenty-five per cent. had no surplus
gains at all.   And this points out the reason of the
proverb that money makes money, and proves that
the greater are a person's gains, the more easy does it
become still further to increase them.   The chief difficulty is in the commencement, for as the profits of
enterprise then comprehend little but a simple salary
from which a person must live, it must be very hard

to save any thing out of it, whereas, this capability must increase in proportion to the surplus gains, which grow in a greater ratio than the capital and business extend.

But this extension of business and accumulation of stock are limited by the extent of the market. Where it is small, no degree of industry and talents can ever make a large fortune, because, beyond a certain point, there is no room for the employment of the gains realized. A person cannot take upon himself a great variety of occupations with much prospect of success, for his attention would thus be too much divided, and hence, the probability of failure in *all*, exceedingly increased. So that when once a man has vested in his own branch of trade all the stock to which the wants of his customers can give employment, there is nothing left for him but to lay out his future gains at interest, and content himself with the net profits of capital. Hence, it is in cities only that large fortunes are ever rapidly made, for there a master can always enlarge his business along with his capital; and if he get credit, even to a much greater extent than his own funds permit. For the same reason, no very colossal fortunes are ever made by *farming*; for there is a limit easily attained, beyond which the constant superintendance of the agriculturist becomes impossible, without which, however, success is necessarily doubtful. The difference between this last case and the former, is this, that the business of farming is limited by its very nature; whereas, in the other instance, it is only the want of customers, and the thinly-peopled neighbourhood which set bounds to the employment of stock.

Supposing then, the trade to be one in which fresh capital can always be vested without losing the personal superintendance of the head of the establishment, and that the market is sufficiently extensive, we have found why the more any business enlarges, the greater is the facility for its further progression, and why the rich man's fortune accumulates in a far more rapid proportion than that of the poor.

And this leads directly to a very important consequence, namely, that the concentration of capital in the hands of a comparatively small number of masters is more favourable to its rapid accumulation, and the increase of national wealth, than its subdivision among a larger body of persons ; and, hence, that a great equality of fortunes, however desirable it may be in other respects, is not the state of things most conducive to the augmentation of the riches of a country.   Thus, taking the example above given, we find that the head of an establishment having a capital of L.3000, would be able, by selling his goods at the moderate gross profit of 10 per cent. to realize his salary and L.90 in addition, forming a fund out of which savings can easily be made.   Now, were this capital split into ten parts, each belonging to a separate individual, we should have instead of *one* capital of L.3000, *ten* of L.300.   But we have seen that a master possessing L.300 of capital, can gain nothing but his salary even in charging 25 per cent. on his merchandise. And as this is the fund for the maintetenance of himself and family, of course his power of accumulating must be very small, and can be possible at all, only by very strict economy. Such is the case of every one of the *ten* small traders, so that their united capabilities of saving must be very limited, as compared with those of the single rich master. And this instance proves the general truth above stated; and were the difference of fortunes greater, the more would the disparity appear between the facilities for amassing wealth in the opposite instances.

This cause of a more rapid accumulation of wealth where large capitals are employed by a few, rather than small ones by many, is quite distinct from another arising out of these different states, but which tends to a similar result; namely, the better direction that can be given to the instruments of production in the former case than in the latter. Where masters have the command of large capitals, they can introduce the most perfect division of labour, they can adopt all the newly-invented and most improved machines for economising it, however costly in the first instance these may be ; and they can afford to lay out large sums in improvements from which little return can be expected for a length of time, as is particularly the case with rich farmers. Hence, the master who carries on the business of production on a large scale, has great advantages over him, whose establishment is limited by the want of funds of his own, or of power to borrow them, and he can generally create a greater return in proportion to the expense. In a word, land, labour, and capital, are more productive in his hands. Consequently, on this account also, the concentration of stock in the hands of a comparatively small number of masters, is more favourable to the increase of national wealth, than its dispersion among many.

Having thus fully allowed the more rapid advance of national wealth to be expected from the concentration of capital, and having stated the causes, arising out of this concentration, to which the more rapid advance is immediately to be attributed, I must be allowed to add a few observations which may tend to limit our admiration for this state of things.

And, in the first place, I would remark, in reference to the cause first mentioned, that although the master who sets in motion an extensive capital, has greater facilities for saving than several minor ones whose united funds are equal to his, yet it does not necessarily follow, that he actually does accumulate more. For we must remember that it is a principle of human nature, that wants increase with the means, desires with the opportunities of satisfying them. Thus, the merchant or manufacturer who in the beginning of his career was satisfied with a comfortable, though humble house, in the commercial part of the city, by and by must have a more spacious mansion, and in a more fashionable situation; his wife perhaps pines for a house in the country, hence, the necessity for two establishments; his daughters must be handsomely dressed, have piano and harp masters, and singing masters, servants to attend them; and for all, equipages are indispensable. Thus it happens in many cases, that the more a man makes, the less he saves; for even if he were himself economically inclined, his family would spend for him. Not only do the desires rise with the increase of fortune, but generally in a far greater proportion, so true is it that Man is insatiable.

On the other hand, the little master-capitalist, whose desires are repressed by the impossibility of gratifying them, generally lives very frugally, and contrives to save even with his limited capability. So that, in practice, the concentration of capital in the hands of a few is not quite so favourable to accumulation, as the causes above stated would at first lead us to imagine.

But even allowing, as I am willing to do, that the concentration of capital is in reality favourable to the amount of national wealth, yet it does not follow necessarily from that admission that it is upon the whole advantageous or desirable. For we must always bear in mind, that the manner in which riches are divided and distributed, is a matter of no less consequence than their absolute quantity. Division and distribution,* not less than production, belong to

* By Division of Wealth I mean Division of Capitals; by Distribution, the Partition of the Gross Produce among labourers, masters, capitalists, and landlords.

political economy. But perhaps this truth has not always been attended to by writers upon this subject so much as it ought to have been, and hence many prejudices have been entertained by the public in regard to the science of wealth. Political economists have often been looked upon as cold-blooded calculators, who, provided the national riches and power increased, were careless of the welfare of individuals, who would be content that the great mass of the population should gain a bare subsistence, if the profits of master-capitalists were thereby augmented, and who could behold with indifference children condemned to toil for ten or twelve hours a-day, in close, over-heated cotton-mills, and adults for fifteen or sixteen, so that the country maintained its character for manufacturing pre-eminence. In this case as in others, the sins of a few have been attributed to many, and even the science itself covered with unmerited obloquy. No doubt, writers may be found whose opinions are not very different from those above stated, whose sympathies are all on the side of the rich masters, and who, provided wealth be produced, care little for the price paid for it, the excessive toil and premature death of the labouring poor. Others, again, also led away by their too exclusive admiration for amount of wealth, have attempted to prove that no such hardships attend the mode in which it is often created, and that a spinner who labours for fifteen or sixteen hours in the atmosphere of a cotton-mill, is likely to enjoy as much health and happiness as the rustic who spends a great part of his life under the open canopy of heaven. All the world, it would appear, have been in error since the beginning of time, in supposing free air and a country situation favourable to human life and enjoyment. When such opinions were broached by writers on political economy, it is no wonder that some degree of discredit should have attached itself to a science, which, as treated by them, seemed repugnant to common sense, and the first principles of humanity.

It is therefore of the greater consequence to attend to the source whence these erroneous views may be supposed to flow. And this I conceive to be, the giving too exclusive an attention to the Production of wealth, as if the Amount thereof were the one thing needful, and the Division and Distribution of comparatively trifling importance.

Now, these last are not only of themselves a matter of the greatest moment, but belong to political economy quite as much as the other. Whatever harsh views, then, may have been taken by some writers, by attending too exclusively to one branch of the inquiry, these form no just objection to the science itself, but only to their too narrow way of considering the subject.

If the question, By what means can the greatest amount of wealth be produced? be *one* grand practical problem which political economy is destined to

solve, another, and no less important one is, What
mode of division and distribution of this wealth would
be most conducive to the general happiness? Therefore, after showing that the concentration of capital
in the hands of a comparatively small number of masters, is more favourable to the increase of national
wealth, than its dispersion amongst a more numerous
body, it does not necessarily follow, that the former
mode of distribution is to be preferred.

If Wealth be of any avail to human happiness—and
who will deny it?—the more people possessed of it,
the better, particularly if we consider that poverty is
a far greater evil, than much riches in the hands of any
individual is a good. It may then be assumed as a
general principle, that the larger the number of persons not entirely dependent upon their daily labour
for subsistence, the better it is for any country. And
though wealth should accumulate more slowly under
these circumstances, than where the inhabitants are
chiefly divided into two classes, that of great capitalists,
and *proletaires,* as the French call those who, having
no accumulated fund, live precariously from day to
day, yet can we for a moment doubt which state of
things is most conducive to the welfare of the great
mass of the population? and therefore to national
prosperity in the only true sense of the word? A
pretty sort of national prosperity would that be, in
which the increase of the general wealth should go
chiefly to swell the already enormous incomes of a few

great master-capitalists, and to enlarge the numbers of a beggarly class of labourers!

Our sister island affords an example of a *prosperity* of this last description. There can be no doubt that the wealth of Ireland has increased exceedingly since the narrow and most unjust restrictions imposed upon its commerce by Great Britain have been done away with. This is proved by the progressive increase in its exports and imports since the Union. Indeed, so very remarkable is this increase, that M. Storch has dedicated a long note to the subject, it being one of the most remarkable instances of rapid advance in national prosperity with which he was acquainted.*

To the inhabitants of Great Britain, who know something of the real condition of the people of Ireland, it cannot but be a matter of astonishment to hear that country brought forward as foremost in the race of improvement. Now, I do not question the facts brought forward by the Russian economist. These facts may be quite true; but what do they prove? They prove the very point upon which I am now insisting, that a nation *may* increase greatly in wealth, and yet the mass of the population be little the better. Notwithstanding this unexampled prosperity, are the peasantry of that country less miserably poor than formerly? Are famines less frequent, epidemics less fatal, riots and murders more uncommon?

* See Note A.

I would not, however, be supposed to mean, that the only consequences of this rapid increase in the wealth of Ireland since the throwing open of its trade, have been the augmentation of the fortunes of those already rich, and an immense enlargement of the population. A great permanent good has undoubtedly arisen to Ireland since its productive powers were set at liberty, which consists in the greater numbers and wealth of the middle classes, in the towns particularly, who, I have no doubt, form a much more important body than they did forty or fifty years ago. The force of the Catholics exerted in the cause of emancipation is one proof of this, for the greater part of the *landed* property of the island is in the hands of Protestants. Still, the country at large has benefited much less from the sudden increase of its riches that followed the Union, than it would have done under a better distribution of the mass of wealth. There can be no doubt that it would be in a far more happy condition, one of much more real prosperity, if a considerably smaller amount of productions were more equally divided among the inhabitants. For, notwithstanding the great wealth of *some*, and the easy circumstances of *many*, the *mass* of the people is the most miserable in Europe. It seems impossible to bring forward a more striking example to prove the importance of that branch of political economy which treats of the Distribution of Riches.

From the principles above expounded, which go to

prove that a concentration of capital is favourable to accumulation, it follows that an equality of partition among all the members of a family, however desirable it may be on other accounts, is not the state of things most conducive to a rapid increase in the wealth of a nation. I do not here allude to the subdivision of landed property, that is a thing quite distinct from the equal partition of capital, and has peculiar inconveniences of its own, while on the other hand it does not follow because the concentration of capital is favourable to accumulation, that therefore that of land is so likewise. The principles which proved that a small number of rich master-capitalists had greater facilities for amassing wealth, than a larger body of poor ones, derived from a consideration of the nature of profits of enterprise, do not at all apply to the case of landholders, considered merely as owners of the soil. In that capacity they neither are capitalists, nor do they exercise any branch of industry. But all the arguments which tend to show that the actual savings of the rich trader or manufacturer will not be in proportion to his facilities for making them, on account of the tendency to extravagance which grows along with his fortune, bear with tenfold force on the case of the great landlord, who, of all classes of persons, is notoriously most apt to live up to his income, and even beyond it, which small proprietors but very seldom do. For these reasons, and others, land and capital must be carefully distinguished, and it is only in reference to the latter that I consider it to follow

as a consequence from the principles above established, that the system of equal division among all the
children of a family, is not the most favourable to the
increase in the amount of national wealth.* Notwithstanding this drawback, the equal partition of
moveable property is highly desirable, the advantages
of such a division greatly outweighing the above inconvenience.

Whatever may be the opinions of an author on any
subject, truth and candour require that he state the
evils attached to that system, which yet, upon the
whole, he regards as preferable to any other.

We now come to another consequence of our principles. If the concentration of capital in the hands
of a comparatively small number of masters, be the
state of things which gives the greatest facilities for
saving, on account of the *surplus gains* being proportionally so much larger as the capital employed increases, it must also afford the most ample means for
the collection of a public revenue. The same arguments which show, that one master who employs a
capital of L.3000 in his business, can accumulate
much more easily than *ten* persons having each L.300
engaged in production, prove also that the former can pay a larger sum to government without
much hardship, than all the others put together.

---

* If subdivision of landed estates leads necessarily to that of farms,
then indeed the same argument may be used. And this, as we shall see
hereafter, is in reality the case. But the very important subject of division of land cannot be treated till after a full inquiry into the Theory
of Rent.

Therefore it follows, that of two nations supposed to possess equal amounts of wealth, the one in which master-capitalists were fewer but richer, (and consequently the class of *proletaires* more numerous,) would be able to raise a larger revenue for the exigencies of the state, than the other, in which capital was more dispersed. Therefore the former would be able to maintain larger fleets and armies, and for a longer period, and on this account would be more powerful than the latter.

In the above case, the two nations are supposed to be equal in riches. The superior capabilities of the one over the other, in raising a public revenue, and maintaining fleets and armies, depends entirely on a different division. But if we consider that the same mode of division which is favourable to a large State revenue, is also that most conducive to a rapid increase of national wealth, as formerly shown, we can easily suppose that that country in which capital is less dispersed, will probably be more powerful, not only from the manner in which wealth is divided, but also from its greater amount. Thus, concentration of capital is both an immediate and remote cause of the greater political importance of that people among whom it prevails. For these reasons, Great Britain is now, and is likely to continue, more powerful in proportion to its extent, than France.

There is still another way in which, it may be thought, a great equality of fortunes is unfavourable, though remotely, to the national wealth, and that is, by its effects upon the spirit of enterprise. A man's activity, it will be said, and truly, depends upon his desires; in proportion to their intensity, will be the energy of his conduct. Now, nothing is more calculated to moderate desire than the circumstance of living in a society, of which none of the members are greatly elevated one above another in point of riches. It is ambition of the honours, luxuries, and general distinction which wait upon great wealth, as well as a dread of the stigma which, in enterprising and commercial communities, public opinion attaches to those not actively employed in the improvement of their fortune, that alone can induce persons already far raised above the fear of want, to engage in industrious occupations. But the greater the equality of fortunes, the less do the advantages, real or supposed, of superior riches, present themselves to view, and the less is the tranquillity of the man of moderate means liable to be disturbed by dreams of grandeur and power. Hence a great spur to enterprise is done away with, or deadened at least, and when once it has become usual for persons of middling fortunes to live upon the interest of their capitals, without toiling to improve them, public opinion becomes changed, and no longer stigmatises such people as idle and useless.

He, who, in a certain situation, surrounded by his superiors in fortune, though not in birth, has been accustomed to consider himself quite a poor man, and could not endure the idea of living quietly upon what he already possessed ; if transported to another country, (without supposing his income to go at all farther in the purchase of necessaries and comforts than in his former place of residence,) might suddenly find himself quite on a par with his associates, and hence his ardour for bettering his condition would certainly decline.   Such is the argument in full that may be argued against a considerable equality of fortunes, as unfavourable to the progress of a nation's prosperity, by deadening the spirit of enterprise.

But however specious it may at first sight appear, upon a nearer view, it will, I think, be found erroneous.   I have been induced to touch upon this objection for *two* reasons ; first, because having had occasion to mention certain effects arising from a great equality of fortunes, which seemed to prove that state of things *not* the one most favourable to a rapid increase of national wealth or national power, I wished at the same time to do away with any arguments against it, which appear to me void of foundation. And, in the second place, I thought that a consideration of this objection might throw some additional light on the nature of the industry exercised by the master of an establishment.

What I consider the fundamental error of the above argument is, the supposing it to be of any consequence to the nation whether capital be employed by its owner, or by any other person, provided it be employed at all. Those persons whose desire of bettering their condition is deadened by the general equality of fortune around them, are supposed to live upon the interest of their capitals, and if so, these capitals must be engaged in some branch of productive industry.* And who can say, they are not likely to be turned to as much advantage by him who borrows with the view of enlarging the sphere of his transactions, as by the owner in person? In fact, from what has been above shown, it follows, that of the two, it is more for the interest of the national wealth, that one individual should charge himself with the management of the funds of several small capitalists, than that each should engage in a separate employment of his own.

It is impossible then that the nation can at all suffer from the want of enterprise in those possessors of capital who are content to live upon the interest of their fortunes, so long as individuals are found able and willing to turn them to account. And if by any chance the numbers composing the former class should increase so much, that a difficulty should arise of finding persons to whom their funds could safely and advantageously be trusted, the rate of interest would fall so low from the increased competition of the lenders, that many of them finding it impossible to exist on it alone, would therefore be obliged to enter into some active occupation. Thus, the evil, if it be one, carries along with it a principle of self-correction.

---

* No doubt capital may be lent to government also, or other unproductive borrowers, but this is not peculiar to any one state of society, and certainly is likely to happen, at least as frequently where much inequality of fortunes prevails, as where they are more upon a par.

Therefore a great equality of fortunes cannot be found fault with on these grounds.

And this brings me to take notice of a remarkable difference between the nature of the labour of the master of an establishment, and that of the common workmen. It can rarely if ever happen that one of these last can do as much as two, far less as *three* of his brethren in the same occupation, but the toil of one master may easily replace that of *ten* or more of his comrades. Who will say that any great manufacturer engaged in the cotton, silk, or woollen trade, cannot just as well superintend the emplòyment of a capital of ten or fifteen thousand pounds, as of one thousand? Consequently, the labour of one person can stand instead of that of ten or fifteen. The same is true, though not to the same extent, of farming. Within certain limits, a tract of land can in most cases be just as well cultivated by one rich agriculturist, as by five or six poorer tenants or proprietors. Now, this economy of labour is the very fundamental cause of the superiority which the great master has been above proved to have over the smaller, both as regards the price at which he can afford to sell his products, and his facilities for saving. Instead of many masters having to get the reward of their trouble out of the united value of the several returns to their industry, one only has to pay himself. No wonder then that he can afford to sell cheaper, and yet have a greater surplus above his salary than all the others put together.

Thus we see that an increase in the numbers of masters of industry, does not necessarily constitute a new fountain of riches; whereas every able-bodied ordinary labourer joined to the population of a country, is a certain addition to the sources of its wealth.

CHAPTER VII.

ON RENT.

IN commencing the inquiry into the distribution of
wealth, I mentioned the different classes of persons
entitled to a share in the gross produce of industry,
and enumerated Labourers, Masters, Capitalists, and
Landlords, as owners of three grand sources of production, Labour, Capital, and Land; the only sources for
the use of which some compensation can be demanded. I also took notice, that it is not until population
has made some progress in a country, that any thing
is paid for land, and therefore concluded, that there
must be causes regulating the respective shares of the
labourer, master, and capitalist, anterior to, and altogether independent of those which afterwards determine the portion of the landlord. Having now investigated the former class of causes, having treated
of Wages and Profits, without any reference to Rent,
this last remains to be considered.

In this inquiry, several points are to be attended
to. First, we must accurately determine what is
meant by Rent.

Secondly, we must state the Causes which give rise
to Rent in general, whether high or low, great or

small, the causes, in short, from which it results, that there is any such thing as rent at all.

Thirdly, it is to be seen what are the Causes which Limit its Amount.

Lastly, it will remain to be known whether the creation of Rent occasions any Change in Wages and Profits, or in the Value and Price of Commodities.

It may perhaps be necessary to repeat, in the first place, what has already been remarked, that it is not the surface alone of the land which affords rent, but also the bowels of the earth, whence minerals are drawn, and internal waters abounding in fish. The very same principles apply to these, but at present I shall confine my observations more particularly to land taken in its more limited and usual signification.*

Rent, in its most general sense, is that portion of the gross produce of the land or waters which remains to the owner of these sources of wealth, after replacing the fixed capital expended, and paying according to the usual rate, the wages of labour, and the profits of the master-capitalist. But though this is the sense generally given to it in Political Economy, it is far from being always taken in this strict signification in the usual intercourse of society. It is constantly mixed up and confounded with the interest paid for

---

* Giving the most enlarged meaning to the word, Mr. Malthus has thus defined land. " The soil, mines, waters, and fisheries of the habitable globe. It is the main source of raw materials and food."—*Definitions in Political Economy.*

the use of capital. Thus, when a farmer takes the lease of a certain extent of ground, the whole sum which he pays to the landlord goes under the denomination of rent, though some part of it may be in reality the interest or net profit of capital previously expended in ameliorating the soil. Another portion of the sum total is probably nothing more than a compensation paid for the use of a house and farm offices erected at the expense of the landlord. Now, the rent of a dwelling-house has nothing to do with the primary distribution of the gross produce, it forms no part of the primitive revenue of the society, for a building of this kind is essentially unproductive. The rent, then, as it is called, which is paid for it, must be drawn from a source of revenue previously existing, whether land, labour, or capital.

Rent being understood as above strictly defined, and not according to the popular and loose signification, it is to be seen how it comes to pass, after paying all the expenses of production, together with the profits of the master-capitalist, that in certain cases, a surplus should remain. What at first cannot but strike us, is, that this seems at variance with the conclusion formerly arrived at, as to the value of commodities being regulated by the cost of raising them. Accordingly, I shall have to point out in the course of the following inquiry, some limitations to which this principle is liable.

Rent of land seems to owe its origin to two causes,

1. The Limited Quantity of land best adapted for Cultivation.

2. The existence of Property in Land.

The land best adapted for cultivation is either that of the greatest natural fertility, or else the most advantageously situated for getting the produce disposed of, lying contiguous to a navigable river, or the sea, or in the neighbourhood of a populous district. Now, land of this description, particularly that favoured chiefly by situation, is in every country more or less limited. In the infancy, indeed, of society, perhaps even for a considerable time subsequent to the commencement of cultivation, land of the best quality may be said to be unlimited in reference to the number of people able to turn it to account. More may still be lying in a state of nature, than there are hands to till it, or mouths to consume the produce which it is capable of bearing. In such a state of things, the best land may be had for nothing, as much as the rain which waters the ground, or the streams which flow from the mountains. The price of agricultural produce, like that of other things, will be regulated by the cost of raising it, it will suffice for wages and profits, but will leave no surplus for rent. If, however, population and cultivation continue to increase and extend, it is evident that a time must come sooner or latter, when the whole of the most fertile and best situated land shall have already been subjected to the plough. What then will be the consequence of a still enlarging demand for agricultural produce? Of course it will rise in price. If there be no other lands capable of cultivation, there will be no means of increasing the supply in proportion to the demand. Consequently, the price instantly becomes one of monoply, and may rise to any height according to the wants of the consumers, and their powers of purchasing.

In the mean time, if those who cultivate the land, have, by the authority of government, been able to appropriate it, they will enjoy extraordinary profits from the high price of corn, &c., which cannot be brought down by competition. Should these gains become great, some of the owners of land might be glad to subsist on a part of them, provided they could find any one to take the trouble of managing the farm, and who, at the same time, would engage to pay them a portion of the produce.

On the other hand, there will probably be found men possessed of some capital, and anxious to employ it in agricultural pursuits, but who are at a loss how to set about it from the want of new land fit for tillage. These are just the persons to suit the landowners desirous of ease and retirement. A bargain is struck between them and the master-capitalists. The competition among the latter will prevent them deriving from the employment of their stock more than the ordinary profits; the rest of the produce, or of its value, will be paid to the landlord under the name of rent.

Rent then is originally nothing else than an extraordinary profit derived from the high price of corn, which high price is owing to the scantiness of the supply as compared with the demand, which again ultimately depends upon the limited quantity of good land. Consequently, in the commencement at all events, rent is an *effect* of high price, not a *cause* thereof. It adds nothing to the national wealth, but as is the case in all monopolies, whether natural or artificial, what is gained by one set of men is lost by another. In the present instance, the high price paid for raw produce by the consumer serves to swell the incomes of the proprietors of land. A portion of wealth is thus transferred from the pockets of one class of persons to those of another, and nothing more.

That rent is not the effect of an addition to the *quantity* of commodities, but to their *value* only, is evident from this, that the very same land, with the very same produce, may at one time afford this revenue, at another not. Land, in the back settlements of America, of the highest fertility, and bearing exuberant crops, gives no rent, while similar soil in England would yield a very high one. We are therefore warranted in concluding that the best soils in the latter country formerly gave none, however abundant may have been the return. By and by, rent will be created on the banks of the Ohio and Illinois, as well as on those of the Thames and Severn.

It seems evident that the existence of rent, as a separate branch of revenue, depends upon both the causes above stated, and not upon one alone. If the quantity of the most favoured land were unlimited, however great the increase of population and the consequent demand might be, still, as the supply could be proportionally enlarged at *no greater cost of production than before*, no reason can be shown why the price of corn should rise any more than that of any other commodity whatsoever. The limitation in the quantity of the best land is therefore a circumstance essential to that rise of price, and hence to the origin of rent. Still, unless the right of property in the soil were generally recognised, no rent as distinct from profits would be paid to any one. Supposing that in such a state of things cultivation could at all be carried on, the present occupier might no doubt derive extraordinary profits from the high price of his produce, but could never be able to let any portion of territory on condition of receiving a part of these great profits under the denomination of rent. For he could not secure to any person the undisturbed possession of the farm even for a year, and every one would think himself as much entitled to it as the occupier. The institution of property in land is then essential to the separation of rent from profits as a distinct branch of revenue belonging to a particular class. Indeed, this is so obvious as not to require being at all dwelt upon, though, for the sake of accuracy, the simple statement of such a cause is necessary.

Having traced the causes which give rise to rent in general, it is now to be seen what are those

which limit its amount. In the preceding observations, it has been supposed, for the sake of simplicity,
that there is but one quality of land susceptible of
cultivation, and on that hypothesis it has been shown
that at whatever period in the progress of society the
whole shall be tilled and occupied, upon a farther demand for raw produce, its price will rise above what
has been called a remunerating price, and rent will
in consequence be created. It is the more necessary to insist upon this point, as it has been imagined that rent essentially depends upon the difference in the fertility of soils. But we have seen
that it may arise where there exists land fit for cultivation of but one quality only, provided it be limited in extent. The circumstance of there being other
soils inferior in point of fertility or situation, but still
capable of affording some produce on the application
of labour and capital, does not give origin to rent on
lands more highly favoured, but on the contrary
limits its amount. Were it not for the existence of
these second rate tracts of country, so soon as the
only land fit for raising corn was all taken in, no limit
could be assigned to the rise in raw produce, and the
consequent increase in rents, but what might result
from a stationary population.* But these inferior
soils set bounds to the progressive rise. After the

---

* I of course suppose the country to be confined to its own resources,
and destitute of foreign commerce, by means of which supplies of corn
may be brought from a distance, so as to keep down prices and rents at
home.

price of corn has advanced to a certain degree above what is sufficient to pay all the expenses attendant on the cultivation of the best lands, it may become profitable to employ capital and labour in the clearing and improving those not quite so good. Thus a fresh supply of vegetable food is poured into the market, and a further rise in its price prevented.

But this increased quantity of agricultural products cannot lower the price to what it once was, for, as by the supposition the lands newly taken in are inferior in fertility or situation to the old, and consequently more expensive in the cultivation, a permanently higher value of corn becomes an indispensable condition of the supply. Were it to fall, these lands would be abandoned, till a deficiency in the quantity of grain brought to market should again elevate its price. This price, then, comes to be regulated by the cost of raising produce on the inferior soils. We have seen that it cannot permanently fall below this, neither can it for any considerable period be much above it, so long as fresh supplies can be obtained from these second-rate lands. These last, it is evident, will afford a profit before the price of grain rises so high as to yield a rent upon them, and this profit will offer a sufficient motive for taking them in. The cultivator will not wait for such an augmentation in the value of agricultural products as may secure him an extraordinary profit ; he will be satisfied with one not inferior to what can be gained in other occupations.   Consequently, the lands last brought under tillage will afford no rent.

Moreover, as the cost of raising produce on these last regulates the price not only of what is grown on them, but also of that which is obtained from the most favoured soils, since it puts a stop for a period to its farther advance, it must therefore limit the rise of rent on the lands first brought under the plough.   Whatever may be the difference in the gross return to equal capitals expended on the respective soils in question, rent cannot go beyond this. If, for instance, an acre of the most fertile ground should yield eight quarters of wheat, while another of second-rate quality with the very same expenditure gives but six, two quarters, or the value of the same, would be the rent paid for the former.   For if six quarters be sufficient to afford a fair profit in the one case, so will it in the other, since by the supposition the capitals advanced were equal.   And the competition among those anxious to vest their stock and employ their industry in the cultivation of the soil, will enable the proprietors of estates to obtain from the farmer all above the ordinary compensation for the use of his capital, for his risk and trouble.   Six quarters being, it seems, in the present state of things, sufficient for these purposes, two will remain over to the landlord.   Thus it is that the rise of rent on the best lands is limited by the cost of raising produce on those in some degree inferior.

It is evident that this series of events may be constantly renewed so long as the demand for raw produce and its price continues progressively to advance, and so long as there exists any land in the country not yet taken in, but capable of being turned to agricultural purposes. On every fresh increase in the price of corn, an augmented rent will be demanded, and can be paid, on soil of the best quality, and the same will for the first time be created on that which previously gave none. This rise in the price of grain, and consequently the amount of this augmented or newly created rent, will again be limited by the price at which corn can be grown with a profit on land still inferior in point of fertility or situation. As before, whatever may be the difference in the return to equal capitals expended on land, that difference will constitute rent. Thus, when soil of the first quality gave a produce of eight quarters per acre, and that of a second-rate nature only six, we found that two quarters would be the amount of rent paid for the former. Should the tracts next brought into cultivation, on an equal expense being bestowed upon them, return no more than four quarters, and yet continue to be tilled, then, it is evident, that at the actual prices, this amount of produce would give a fair, that is, the ordinary rate of profit. But if it does so on one sort of land, so will it on another, the capitals expended being still supposed the same. Consequently, the farmers who cultivate the superior soils will not be able, on the expiration of their leases, to keep for themselves more than four quarters; the surplus will go to the landlords. This surplus in the one case will now be four quarters, and in the other, where no rent was formerly paid, it will be two. Still, the land last taken in affords none.

This series of changes may be repeated again and again, until there remain no more new land capable of bearing crop, and no possibility of further improvement of the old. For it is clear, that a fresh supply of grain, whether obtained from virgin soils, or by the application of more labour and fixed capital to those already under tillage, will equally have the effect of putting a stop to the further rise of prices and rents. Until both these means of increasing the produce are exhausted, its price cannot be permanently elevated above that which is sufficient to remunerate the grower who gets the smallest return in proportion to the expense. Should cultivation ever extend to such a degree, that no more corn could in any way be raised from the soil, then indeed (always supposing foreign supply out of the question,) there would be no limit to the possible rise in the price of grain, and consequently in rents, except a stationary or decreasing demand resulting from similar states of the population. Then the price of corn would be that of an unlimited monopoly, whereas formerly this monopoly had its bounds. In such a state of things, even the land last taken in might afford rent, for what is to prevent the price of its produce rising above that which is simply sufficient to remunerate the farmer?

As soon as it does get beyond this, the landlord will demand a rent, and cannot fail of finding persons able and willing to pay it.

That the condition of China is not far removed from this, seems not improbable, more particularly as the policy of its government, as we know, is so much opposed to foreign commerce. But though we are obliged to turn to China in order to find an example of a country, in which the whole of the territory capable of bearing the most ordinary products is cultivated to the utmost, yet we may find states nearer home, where all the land on which certain peculiar crops can be raised, has long been made the most of. This is the case in France, and in other wine countries, with those soils which give grapes affording a liquor of singular excellence. The territory whence such choice wines can be derived is never extensive, and sometimes exceedingly limited. These lands having long been so highly cultivated, that no more produce can by any means be drawn from them, its price has by degrees been elevated far above what is sufficient to pay the expenses of raising even that portion of it which has occasioned the greatest outlay. All this land, then, even the least productive, yields a rent to the proprietor.

This instance is exactly in point, and proves what would be the case with wheat and barley lands, potatoe grounds, &c., supposing that all the territory capable of raising these crops should in time be fully cultivated. The only difference is in the immensely greater surface calculated for such products, which must put off to a far distant day, the period when no farther return of them can by any means be drawn from the soil.

Having now traced the causes which give origin to rent, and those which set limits to its rise, it remains to be seen, rent being once created, whether it in any manner affects the value of the products of the soil.

Since it has been shown that rent is the *effect* of a high price of agricultural produce, not the *cause*, this question may appear already decided. Prices and values, it may be thought, are quite independent of rent.

But though this is true of rent in its origin, and in respect to those commodities the price of which first rises high enough to afford such a revenue, still it is possible that it may *afterwards* influence the value of other agricultural productions.

Whatever the most ordinary food of the people may be, since this is required in a greater quantity than any thing else, it will soonest reach that price at which rent may be paid. The lands then on which such food is raised, will be the first on which this income is created. But though the demand for the principal article of consumption increases much faster than that for any thing else, particularly in the early stages of a nation's progress, yet as society advances in wealth and population, a demand for other productions which mainly depend on the soil, arises and extends with more or less rapidity. The chief of these are animal food for man, and grass and other vegetable substances required for the maintenance of cattle, and of the numerous horses, oxen, &c. employed in the business of agriculture, for the transport of merchandise, in travelling and war, for ease and luxury.

In the first periods of national advancement, the demand for animal food is usually very limited, and can be supplied by merely catching the wild creatures peculiar to the country, which roam through the woods, or over the open plains. In such circumstances, the price of these animals is regulated entirely by the labour necessary to take or slay them, and may be very low indeed. " At Buenos Ayres," says Adam Smith,[*] " we are told by Ulloa, that four reals, one and twenty pence halfpenny sterling, was forty or fifty years ago, the ordinary price of an ox chosen from a herd of two or three hundred." " An ox there," he says, " costs little more than the labour of catching him." Nay, we are told, that even beggars are sometimes seen on horseback in the streets of Buenos Ayres.

By and by, however, all the animals which can be procured in this way no longer fully supply the increasing demand for butcher's meat. The price of cattle rises accordingly, and may continue to do so for some time. A greater number of persons, no doubt, will be induced to employ their skill and labour in hunting, and thus the market may for a period be in some degree more amply provided. But the progress

* Wealth of Nations, Book i. Chap. xi.

of cultivation driving away the animals from the im-
diate neighbourhood, their pursuers must extend the
range of their excursions, and, therefore, it will every
day become more difficult to obtain a supply to meet
the constantly increasing demand. The price then
cannot but rise. In consequence of this, the occupiers of land will, in the course of time, find it their
interest to catch some of these wild creatures when
young, in order to tame them, and establish a domestic race of cattle, ready always to be brought to market. With this view, it is necessary that some land
should be set apart for grazing, and the beasts prevented from straying, either by a suitable fence, or the
presence of a herd-boy or shepherd. But what are
the lands which will be employed for this purpose?
We cannot suppose that the cultivator will give up
some of his best corn fields in order to feed cattle,
which now, for the first time only, are thought worth
rearing at all. The higher the price of corn, the more
will this be out of the question ; and if rent be already
paid for these soils, it must be quite apparent that
they cannot be abandoned to live produce, which by
the supposition begins to afford a profit only, on the
taming and keeping. The lands then set apart for this
new scheme, must either be those which have never
hitherto been considered worth cultivating, or at all
events, the least fertile of those already under tillage.

For a considerable time, it is probable that the
former only will be devoted to this use. The beasts
will be allowed to roam over a certain extent of coun-

try, as they do at this day in the Highlands of Scotland. The price of cattle will be regulated chiefly by
the quantity of labour employed in tending them, and
also, in some degree, by the expense of food and shelter required during the most severe part of the winter. In some parts even of Scotland, however, the
cattle remain out all the year. This is particularly
the case in the Western Islands, where the proximity
of the sea greatly tempers the climate, so that snow
scarcely ever lies long on the plains.

But as population increases, the supply of animal
food obtained in this manner is insufficient to keep
pace with the constant enlargement of the demand.
Its price in consequence again rises, till at length it
becomes worth while to convert some of the poorest
corn-lands from tillage to pasturage. Enclosures will
then be introduced, and capital expended for increasing the quantity, and improving the quality of the
herbage.

Another effect of this rise of price will be, that some
rent, however small, can be paid for the uninclosed
and unimproved wastes, supposing them to be private
property; for if even at the old value of cattle a suitable profit could be made on the rearing, there must
now be something more than this, which will become
the revenue of the landlord. As the gross produce of
these districts is itself but very small, of course that
part of it which goes for rent must be little indeed,
but still, over a large tract of country it may amount
to something.

Thus, by means of the increased demand for animal food, the landlords derive a revenue from those
districts, which otherwise would perhaps never have
afforded any rent whatsoever, nor even profit. Nothing
can well be conceived more barren than the mountains
in many parts of Scotland, yet they bring in some income to their proprietors, from the high price of the
cattle and sheep which they maintain, which again is
owing to the great demand from the populous regions
of the south. We cannot suppose that these hills
could ever have yielded a corn rent. I am aware
that it has been asserted that the rents given by
Highland tenants are owing to certain fertile spots,
adjacent to rivers for instance, forming a part of their
farms, so that the valley pays for the mountain.*
This of course may sometimes be the case, but that it
is always so, is certainly incorrect. Every one at all
acquainted with Scotland must know, that rents are
paid by many hill-tenants whose whole farms consist
of moorland only, except perhaps a patch of indifferent oats or barley grown about the door. To suppose that rents of a hundred pounds or more could
ever be paid out of this sorry produce, is quite out of
the question. In fact, it is well known that cattle is
often the only thing looked to for this purpose.

We see, moreover, from what has been said above,
that uncultivated districts will probably be the first to
pay a cattle rent, because they are the first that can be
dedicated to this branch of production, (the rest of the

* See Mr. Mill's Elements of Political Economy, Ch. ii. Sect. 1.

country being, by the supposition, already engaged by tillage.) The case is exactly the reverse of that of corn lands, of which the most fertile afford this revenue prior to all others. It must be remembered that this rent is exceedingly small, however, and becomes important, only from the extent of territory over which it is levied. Neither can we suppose that all waste lands will pay rent, for some are so wet, others so stony or sandy, as to be good for little or nothing.

As the supply obtained from these unimproved regions is after all but scanty, and can by no means suffice for a large population, the price of cattle continues to rise until it becomes profitable to turn some of the inferior corn lands into grass. As soon as grazing is introduced into cultivated districts, inclosures become necessary, and means will be taken to improve the pasture so as to rear as great a number of beasts as possible on a certain space of ground. Still, as the amount of human food which can be drawn from a cattle field is very much below that which the same land would give in corn, no soils will be thrown out of tillage, till the deficiency in the Quantity of live produce shall be amply compensated by its high Price. It must therefore rise very considerably above that of corn, before it can be substituted for the latter. Thus, the price of cattle comes to depend, in part, upon that of corn.

To some this conclusion may at first appear singular. It is only in the very early periods of society that the price of bullocks, sheep, &c. is regulated like

that of most things, by the cost of procuring them.
At first, as we have seen, they cost nothing but the
labour of catching, and their price must have been
regulated accordingly. By and by, this is determined by the expenses of tending cattle over large uncultivated districts, and taking care of them during the
winter. Thus far then the general law as to value
and price holds good. But afterwards it is not so.
If the price of live stock did not rise far above what
it costs to rear them, no tolerable corn-land could ever
be given up to the feeding of cattle. Though the revenue of the cultivator might be greater in proportion
to his expenses, yet the gross produce would undoubtedly be much smaller, and consequently the sum total
of his profits. No corn-land therefore can be turned
into pasturage, until the price of cattle has risen, so
that a pound of meat shall be far dearer than the same
weight of bread, the value of the product making up
for its very inferior quantity. The higher *rate* of
profit will then compensate the farmer for the smaller
amount of it which can be drawn from the same extent of ground.

After much of the poorer corn land has been turned into pasture, should the demand still continue to
increase faster than the supply, the price of cattle
would rise still higher. Rent, it is evident, will then
begin to be created on those grazing farms which,
when in corn, afforded none. In fact, we may suppose
that the period when rent is first paid for them, will
be almost contemporaneous with their being turned

into grass, or at farthest, at the expiration of the existing leases. For it is only the extraordinary *rate* of profit which tempts the tenant to leave off the cultivation of corn, the gross produce of which is so much greater. But this high profit can last only so long as the present leases. Afterwards a part of it will be demanded as rent. Thus, the introduction of grazing consequent on the high price of cattle, though it diminishes very much the quantity of human food which can be raised from the soil, does yet increase that proportion of it which comes under the head of Net Revenue, and so gives origin to rent on lands which, when in corn, paid none. This result is seen very clearly in the higher country of Scotland, where the change from corn to pasture, from small arable farms to large grazing ones, can be accounted for only by the greater rent obtained by the landlord from the substitution of cattle for grain. That the gross produce of the soil has much diminished there can be no doubt, for the population has fallen off very much in those parts. The landlords are those most interested in this change, and who therefore promote it as much as possible.

As to the better soils which do already afford a revenue to the proprietor, it is evident that corn will continue to be raised upon them, until the increasing demand for meat, and the inadequate supply obtained from the inferior lands, shall have raised the price of cattle to such a degree, that live stock will afford a greater rent than grain. Good arable ground cannot be turned into pasture until this happen.

Thus the price of cattle comes to be regulated, in part, by the rent paid on corn-lands, and ultimately by the price of grain.

Even the very best lands may in time be given up to grass, which they certainly could not, had not the price of live stock *previously* risen so high as to afford a rent at least as great as might be drawn from the same soils if under tillage. Thus we see that the price of cattle, unlike that of most things, does not depend entirely upon cost of production, except in the infancy of society, that afterwards it rises far above this, and at last becomes regulated by the rent already paid on arable grounds. A price sufficient to give this rent becomes essential to the continued supply. The rent that might be paid by the best land now in pasture, were it devoted to corn, serves for the time to regulate the price of cattle. If it got above what is sufficient for this purpose, more of this quality of soil would be thrown out of tillage into grass; if it fell below it, a contrary effect would follow. In one way or the other, then, by an increased or diminished supply of animal food, the former ratio between it and grain would be restored. Thus it appears that the rent paid for corn land is truly the cause of the high price of cattle.

From all that precedes the conclusion, then, is the following:—Although rent unquestionably owes its origin to a high price of corn, or whatever may be the principal vegetable food of the people, yet when once created, it prevents the supply of other productions of the soil, such as animals, and grass for the subsistence of animals, from becoming immediately equal to the demand, and so keeps up their price until they rise sufficiently to give as good a rent as corn. In this manner the rent paid for one species of produce becomes the cause of the high value of others. Rent, then, in its origin, is an *effect* of high price, but afterwards becomes itself a *cause* of the high price of various objects of rural industry.

We have seen also that some small rent will probably first be paid from the cattle reared on uncultivated wastes, before any land already under tillage can be given up to the feeding of live stock, and that the poorer corn fields will be dedicated to this purpose previous to the more fertile, and will sooner yield a cattle rent. Nor in this conclusion is there any thing contradictory to that arrived at in treating of the origin of rent, when it was proved that the most fertile soils first afford this revenue. It only shows that when once land has been cultivated for corn, and rent created, a new class of facts is introduced which have a powerful influence on the future progress of rural industry, and on the rent derived from other products. If the country were occupied for the first time by a purely pastoral people, then no doubt it might be supposed, that the best lands only would for a period be devoted to the feeding of cattle, and on these, just as in the case of corn, that rent would first be created. But after great part of the territory is already dedicated to the raising of

grain, the case becomes very different. Lands which
return a considerable amount of profits, and perhaps
of rent also, cannot be given up at once to the feeding of a few head of cattle. Before this becomes possible the price must rise very much, so much as to
afford some rent even on waste grounds,—very small
at first, no doubt, in proportion to their extent, but
likely to augment with the increasing demand for
animal food. We may remark, too, that the cause
of rent in the present case is similar to that which
gives origin to a corn rent, namely, the limited
quantity of land which for the time can be turned to
the rearing of live stock. The only difference is, that
in the former instance this limitation depends upon
nature, in the other it is the effect of art, that is, of
cultivation. In consequence of this difference, the
operation of the general cause in the two cases in
question, is first felt by lands of very different, nay,
opposite qualities.

We must also bear in mind, that there is a wide
diversity between corn and cattle, in this respect—
that the expense of raising the former increases exactly in proportion as the fertility of the soil decreases, while with the latter it is not necessarily so.
Of course good land will always feed more animals
than bad; but it does not follow that in proportion to
their number, those bred on the latter cost more
than others reared on the former. In a populous
district, no doubt, where corn and grass are inter-
mingled, and where consequently grazing requires

either fences or constant tending, the poorer the soil, and therefore in proportion to the beasts fed on it, the larger the space, the more may be supposed to be the expense of enclosures or of labour. But in a country like the Highlands of Scotland, where there is little or nothing to injure, no fences and very little tending are required. The cattle are allowed to roam over an extensive region, and if the owner merely send a man or boy from time to time to see that none have strayed beyond due bounds, it is sufficient. The chief expense is in winter, so long as snow lies on the ground, when the animals must be housed and fed. But, as formerly observed, there are parts even of Scotland, where, from the mildness caused by the neighbourhood of the sea, this is not necessary. Still less in southern countries, can shelter in winter be required. Besides, even if indispensable, it is an expense not peculiar to any one soil, but common to the rich and poor, the improved and unimproved. It is probable, therefore, that no where are cattle and sheep reared at less cost than on these uncultivated wastes. Consequently, though the produce may be small, yet rent will form as large a proportion of the whole as on the best grazing farms in the country. We need not then be surprised that the landlords should so soon begin to derive a revenue from these districts.

As a farther illustration of the above principles, we may take the instance of wood. Wood we know is

found in such abundance in most new countries, that
nothing can be obtained for it in exchange. Far
from being an object of wealth, it is regarded merely
as an incumbrance to be got rid of as speedily as possible. Even in this state of the country, there may
be some particular localities, however, in which not
only a profit, but even a rent, may be drawn from
timber. Although wood is of no value at home, yet
abroad it may bear a high price; therefore, if there
be any ready means of transport, some gain from it
may be derived. Forests, then, situated near the
sea, or a navigable river, will afford a profit to their
proprietors in proportion to the expense of cutting
and bringing down trees or planks to the port. And
if the quantity of wood in such favourable situations
be of limited extent, no reason can be shown why
the price at the harbour may not rise high enough
not only to recompense the owner for his outlay of
capital, but also to give a surplus which properly
speaking is Rent. These forest lands are exactly analogous to the most fertile or best situated corn fields,
on which we found that rent first begins to be created. If the price rises as high as we have supposed,
persons will easily be found willing to take these
woods on lease, paying to the proprietor a portion of
the return, or of its value, as rent, just as in the case of
the arable districts. And the cause of this high price,
and consequently of the rent, is the same in both
cases, namely, the limited quantity of land best
adapted for the growth of corn or of wood, or best

situated in respect to markets. In both instances, also, it is necessary that the lands be appropriated, for no one would pay a rent for what was common to all. This evidently is supposed.

As a proof from experience of the truth of these principles, I may mention what is stated by M. Storch, that the woods of the Russian provinces having a free communication with the Baltic, find in the other countries of Europe a market which they could not enjoy on the spot, and that in this way they often afford a very considerable revenue to the proprietor. According to a calculation made in 1799, it appears that the rent given for the woods situated on the Dwina and its tributaries, amounts to a sixth part of the price which foreigners pay for the timber at the port of Riga. Now, the above writer observes, that few agricultural productions yield a greater.* Adam Smith also states, that the forests of Norway afford some rent.

This high price of wood is confined to certain localities, however. In the interior of new countries where forests prevail, it is from its abundance, destitute of all value in exchange. Such is the case in the back settlements of America, where every man can take away as much wood as he pleases to cut down, and if the lands be appropriated, the owner will be but too happy to get rid of the encumbrance. But in proportion as the country advances in popula-

---

* Cours d'Econ. Polit. liv. iv. ch. xiii.

tion and cultivation, the forests gradually disappear,
partly by the extension of tillage, partly from the injury done to the young trees by the numerous herds
of cattle kept by the inhabitants. It is in this latter
way that the forests which formerly covered many of
the mountainous districts of Scotland, have been totally destroyed. No sooner does the young plant
appear above ground, than it is browsed upon or
trodden under foot by cattle and flocks of sheep.
Nay, so injurious are trees to the herbage, that graziers are most anxious to get rid of them, and thus a
general destruction ensues. I have myself seen on
the mountains of Savoy, the recent remains of most
splendid pine forests, which had been hacked and
ruined more than cut, with a view to their decay, and
the improvement of the pasture. Thus a tract of hill
which previously scarcely supported a score of milk
cows, now easily maintains four times that number,
besides many goats.*

The scarcity of wood thus produced, as well as the
increasing demand for it, to supply the wants of a
larger population, whether for firing, or for building
and rural purposes, cannot but give a value to that
which at first had none. Thus the price of wood
gradually increases with the progress of society.
Now, if some natural woods still exist, it is evident

---

* The keeping of cows is a principal branch of rural industry in the
Alps. There is a much better market for butter, but especially cheese,
than for butcher's meat. In Savoy, the price of the latter is not more
than twopence halfpenny the pound, about double that of bread.

that the owners will in time come to derive a revenue from the sale of the annual cuttings. At first the price will be only sufficient to afford a profit on the expense necessary for felling and transporting the timber, but as the value of wood farther rises, something more than this will be obtained, which surplus will constitute rent. Rent then in this case, exactly as in that of pasture grounds, will first be paid by the lands worst adapted for corn, which have not been thought so well worth cultivating as others. No doubt, this will in the commencement be very small, but as population advances, it will gradually increase.

The causes, moreover, why rent is first paid by these natural woodlands, are the same as in the former case of uncultivated wastes. Land already bearing crops of grain, supporting a population of labourers, yielding profit to the cultivator, and perhaps rent also, cannot all at once be given up to growing trees.* The price of timber must rise very considerably before this can be advisable, and in the mean time, some rent may be created on the formerly neglected tracts, from a produce which owes its existence to the bounty of Nature alone. So far, then, these last enjoy a monopoly, the result of the general cultivation of the country, but which of course has no bounds.

Secondly, no where can timber be obtained at a

---

* More especially must this be true where the owner of the land is also the cultivator, and therefore derives a revenue from profits as well as rent. But this will be shown at large by and by.

smaller cost than from such lands. There are the woods already grown without the aid of man, without the outlay of capital necessary for trenching, planting, draining, or fencing. Because some rent can be got from such natural woods, it by no means follows that it would be worth while for any proprietor to be at the expense of raising them by art. The price might not be sufficient to pay the profit on such an outlay, far less to leave any thing over. Notwithstanding the general destruction of the Scottish forests, some have been saved from the general wreck, and the primeval firs of Braemar and Strathspey afford some rent to their Highland lords. In Scotland, natural oak copses are found very generally upon the steep banks of rivers and lakes, and from the high price of the bark so useful in tanning, yield, in time of war especially, a very considerable income to the proprietors. The wood, moreover, grown upon hills is generally of a superior quality to that raised upon plains, being harder and more compact, though perhaps of less bulk. The soils most adapted for corn are not the most proper for other productions, for this in particular, and I may add, the vine. The best wheat field might make the worst vineyard.

But if the natural woods still remaining in the country are not sufficient to meet the increasing demands of the population, it is certain that the price will rise, until it may become profitable for proprietors to lay out some of their poorest lands in plantations. That the poorest lands only would at first be set apart for this purpose, is clear, for it would be advantageous to employ inferior soils in this way, long before the price rise high enough (if ever it do,) to tempt the owners to convert good corn-fields into woods. Should the country be one not possessing any extensive tracts of moorland or mountain, the price will the sooner reach that point at which it may be profitable to turn arable lands into forest. It is evident, however, that no arable land will be thus dealt with, until the price of wood be such as to give a rent at least equal to that paid by the same soil when under corn. A price sufficient for this rent becomes an indispensable condition of the supply, supposing all the waste spaces fit for wood already occupied by that production. Until it reach that height no fresh supply can be obtained. Thus, the price of wood, as formerly we found in the case of cattle, comes in the progress of society to be influenced by the rent of corn-lands. First, it is regulated by the rent of inferior soils, and if these suffice not for the demand, it will rise until it can give a rent equal to that already paid by those somewhat superior.

There can, I think, be no doubt, that the high price of fire-wood in France is owing to this cause. The extensive tracts of territory allowed to remain in forest must pay a rent as high as corn-lands of equal fertility, otherwise they would quickly be cleared and cultivated. This rent becomes a condition of the supply quite as indispensable, as that the price of wood should

be sufficient to pay the wages and profits of the labourers and master-capitalist employed in cutting
down, and transporting it from one place to another.

I may remark here, that as wood is a much more
bulky commodity than corn, it is far easier and less
expensive to procure the latter from abroad, than the
former.   From this it follows, that as the population
of a country advances, a period will necessarily arrive
(particularly if there be no mountain tracts fit only
for wood,) when wood-land will have a tendency to
encroach upon the corn land, it being more advantageous to get the latter in part from abroad, and
raise the former at home.   Thus, the process which
took place in the infancy of society is reversed.   It is
evident that this tendency will be greatly increased,
if wood form the principal fuel of the inhabitants.
This circumstance cannot but make an immense difference, inasmuch as the consumption must be far
greater in this way, than in all others put together, it
being both so general and so rapid.   Many proprietors in France derive a great part of their income
from woods, which, being cut periodically, and allowed to shoot up again, afford them an annual rent of
the most constant kind.   Now, if this continue to be
the favourite and general fuel of the country, it is
clear, for the reason above stated, that a greater and
greater portion of the present corn-land must in time
be turned into forest.   It is comparatively easy to get
corn from foreign countries, whereas the cost of bringing fire-wood would be immense.   As the price of the

latter rises in proportion to the increasing wants of the population, it will become more and more profitable to plant trees than to grow corn, which last must therefore be sought for at a distance from home.

Nothing can prevent this consummation, (supposing France to progress in population and prosperity,) except the substitution of coal for wood; which in all probability will take place, if not universally, at least to a great extent. The increasing price of the latter will hasten this result; the higher it rises, the greater being the temptation to use coal in its stead. For, according to the principles above laid down, the price of wood will not fall, although the supply be increased so as to meet the wants of the people, for, if to procure this greater supply, it be necessary to turn good corn-land into forest, the price must continue permanently high, so as to afford as much rent as before. Indeed, within these few years, coal is much more burnt in Paris than formerly. At present, the difference in the expense of the two is not great, though rather in favour of the last. This difference will probably become greater, however, the one, as we have seen, having a tendency to rise, while the other will probably fall from increased facilities of communication.*

* Coals are very dear in Paris, thirty francs, or twenty-four shillings being usually paid for a thousand pound weight. This is at the rate of about fifty shillings the ton. In many places of Great Britain, they can be had for ten. If even at this price they are cheaper than wood, it may be judged how dear the latter must be. The transport of wood to Paris costs less than we might suppose for so bulky a commodity, it being floated down the Seine and its tributaries, much of it without boats, but merely formed into rafts. Therefore, we may conclude, that the price

What has been said of the tendency of wood to take the place of corn, as a country becomes densely peopled, is still more evidently true of cattle, and grass for the use of cattle and other tame animals. The transport of sheep and oxen by sea, particularly for long distances, when so much space must be occupied by their necessary food, is a matter of great inconvenience and expense. The introduction of steam-boats by shortening the time of passage, has no doubt diminished this difficulty, as is proved by the quantity of live stock now exported from Ireland ; but for long distances, it must still exist to a great extent. I understand that the expense of transporting cattle by these conveyances from Scotland to the London market is very considerable, so that none but prime beasts can be sent in this way. It appears, moreover, that the animals suffer much in their condition from a sea voyage of not more than fifty hours.* For cattle, then, bred at home, for milch-cows, for the numerous horses employed in agriculture, internal commerce, travelling, or kept for state and amusement, it is evident that a greater and greater quantity of grass, hay, or other substances on which these animals are generally supported, must be required. But hay being an article of great bulk, is brought from foreign countries at an immense expense as compared with corn.

on the spot where it is grown must be considerable, a great part at least of which makes up the rent of the landlord.

* See House of Commons' Report on Railroads. Slaughtered animals, however, are now sent up from Scotland to London in great quantities, during the winter.

Therefore, it will be the interest of the nation more and more to turn its corn-lands into pasture and hay-fields, and to procure a constantly increasing supply of corn from abroad.

That such is the tendency of things in England at the present day, there can be no doubt. Grass is every where increasing at the expense of corn. This is more particularly remarkable in the neighbourhood of large towns, such as London. The great quantity of grass required for the consumption of the numerous cows which supply the metropolis with milk, of the cattle who are brought up to be slaughtered, and of the horses employed either for trade or luxury within the capital, and in its immediate vicinity, all occasion a constant demand for that sort of produce which, from its bulk, cannot be brought from the more distant parts of the country without a very great expense.*

If this expense be so felt even within the country itself, a country too whose means of communication are equal, if not superior to any in the world, how much more must it become sensible when this com-

---

* Fresh milk being an article which evidently cannot be brought from far, the extent of land from which it can be procured for the supply of an immense town like London is very inadequate, so that although every expedient is resorted to to increase this supply, by augmenting the quantity of food drawn from the soil dedicated to the support of cows, yet the market is after all but badly provided with this necessary. Hence, its very high price, and the consequent temptation to adulterate. What wretched stuff is London milk ! Matthew Bramble scarcely exaggerated when he called it a miserable compound of chalk and water. Railroads, however, from the *quickness* with which they can transport produce, will open up a new district for milk at a greater distance from the metropolis, and so tend to bring to market a more genuine juice of the cow. See House of Commons' Report on Railroads.

modity is to be brought from foreign lands. It is probable, then, that the whole surface will gradually resemble the district immediately surrounding the metropolis, in which grass-fields greatly predominate over corn. As the neighbourhood of the capital enjoys in this respect a natural monopoly, which can hardly be broken down by the competition of the more remote provinces, so does the whole land of the country in reference to foreign states. The consideration of this natural monopoly, which must always keep up the price of cattle, and the food of them and other animals, may serve to reconcile the landlords to the abandonment of the artificial monopoly of corn.

There is one case of rent, as it is called, which I may mention, in order to show the distinction between it and rent properly so denominated. This is the revenue which many proprietors in the Highlands of Scotland now derive from letting their moors for the shooting season. An income of this kind is evidently quite different from rent, as it is not paid out of the produce of the soil, for the game killed is not looked upon as an article of gain, nor brought to market. The pleasure of killing is alone regarded, not the profit which might be made. As the rent given is not drawn from the produce of the soil, it must therefore be taken from some other source, that is, from some independent branch of national industry. Consequently, this revenue is not a *primary* but a *secondary* one, according to the meaning I have before affixed to these words. It is not in the least dependent on the price of grouse or deer, but simply upon the proportion between the quantity of shooting grounds to be let, and the number and wealth of those who are eager to hire them for the sake of sport. Still, even this revenue is *ultimately* owing to causes similar to those from which rent, properly so called, originates, namely, the limited quantity of land fit for raising certain sorts of produce, and the existence of the right of property. Were grouse lands unlimited or unappropriated, no one, of course, would give any thing for the use of them.

But to return. We have found that the price of certain rural products, such as cattle, hay, and wood, rises in the progress of society far above the cost of production, and comes at last to be regulated by the rent paid for corn lands equal in fertility to the best soils dedicated to grass or wood. For, when arable fields are given up to wood, hay, or pasture, they are abandoned to these purposes entirely, and cease to be subjected to the plough. At least, this is generally the case. There are pasture lands, no doubt, in Scotland for instance, of which the herbage deteriorates after a certain number of years, and which therefore require to be ploughed up from time to time, and again are laid down in grass, after having given one or two crops of oats or barley. Still, the pasture is the chief thing looked to for paying the rent, the rest is only occasional, and at distant inter-

vals. Where the soil and climate are more favourable, as in England, the oldest grazing fields are considered the best.

No arable lands, then, can be devoted to wood,
hay, or pasture, and so withdrawn entirely or chiefly
from the dominion of the plough, until wood, hay, or
cattle will give as good a rent as corn grown on
fields of equal fertility. There are, however, other
products of the earth, some of them intended for the
food of animals, which, as they do not require the
soil to be given up solely or principally to them, may
be grown even on the best lands, although their
price be not sufficient to pay any rent, such as turnips, vetches, tares, potatoes, &c. The soils even best
adapted for wheat or other grain cannot always bear
these without being exhausted; rather than let the
lands lie altogether idle, the farmer will then cultivate
the other sorts of produce in the interval of his corn
crops, if their price be but enough to pay the necessary expenses. He looks to the wheat for the payment of his rent, though from the rest he may derive a suitable profit for himself. The price, then, of
these last will not at all depend upon rent, but upon
cost of production alone. The same observation applies to oats and barley, raised in the interval of
wheat crops. As, however, the demand for these objects of agriculture increases with the progress of society, the supply obtained in this manner from the
best soils may not be sufficient, the price will rise,
and they also will begin to afford a rent, which, just

as in the case of wheat, will be limited by the expense of growing them on soils somewhat inferior. Indeed, it is well known, that in a due rotation of crops lies one of the principal secrets of good farming. Since the improvement of agriculture, fallows have become much less frequent than they used to be. In the instances last mentioned, rent, it is clear, is the *effect* of high price, not the *cause*.

Hay is a crop peculiar in this respect, that it is grown both naturally and artificially. Thus we have meadow grass and rye grass, for which last the land must be prepared by tillage and sowing. So long as the quantity raised in this manner from arable fields in the interval of corn crops, and the meadow hay obtained from wet places along the beds of streams, are enough for the consumption, so long will there be no temptation to give up good soils entirely to grass. But as the demand increases, the supply thus procured is not sufficient, therefore the price rises until grass alone will afford a rent equal at least to that hitherto paid by some corn lands. Grass lands will then give a rent as great as that of corn lands of equal fertility; neither, it is evident, can they yield much more, otherwise the quantity of them would be increased, until the supply of hay should in some degree bring down its price.

From what has been above said, we should expect to find the greatest extent of meadow land in the richest and most populous countries. Accordingly, in England and Holland, there is much more than in

France or Scotland. In the last, there is very little meadow ground. Enough of hay to meet the consumption is obtained, we may suppose, by an occasional crop, without devoting much land to the express purpose. The use of this article must indeed be far less in proportion to its population in Scotland than in England, so much poorer is it, and consequently so many fewer horses are kept for the pleasures of the rich, and so much less does butcher's meat form part of the food of the people. Besides, the great extent of waste country fit only for cattle and sheep, must render less necessary the conversion of good corn land into grass.

One consequence of the increase of pasture at the expence of corn, which arises as a country advances in wealth, and particularly as manufacturing and commercial industry extend, is the enlargement of farms, and the diminution of the rural population. Supposing the income to be the same, or nearly so, landlords generally prefer letting their lands in large farms, because there is much less trouble in collecting rents from a few, than from many; and also because they consider themselves more secure in having to do with persons of considerable capital, than with little tenants, who have seldom much funds in reserve in case of a failure in the year's crop. Should then the rent derived from letting to a few not be quite equal in nominal amount to what they might obtain by a more minute subdivision of holdings, yet the greater certainty, and the diminished trouble, would make landlords partial to the former system. Much more, therefore, will they prefer large farms, if they hope to get a higher rent from them than from small. Now, the substitution of pasture for corn facilitates greatly this change. It must always be much more easy to undertake a large cattle farm than a large arable one. Though, no doubt, a considerable capital is required to stock it in the first instance, yet the degree of personal superintendence which it demands, is small in comparison, and therefore it may embrace a much larger space. To manage a very extensive arable farm is a matter requiring more than ordinary ability, great experience, and continual attention, so numerous and complicated are the processes of husbandry, but the business of grazing is much more simple and uniform. Besides, when once stocked, a pasture farm requires much less labour and other expenses than an arable. For all these reasons, it may be far larger.

Upon the increase in the price of cattle, then, the landlords will be well disposed to take advantage of it, by turning out the present little tenants at the expiration of their leases, and concentrating their lands in the hands of a few, who will employ them chiefly for rearing live stock. This consummation will the more readily take place, if the soil and climate be better adapted for pasture than for corn. Thus it has happened, that very many districts in Scotland which formerly bore crops of grain, and were occupied by a considerable number of people supported on the pro-

duce of the soil, are now turned into sheep-walks and
cattle farms, and have become nearly destitute of population. Nothing is more common in the upland
parts of that country, than the remains of single
houses, and even of small villages. For the number
of persons required to take care of a large grazing
farm, is very much less than is necessary for the same
space divided into small arable holdings.

And this brings me again to remark another consequence of the conversion of corn land into pasture,
which is the decrease in the quantity of food raised
from the soil. There can be no doubt that the annual return to a cattle and sheep farm would feed a
much smaller number of persons than the same district under grain.* But the rent of the landlord,
which is all he looks to, must be as great at least as
formerly, otherwise he never would consent to the
change. In all probability it will be greater. This
high rent, then, must be owing to the *value* of the
produce making up for its deficient *quantity*. The
cause of this high value has been already explained.

Still, even the total value of the produce may be,
and in most cases really is, inferior to what it was
before. For, since the pasture land requires less labour and other expenses than are necessary for cultivation, of course a smaller value will replace this
smaller outlay, and give as high a *rate* of profit as

---

* Adam Smith says, " A corn field of moderate fertility, produces a
much greater quantity of food for man, than the best pasture of equal
extent." Wealth of Nations, book i. ch. xi.

formerly. Nor can the grazing farmer hope long to enjoy a higher rate of profit than the corn grower. Therefore, if the rent be about the same, or at most not very much higher, it is clear that the total value of the produce is less than before. And the quantity of food, as just observed, is certainly diminished.* Therefore, in every sense of the word, the gross produce of the soil is lessened by the conversion of corn land into pasture.

Were any doubts entertained as to the inferiority, even in point of value, of the total annual return to a cattle farm, they would be at once dispelled from the experience we have of tithes. It is well known in England, that landlords have it in their power, by turning their estates into grass, very much to reduce the income of the clergyman. This proves that the tithe is greatly lowered in value, and if the tenth be less valuable, so must the whole. But as the rent has certainly not fallen, and the *rate* of profit may well be supposed the same, it follows that the two together must form a larger proportion of the gross produce. Still, since the sum of profits has declined, unless rent greatly rises, the absolute amount of both, whether estimated in quantity or in value, will be diminished. Thus, not only the gross, but even the net produce of the soil may be less.†

---

* Were we to compare the whole weight of the butchers' meat with that of the corn, the difference would be still greater. But that is of little consequence, the quantity of nourishment being alone important.

† See more on this subject in the chapter on Revenue.

This falling off in the quantity of human food raised from the soil, must render more and more indispensable the procuring a supply of corn or other materials of subsistence from abroad. The extension of manufactures, which has been one principal cause of the increased demand for butchers' meat, and consequently of its high price, affords ready means of purchasing such a supply from foreign states, provided the government at home do not interfere to prevent the free importation of grain. The condition of England, at the present day, is precisely that above described. The immense increase in the wealth and population of the country, consequent upon the rapid extension of manufactures within the last fifty years, has rendered it more and more profitable to convert corn land into pasture, if we except a certain period during the war, when the exceedingly high price of grain tended for a time to counteract this effect. This increase of pasture is still going on, and is checked only by the restrictions upon the free introduction of corn from abroad, which keep up its price at home. These restrictions being supposed the same, there can be no doubt that the conversion of arable into grazing land, would have been even more checked by a still higher price of grain, were it not that England does in reality enjoy a free trade with one country in its immediate neighbourhood, and one too most favourably circumstanced for growing and exporting corn, namely, Ireland. Accordingly, the annual supply thence obtained, has of late years been rapidly increasing. This it is which has tended to break down the monopoly, which the landlords did all they could to establish in their own favour. The liberal spirit of the age no longer permitting Ireland to be treated as a conquered or a foreign country, it was impossible to prevent the establishment of a free commercial intercourse between it and Great Britain. No doubt the Union was the immediate cause of this result, and therefore in this way immense good has flowed from that measure. Indeed the wealth of Ireland, the amount of its exports and imports, have increased since that event in a most unexampled degree. How could it be otherwise, its resources being naturally so great, and the richest market in the world close at hand, now open to receive its productions?*

Ireland too is a country most particularly well adapted for exporting corn, both from its fertility and the condition of its population. Its lands are considered more rich than those of England, and its people are beyond all comparison poorer. Potatoes, sometimes with milk, more frequently without it, form the sole subsistence of the great mass of the peasantry, too ill off to purchase wheat or any species of corn. No market then being found at home for these products of the soil, they are naturally sent to England in large quantities. This state of things, a fertile territory and a poor people, is exactly that parti-

---

* See chapter " On the rate of Gross Profits in different employ-. ments," and Note **A.**

cularly calculated for favouring the export of the
more costly kinds of agricultural produce, such as
wheat and cattle, if for the latter a near enough market can be found.

Poland and Ireland are precisely in the condition
above described, and accordingly they are greater
exporters of grain than even new countries, such as
the United States of America, where the abundance
of fertile and unoccupied land so greatly favours the
increase of agricultural wealth. But as the inhabitants themselves live upon the more costly sorts of
food, the home market becomes of far more importance than the foreign. What is left for sending
abroad, after satisfying the wants of the natives,
forms but a very small part of the whole.

From these causes it arises, that the increasing
demand of England for corn has been met in a great
degree by a copious supply from the sister island,
and thus the operation of the laws restricting its importation from abroad have been much counteracted.
These laws have of course been all to the advantage
of Ireland, as they have given it the exclusive privilege of selling its produce to Great Britain. This
supply of wheat and other grain has allowed things
in England to take their natural course, at least to a
considerable extent, and has admitted of pasture being substituted for corn in very many places, as no
doubt it would have been still more generally, had
no prohibitory regulations existed.

Of late years, indeed, the invention of steam-boats,

by greatly shortening the time of passage, has rendered possible the sending of cattle also from Ireland to the opposite coast. Great numbers of bullocks and pigs are daily exported from Dublin to Liverpool, whereas formerly salted meat alone could be conveyed to England. This must tend somewhat to discourage grazing throughout Great Britain.

One consequence, as we have seen, of the change from corn farms to pasture, which arises from the increase of national wealth, and particularly from the spreading of manufactures, is the diminution of the agricultural population. This of course must cause a still farther increase in manufacturing and commercial industry, for the labourers thus thrown out of employment in the country must now resort to towns to earn their subsistence, and will therefore swell the ranks of those already employed in the above branches of production. Thus the number of persons engaged in such occupations constantly tends to increase at the expense of those who live by agriculture. That this in particular would be the result of a total abolition of the corn laws, there can be no doubt. If such an abolition should produce any effect upon prices, or at least any effect of consequence, it is quite certain that some lands which now bear corn could no longer be so cultivated; all those for instance which at present barely pay the expenses with a profit, but afford no rent. Whatever might become of those lands, whether they would be left waste, or, as is more probable, be turned into wood or pasture; it is in all cases certain, that a part of the labourers formerly employed upon them would no longer be wanted; and therefore that they must either be supported by the parish, or resort to towns in quest of occupation. These consequences of an abolition of the corn laws, namely, first, the evils resulting to the present agricultural population from the services of some of its members being no longer required; secondly, the permanent diminution in its numbers, which, of course, must follow, are very necessary to be kept in mind in considering this great question. We see that it is a question affecting not the landlords only, as some have said, but bearing most materially upon the interests of the great body of the peasantry. How far it is a consummation devoutly to be wished, that the manufacturing population of England should be still farther increased at the expence of the agricultural, may well be doubted.

As I am treating of rents, it may not be foreign to the subject, to remark, that the turning of corn-land into pasture, will be materially hastened or retarded by the manner in which territorial property is held throughout the country. Where land has become the possession of a comparatively small number of individuals, and where, consequently, estates are large, the above change will much more readily take place, than where the soil is greatly subdivided.

As we have seen above, that portion of the national revenue which constitutes rent may increase, when the gross produce of the earth actually diminishes, not merely in quantity, but even in total value. Now, since a great landlord, who lives entirely upon this branch of revenue, cares little what may be the amount raised on his farms, except in so far as it influences rent, he will of course adopt any system which tends to swell the last, though the quantity of human food produced may be much lessened. And as in the progress of society, grass comes in many situations to afford a higher rent .than corn, he will of course let his lands for pasture, though in this way they will no doubt support fewer people than before. But the case of a small landed proprietor is very different. One of this description, such as France abounds in, combines in his own person the character of labourer, master, capitalist, and landlord; and, therefore, it is evident, in the last capacity he has only a partial interest, which may be inferior to the united interests of all the other three. So great a part of the produce of his farm is consumed by himself and his family, the members of which are often the only labourers employed upon it, that the *quantity* of human food raised becomes the matter of chief importance, rather than its *value* on which high rents principally depend. Now, the quantity of food which can be drawn from a small property by the constant toil of its owner, applied to the cultivation of corn, potatoes, and other vegetables, is immensely greater than he could obtain from it if in pasture. Nobody is so industrious as a small landed proprietor. The knowledge that the produce is all his own, greatly stimulates his exertions to derive as much as possible from the soil. No labourers hired by the day can be expected to do nearly so much. As a proof of this, the example of France is before us, where the numerous small proprietors, it is well known, are industrious in an eminent degree. They do not grudge their labour as a hireling does; to obtain but a small additional return they submit to great exertions. The superior ease which they would enjoy if their arable fields were converted into pasture, cannot induce them to adopt this change, first, because they could not in this way raise food enough for the subsistence of themselves and families; secondly, because, as I have said, they do not nicely calculate their labour, but give it cheerfully, knowing that the produce will be all their own. Supposing a small proprietor to derive from his fields if turned into pasture, as high a gross profit on his little capital and enterprise, and as much rent as when in corn and potatoes, or even more, yet he would miss his own reward as a labourer, and that of the grown up members of his family, which may form a great part of his annual income. This circumstance is essential. His interest, and that of his family as labourers, balances, and may even predominate over that of master, capitalist, and landed proprietor, which characters in him are all united. It is this circumstance which will prevent him from substituting grazing for tillage.

But without supposing the surface to be subdivided to such a degree that the proprietor should em-

brace in himself the four characters above enumerated, it will still be much less the interest of the small
than of the great land-owner to convert his estate into pasture. If we suppose the soil to be occupied
chiefly by a class once so common in England, that
of yeomen, or persons uniting in themselves the proprietor and farmer, we shall find their case to approach that last discussed. These men derive their
income not from rent exclusively, as the great owners
do, but also from profit; and, on this account, their
interests in the management of their possessions are
not always the same.

The great landlord regards only, 1. The amount of
rent; 2. The ease and security with which it can be
collected. On these accounts, he will always be partial to large pasture farms, as soon as the price of
cattle rises high enough to give a better rent than
corn, or even as good. But the yeoman looks to the
amount of profits as well as rent, they being received
by the same individual. Now, we found that one
consequence of the change from corn to pasture is the
diminution in the gross produce of the soil, not in
quantity only, but even in total value; and that
though the *rate* of profit remain the same, yet the
amount of it must be lessened, because the annual outlay from which it results is not so considerable.
Therefore, by the above change, the *amount* of the
yeoman's profit will be lowered, though the portion
of his income which properly constitutes rent, may
be rather augmented. And that diminution in his

profits will probably, for a long time, more than counterbalance this advantage. Were he to convert his
arable fields into pasture, a portion of his capital at
present profitably invested would cease to be employed, and therefore he could derive nothing from it,
except by letting it out at interest, which would be
impossible however, were it fixed in barns, thrashing-
mills, and agricultural implements. Where, on the
other hand, these expenses have been undertaken by
a tenant, this sacrifice of capital no way concerns the
great landlord; if, at the expiration of the lease, he
can by a different system of husbandry obtain a higher
rent, it is all in which he is interested.

There is another circumstance also in which the
case of the yeoman agrees with that of the small proprietor, rather than with that of the great, which is,
that he is considerably affected by the quantity of the
return, independently of its value. The amount of
produce consumed on the spot without any exchange,
by himself, his family, his friends, and his labourers,
forms no contemptible part of the whole annually
drawn from his farm. Now, by the change from corn
or other vegetable aliment of man to pasture, the
quantity of human food is much diminished. Consequently, the rearing of cattle exclusively can never be
so advantageous to the small yeoman, as to the lord of
thousands of acres. A farmer will generally find it
his interest to raise sufficient vegetable food for himself and those immediately surrounding him; there-

fore, the more land is divided into small properties
and holdings, the greater will be the number of families thus provided for, and consequently the larger the
extent of surface almost necessarily devoted to tillage.

There are, on the other hand, two circumstances
arising out of the subdivision of landed property,
which will materially lessen the demand for butcher's
meat, and hence diminish the temptation to convert
corn into pasture. First, where territorial possessions, and consequently farms also, are small, opportunities for accumulating large capitals in the hands
of individuals can occur much less frequently. Consequently, fewer considerable capitals will find their
way to be employed in manufactures, without which
these cannot make any great progress; and the number of persons engaged in them, or who arrive at
wealth and comfort by their means, will increase the
more slowly. Therefore, the demand from this quarter for agricultural productions in general, and for
butcher's meat in particular, will be limited. A manufacturing population living in towns always consumes much more animal food than the same number
of country labourers.

Secondly, in the state of landed property here supposed, the extension of manufactures, at least of the
finer kind, which chiefly give a stimulus to foreign commerce, and have a tendency to multiply with rapidity,
is checked by the want of demand for them at home.

The demand for manufactured goods in any country, must mainly depend upon the surplus of agricultural products which remains, after feeding all the people employed in raising them, and replacing the various elements of the farmer's fixed capital consumed in the work. This surplus is a fund from which an effective demand is created for articles of convenience or luxury such as the cultivator does not himself produce, and which are either fabricated at home, or obtained by commerce from abroad. It serves, at the same time, to support the people engaged in these occupations. Upon its amount then must depend the amount of manufacturing and commercial industry in any country, at least in the commencement, for after manufactures have been perfected and extended, they can find a market for their products at a distance, and feed their own people, by means of foreign supplies. For a long time, however, they must principally depend upon this surplus. It therefore becomes an important question, what state of things best promotes its amount, that in which the land is in the hands of a few proprietors, and where farms are large; or where proprietors are numerous and farms consequently small. Where proprietors are few, farms may or may not be large; but where estates are numerous and small, farms must be so too, as they are generally cultivated by the owners.[*]

Now, a small proprietor has in every respect a great advantage over a small tenant, having so much

* This will be shown more particularly hereafter.

greater an interest in the land, which being his own,
every amelioration redounds to the exclusive advantage of himself and family. Besides, the very feeling
of being a proprietor gives him heart to work, and
makes him prudent in his expenses. Whatever advantages, then, attend cultivation in a small way,
must be found in perfection where the little farmers
are also owners of the soil. A system of husbandry
by small *tenants* must be very inferior, though of
course the difference can lie only in the superior dili-
gence and prudence of the former; the general plan
of operations on the land being necessarily the same.
In both cases, cultivation is carried on on a small
scale. Herein they agree. The question, then, lies
between great proprietors with large farms on the
one hand, and small properties farmed by the owners
themselves on the other.

Without supposing any difference in the sorts of
produce raised in either case, it seems probable that
the quantity thereof will be greater in the latter state
of things than in the former. More labour will certainly be bestowed upon the land, both as to the
number of labourers, and its intensity and duration, so
little does a small proprietor, as before observed,
grudge his own exertions and those of his family, in
ameliorating his little spot of ground. The advantage of constant personal superintendence will also
be his; nor will his mind be distracted by a multi-
plicity of objects, and the complication of an exten-

sive concern. Where, on the other hand, lands are
let in masses to wealthy farmers, who cultivate them
with large capitals, as less labour is bestowed on the
soil than in the former case, and there is less anxiety
to make the most of every foot of surface, it is probable that the quantity of the total produce will be
inferior; though the greater skill with which labour
is applied, and the use of the most improved implements and processes of husbandry, will serve in part
to prevent this effect. Under this system, though
the gross produce may still be smaller, yet it is certain that the surplus which remains after feeding the
labourers employed, and replacing the fixed capital
consumed, will bear a larger proportion to the whole,
on account of the superior skill, and the power of
adopting all new inventions which may require a considerable command of funds. Therefore we arrive at
this result, that in the instance of the small proprietor, the gross produce is greater, but under the opposite system, the surplus above defined is a larger
part of the whole. It still, however, remains unde-
termined in which case the *amount* of surplus is most
considerable, nor, it may be thought, is this a matter
very easy to decide. But I should be inclined to believe that it would be greater on the large farms than
on the small, always supposing that the kinds of produce are the same in both cases, and that corn, not
pasture, is the principal object in each. For, of the
diminution in the gross produce, not in quantity only,

but also in value, consequent on the substitution of
pasture for corn, and of the tendency of large properties to favour this change, I have before spoken.

On this subject I cannot, I think, do better than
extract the following passage translated from M.
Say.* " One would not perhaps believe, if we did
not take pains to reflect upon it, that the plough, the
harrow, and other similar machines, of which the
origin is lost in the night of time, have powerfully
contributed to procure for man a great part, not only
of the necessaries of life, but also of the superfluities
which he now enjoys, and of which probably he would
otherwise never have had even an idea.   If, however,
the various operations which the soil requires could
be performed only by means of the hoe, the spade,
and other instruments as little expeditious, if we
could not bring animals to concur in the work, which
in political economy are considered as machines, it
is probable that in order to obtain a quantity of food
sufficient for our present population, it would be necessary to employ the whole number of hands which
are now engaged in manufactures. The plough, then,
has permitted a certain number of persons to give
themselves up to the arts, even those of the most
futile description, and what is better, to the cultivation of the mental faculties."

Now, what is true of spade husbandry in particular, is so likewise, though not in the same degree, of

* Traité d'Economie Politique, liv. i. ch. vii.

cultivation by small proprietors or tenants in general, as compared with farming carried on on a larger
scale by rich capitalists possessing the means of
adopting all new improvements in agriculture. The
surplus which remains to the latter, after feeding all
the persons employed, will be not only proportionally, but absolutely greater, though the gross produce
be less.

Supposing, then, this surplus to be more considerable on the large farm system than on the small, it is
clear that the fund from which an effective demand is
created for manufactures, and the means of supporting a larger population employed in fabricating them,
are so much the more copious. Therefore, there is
reason to believe that this branch of industry will increase the more rapidly on that account, and hence
that the period will the sooner arrive, when the demand from this quarter for butcher's meat will encourage the conversion of corn land into pasture.

But should we even suppose the surplus fund above
mentioned to be pretty much the same in the two
opposite modes of industry, still there would be a
great difference in the distribution thereof. In the
one case, it would come into the hands of a comparatively small number of persons, tenants, and landlords; in the other, it would be divided amongst an
immense body of small proprietors. But the wants
of the latter class are very different from those of the
former. They are confined, as may easily be imagined, so far as manufactures are concerned, to

those of a coarse description, whereas, great landlords and even wealthy tenants, spend a considerable part of their incomes in articles of a finer and more costly nature. Their demand will consequently encourage the setting up of a greater variety of manufactures, in some one or more of which there will be the stronger probability of arriving at perfection, so as to permit of the products being sent abroad, which new market must favour the further extension and improvement of such branches of industry. Besides, the finer kinds of wrought goods are those best calculated for the foreign trade, as containing great value in little bulk.

For these reasons, from the amount of demand as well as its nature, I consider the concentration of landed property and farms more favourable than their subdivision to a rapid growth of the manufacturing business of the country, and consequently of its commerce also. And it is the extension of these branches of production which chiefly creates an increasing demand for milk and butcher's meat, and renders it in certain situations advantageous for landlords that grass should be raised in preference to corn.

I also observed above, that the subdivision of landed property being unfavourable to the accumulation of large capitals, was on this account adverse to the progress of manufactures, and therefore again to the demand for meat, milk, &c.

We likewise found, independently of all difference in the demand for these agricultural products, that it must generally be much more advantageous for a small proprietor to cultivate his land chiefly for corn, potatoes, or other vegetable food, than to lay it down in grass, while the interest of the great landlord may be just the reverse. Therefore, on every view of the question, the subdivision of landed property and farms is opposed to the extension of pasture at the expense of corn.

The example of France offers a strong corroboration of the truth of these remarks. In that country where the soil is so much divided, of meadow or pasture land there is very little. What cattle there are, are kept almost entirely within doors, except for a short period at the close of autumn, when they are let out to the fields for an annual excursion, to browse on the scanty gleanings of the crop. Hence the use of artificial grasses is universal. Even in the neighbourhood of great towns there is little or no pasture or meadow to be seen. Up to the very walls of Paris, the whole surface is under tillage,—a most striking contrast to the country near London.

Some of the consequences of a concentration or subdivision of properties and farms, considered as influencing the change from tillage to pasture, the numbers of the agricultural population, and the progress of manufacturing and commercial wealth, I have thus endeavoured to trace.

As a convincing proof of what has been above stated, that the owners of very small landed proper-

ties consider the principal, or at least a very important part of the advantages thence derived, to arise
to them not in their capacity of landlord, capitalist,
or master, but of labourer, I may remark the very
high price paid for the possession of the soil in those
countries where it is greatly subdivided. In many
parts of France, forty years' purchase is commonly
paid for land, at which price the rent would give but
two and a half per cent. on the money, whereas the
ordinary rate of interest in that country is certainly
above five per cent. Indeed, I am told, that to all
but government, and individuals of the very first security, it is far higher.*

It is evident, then, that the buyers of these small
spots of ground do not look either to rent or profits
for their sole or principal support, but to the fruits
of their manual labour. Land is considered advantageous chiefly as a never-failing source of employment for themselves and the more advanced members
of their families, and hence as a security against
want. This alone can explain the very high price
given for it, and the fact that when a property in
France is sold, it is generally found better to dispose
of it in lots than undivided. This high price, in con-

---

* I have seen it asserted that little proprietors and manufacturers pay
eight, ten, and even twelve per cent. Six per cent. at least is said to be
commonly given with the first landed security. An inquiry was set on
foot at the time of the creation of what is called the " Caisse Hypo-
thecaire," when it was established that the real interest on mortgages
varied from five to twelve, and even fifteen per cent. Thus the mean
is about eight per cent.

junction with an elevated rate of interest, is certainly very remarkable. Before the Revolution, as we learn from Adam Smith, twenty years' purchase was commonly paid for land in that country. Nothing can more forcibly prove the effect produced on its value by splitting it up into small properties.

Our sister island affords us an example of a state of things which in some respects bears an analogy to that just mentioned, though in others it differs. The very high rents paid for land in that country must be explained on a principle similar to the above. Instead of the face of the soil being occupied by a number of small proprietors, as in France, it is held in lease by a host of petty tenants, who pay an exorbitant rent. Land is frequently let and sub-let to an astonishing degree, so that sometimes, as I am told, no less than ten different persons have an interest in it, as receivers of part of the produce, before we arrive at the actual cultivators. Each of these must be regarded in the light of a landlord, and his revenue must be considered as derived from rent, for it arises neither from his labour nor his capital. The head proprietor lets his domain to the first tenant for a small rent, this one to another, and so on till it comes into the hands of those who actually turn it to account. Though the rent received by each may be small, yet upon the whole it amounts to a great proportion of the gross produce of the soil, all of which is paid by the cultivators to those immediately above them.

In fact, the rents given in Ireland are immense, far greater than the same quality of land affords in most other countries. The causes of this, it will now not be difficult to explain. They seem to be three in number, first, the over-population of the agricultural districts; secondly, the custom of sub-letting; thirdly, the use of potatoes as the common food of the people.

From the first of these causes it arises that the price of rural labour is in Ireland extremely low, and the demand for it precarious. Hence, the practice of sub-letting being once introduced, the occupation of a small patch of ground became the principal means of gaining a subsistence, and the only tolerable security against starvation.

Again, from the immense number of persons eager on this account to obtain land, the proprietor or his representative has it in his power to drive a very hard bargain with them, leaving to the cultivator but a small part of the annual produce, the rest being all paid to himself as rent. These poor people do not take a farm with the same view as a rich English capitalist, who considers it as the means of employing his stock and his abilities to the best advantage, and who therefore never consents to pay his landlord more than he expects will remain after a due compensation for his skill, trouble, and expenditure. Such is not the case of a poor Irish cotter. Land is to him the sole source of subsistence, his only hope against want. Obtain it he must, at whatever cost, even

though he should promise to pay a rent so great, as
to leave him but a miserable pittance, out of which
to obtain both his profits and the wages of his labour.
It is much more as the means of constant employment for the latter, than as a source of profit, that
he looks upon land. In this respect his case bears a
strong resemblance to that of the small French proprietor. As the one consents to disburse a large sum
once for all, to purchase the soil, so the other agrees
to give an immense annual payment for it, and both
for the same reason, namely, that they regard it principally as something on which their labour may be
constantly employed; while the great competition
arising out of this view of the matter, in the one case
of small buyers, in the other of petty tenants, prevents them getting it on more reasonable terms.

Thus far there is an analogy between the case of
the small landed French proprietor and the little
Irish tenant, though of course I do not mean for an
instant to compare their situations in other respects.
The one having been in possession of funds, his lay-
ing them out in purchasing land was a matter of option, whereas the miserable cotter must engage to
pay an exorbitant rent or starve. The former, having
once got possession of his little estate, has all the
produce to himself, whereas the latter is obliged to
give away the greater part of it to his superior, or
else run the chance of being turned out houseless
and pennyless. No doubt, in the case of the small
French proprietor, the pride of possessing land, the

difficulty of placing funds from the want of provincial banks, and the scepticism of the peasantry as to the security of government stocks, all tend, in conjunction with the circumstances above stated, to account for the predilection shown for the soil, and consequently its high price.

Because rent in the case we have just considered swallows up a great part of the whole produce of the soil, it is not, I conceive, less properly so called on that account. According to the definition given in the commencement of this inquiry, rent is that portion of the gross produce of the land, which remains to the owner of that source of wealth, after replacing the fixed capital expended, and paying, according to the usual rate, the wages of labour and the profits of the master-capitalist.

Now, the high rents paid in Ireland agree with this definition perfectly. The reason of their being so high has just been explained, it is principally because the wages of labour are so very low, particularly those of the miserable cotter tenants, while, from the great competition for land, the advantage of these low wages is felt not by the master-capitalist as in other countries, but by the landlord. Consequently, a much larger proportion of the whole produce remains over for rent after paying that labour, even though we should suppose the profits of the petty farmer not to be at an unusually low rate. As he combines in his own person the characters of labourer, capitalist, and master, it is not easy to say how much of his petty income belongs to him in the one capacity, how much in the others; certain however it is, that his remuneration altogether is exceedingly scanty, as compared with the reward obtained in other parts of the world, from the union of as much capital, skill, and labour. Therefore, a much larger share of the produce must go to form the rent of the landlord.

But there is still another circumstance which contributes to swell this proportion. This is the third cause above stated, namely, the use of potatoes as the common food of the people. From what was said under the head of gross profits, it appears that the productiveness of agricultural industry, is a main cause on which they depend. Now, as the quantity of human food raised at a given cost from a field of potatoes, is very much greater than could be drawn from the same soil if under wheat, it follows, that if the people subsist on the former, a far smaller proportion of the whole produce will suffice for maintaining the labourers employed. Therefore a larger proportion will remain for the master-capitalist. On this account, profits ought to be higher in those countries where the common food of the people is potatoes, rice, Indian corn, or any other plant which gives an abundant return. But as in Ireland, from the circumstances above explained, great part of these high profits go to augment rent, it follows, that the latter branch of revenue, not the former, is benefited by the cause now under review.

If the small farmer cannot pay his landlord without trenching upon his fixed capital, then indeed it
would be quite improper to consider as rent all that
should come into the pockets of the latter. Part of
it at least could not agree with the definition given
above; it would not constitute a surplus remaining
after replacing the fixed capital expended, and paying wages and profits, but would be a deduction from
the first. If, again, wages and profits were so low as
to be insufficient to maintain the present labouring
and farming population, and to enable them to bring
up a race equally numerous and strong to replace
them, then the whole of rent could not be regarded
as net revenue. But that is quite another question.
The subject of net revenue is distinct from that either
of profits or rent, and must be treated in its proper
place.

Before concluding this subject, I cannot help re-
marking, that never in any country was a system devised so well calculated to squeeze the last drop out
of the orange as that just described as prevailing in
Ireland. It is impossible to conceive a plan more
ingeniously contrived for the oppression of the miserable tenantry than that of sub-letting through
many degrees. It arose, no doubt, in part from the
great poverty of the people, in part from the troubled
state of the country; and, so long as it lasts, must
prevent the formation of any thing like a class of independent capitalists. When land is let, as in Eng-

land and elsewhere, by the proprietor, directly to
those who occupy and cultivate it, whatever is paid
as rent becomes the possession of one individual, who
has therefore a sole and great interest in the soil
which is truly and properly his own.   Now, as most
men are inclined to look with complacency on what
belongs exclusively to themselves, a part of the agreeable feeling with which he regards his woods and
fields becomes reflected upon the farmers and labourers employed upon them.   Hence, in the natural
course of things, an amiable intercourse springs up
between landlord and tenant, and in times of difficulty from the failure of crops, or an unusually low
price of agricultural produce, some remission of rent
is very frequently accorded.   Instances of this are in
England of constant occurrence.   But under the sub-
letting system of Ireland, nothing similar can take
place.   So many people have an interest in the soil
as receivers of rent, that no one in fact has a right
to consider himself in particular as the proprietor,
and therefore no one can have the feeling of exclusive possession, which attaches a man not only to the
land, but also to those who till and occupy it; nor
does any person consider himself alone responsible
for the condition of the peasantry and tenantry who
dwell upon the ground.   Besides, it by no means follows, that a proprietor has it in his power to relieve
the cultivators by a diminution of rent in times of
difficulty.   The individual who most properly is the
owner of the soil, that is the head landlord who lets

the estate in the first instance, does not, as the case supposes, receive his revenue from them, but from some middle-man who sub-lets to another, and he perhaps to a third, and so on till at last it comes into the hands of those who really turn it to account. However desirous then the original landlord may be to alleviate the condition of the resident tenantry, he has it not in his power, for he has no transactions with them, he has nothing to do with them.*

The only persons who come in contact with the occupiers are those under whom they immediately hold their farms. Now, those persons cannot, if they would, grant any considerable reduction in difficult times, for they also have their landlord or superior tenant to pay, and unless they can force the wretched cultivator to come forward with the whole amount of his rent, they must themselves fail in their engagements. Thus does this system of sub-letting and middle-men not only prevent the original owner from taking any great interest in his estate and tenantry, and put them completely in the power of others who, properly speaking, are not proprietors at all, nor have the feelings of proprietors; but also it

* The Marquis of Lansdowne, the Duke of Devonshire, and other great English lords who have vast estates in Ireland, are in this condition. Nominally, they are proprietors of the soil, though in reality but a small part of what is paid as rent comes into their pockets. The troubled state of Ireland, after the great confiscations, rendered the English who obtained lands in that country glad to let them on very long leases, and at a very low rate, to any one who would take the trouble of managing the property. These again have sub-let them, and so on.

hinders any one in the chain of those who let or sub-
let, the great lord downwards, from having the *power*
to relieve the occupiers, even if he had the *will*. It
seems impossible to conceive any system more calculated for oppression.

CHAPTER VIII.

ON THE DIVISION OF LANDED PROPERTY.
ECONOMICAL CONSEQUENCES.

In terminating the investigation into the subject of Profits, I took occasion to make some remarks on the respective advantages or disadvantages of a Concentration or Subdivision of Capital in the hands of Masters of Establishments, so far as the amount of national wealth is concerned. At the same time I took care to separate the case of Division of Capitals from that of Division of Land, and mentioned that the latter would more properly come to be treated, after the doctrine of Rent. Now, during the discussion of this last subject, the question of the effects of a Concentration or Subdivision of Landed Property has already been touched upon. Still, before entirely quitting this branch of our inquiry, it may not be considered out of place to enter more fully into this very important topic, and in particular to apply to it those principles already established when treating of Profits.

Subdivision of Landed Property is in itself certainly a very different thing from the Subdivision of Ca-

pital, and of Industrious Occupations, for the Land-
owner, as such, is not necessarily either a possessor of
capital, or one who employs it productively.   But we
shall find that the former unavoidably brings about
the two latter.

When land comes to be much subdivided, it is quite
impossible that the proprietor can live upon the rent
alone, for his estate is too small to afford a revenue
of this kind sufficient for the maintenance of himself
and family.   He is therefore obliged to turn farmer,
if not labourer also, in order to swell his income by
uniting Profits and Wages to Rent.   Whatever little
capital he may possess will then be employed in the
cultivation of his ground.   Now, when all the land of
a country is divided among a number of small proprietors, each being the farmer of his own small domain, of course there can be no place for culture on
a great scale, for where is the rich capitalist to turn
for soil to occupy and till?   And though all the land
should not be in this condition, yet the greater the
extent of territory much subdivided, the less can there
be in the possession of those owners whose large
estates permit them, either to cultivate them in person on a great scale, or else to let them to wealthy
tenants.   Therefore, the subdivision of landed property necessarily tends to exclude cultivation by rich
and enlightened farmers, and to enlarge immensely
the number of agricultural establishments.   Besides,
when a farmer divides his land among his sons, he
cannot but make a partition of the stock upon it, (un-

less he intend that one or more of them should sell or let his portion,) for it would be absurd to leave small patches of ground, without the means of turning them to account. If he divide his land, he must then divide his capital also, more or less equally; and of course the same sentiment that prompted him to bequeath his immoveable property in equal lots, or nearly so, would induce him to make a similar distribution of his moveable wealth. If, indeed, the property was large enough to be split among his sons, each of the shares remaining still sufficient to maintain its owner from the rent alone, then the father might accumulate his personal riches upon one of his children in preference to the others. But when the estate is too small for this, when each of the survivors, in order to live by his land, must cultivate it himself, there is no choice; if the family acres are divided, so likewise must the capital necessary for their due improvement. Thus, we see, that a subdivision of landed property leads directly to a subdivision of farming establishments, and renders unavoidable a similar partition of the capital employed in agriculture.

Now, in order to discover what may be the effects of this on national wealth, we have only to refer to what has been already said under the head of profits, in respect to the division or concentration of capital and employments. We there found that, so far as the mass of riches in any country is concerned, it was more advantageous that the productive stock of the society should be managed by a few great masters, than by many small ones. It is not necessary again to go over the arguments which prove this, it is sufficient to turn to them as stated in their proper place. Whatever was there shown to be true of productive industry in general, must of course apply to agriculture, as well as other employments. It only remains then to be seen, whether there are any Circumstances peculiar to it, which tend either to limit or extend the effects of the General Causes.

Among the circumstances peculiar to agriculture that *limit* the effect of those general causes which influence all occupations, I may, in the first place, mention, that, from its very nature, farming is a business which cannot be carried on on so extensive a s ale as commerce or manufactures. The extent of surface over which a large farm spreads, is a main obstacle to this. The larger it is, the more difficult for the eye of the master to be everywhere present, without which, the probability of success in his undertakings must always be greatly diminished. This is a hindrance which evidently does not apply to any manufacturing establishment, necessarily confined to the walls of a building, or the enclosure of a court. Even the merchant is not obliged to make any longer journey than from his counting-house to the wharf, for by means of letters he can manage his affairs at a distance; though of course he must always be more at the mercy of others than the manufacturer, whether he deal in a small way or in a great.

Besides this, the business of farming is one that peculiarly requires the vigilant superintendence of a master, for it cannot be reduced to the same routine as many others. Go into a cotton mill, and you may be sure that what you see to-day, is a specimen of the whole year; spring or autumn, summer or winter, makes no difference. One unvaried routine perpetually goes on. But on a large farm there is a constant change, always some accident to be guarded against or remedied, its condition depending upon that most uncertain of all things, the weather. A sudden flood comes on, or a violent storm of wind or snow, crops, cattle, and fences are in danger, prompt measures must be taken, or all is damaged or lost. Neither is all land alike ; the same treatment will therefore not do for all, nor will they raise with advantage the same produce. To these differences the farmer must attend. He must be ever on the alert to see his ground well cleared of weeds, his fences in order, his drains kept clean, above all, he must lose no opportunity of housing his hay and corn before bad weather sets in. Besides, a great deal of practical knowledge is required in order to determine the rotation of crops best adapted to the soil and climate, and to change it if necessary. So that the business of a farmer is one demanding not only very considerable skill, but also perpetual watchfulness and readiness to adopt expedients fitted for the occasion. No wonder then if good farmers are rare as compared with the number of bad or indifferent ones, and if consequently they are

highly valued.   But all these difficulties must increase with the extent of land superintended by one
man, and a limit is therefore soon attained, beyond
which an increase in the size of farms becomes no
longer advisable.

Again, if the farm were very large, too much time
and labour would be wasted in removing each day the
instruments of agriculture to the extremity of the
ground, and in bringing home the corn and other produce.   Of a necessity, therefore, some minor establishment would be formed, for the convenience of
the remoter districts, and thus the farm would in
reality become split into two or more, neither of
which, however, would have the benefit of the exclusive superintendence of the head.*

For all these reasons, agriculture cannot with advantage be conducted on a scale so extensive as either
manufactures or commerce; and therefore in the case
of the former, more moderate establishments are preferable for national as well as individual wealth.

The above argument only goes to show that the
business of agriculture, as conducted by any individual,

* Another cause which renders large capitals of much less utility
in agriculture than in manufactures, is this, that division of labour cannot be pushed at all to the same extent in the former as in the latter;
for this simple reason, that, whereas in the one all the necessary operations can be carried on simultaneously by different individuals; in the
other, they must follow in rotation, according to the change of seasons.
Therefore in agriculture, the same person must successively put his
hand to many occupations, and, consequently, one advantage of large
capitals, which consists in favouring a minute division of labour, is, in a
great measure, lost.

is limited not merely by the amount of capital which he can command, but also by the very nature of the occupation; but these limits may still be sufficiently wide to make an immense difference between the largest extent of ground which can be managed with advantage by one man, and the smallest farm in any country.

The next argument, if good for any thing, tends to prove the superiority of the small farming system over the great.

In discussing the doctrine of rent, we came to the conclusion, for reasons there laid down, that the system of all others most favourable to the amount of the gross produce of the soil, was that of cultivation carried on by a number of small proprietors, each working his own little bit of land: and that the further this subdivision of property and farms was carried, the greater was likely to be the total return, spade husbandry giving the most ample of all.

It cannot, indeed, be denied, that very remarkable effects may be produced in the course of ages by the labour of man under the small culture system, even when applied in the most disadvantageous circumstances. The whole country extending from Ghent to Antwerp, called the *Pays de Waes*, is cultivated in this manner, looking like one vast garden more than an arable district, and is abundantly prolific. The fields are all small, each raised towards the centre, and surrounded by a pretty deep ditch, expedients necessary in that low land. Yet the soil by nature was nothing but a barren sand, as is evident from every spot which has escaped cultivation, such as the sides of the roads universally, and occasional tracts here and there not yet reclaimed. They begin by planting firs, which in so poor land arrive at no great height, but serve by the falling of the leaves to give a commencement of fertility. Thus by little and little has the district been brought to its present very rich state. The same is the case around Bruges, where the soil originally was nothing but sea sand, but by the art bestowed upon it for centuries, it has become covered with a fine vegetable mould. In many places, however, the sand may still be seen peeping up at the surface. There can be no doubt that nothing but the system of small farms could have wrought so wonderful a change. In the Pays de Wäes I was told that the largest were those of two horses. It never could have answered the purpose of a great capitalist, who looks to profits alone, to have attempted to improve so unpromising a soil. But the small farmer, especially if at the same time proprietor, is quite differently situated. He is naturally attached to the spot on which he has spent his youth, and which is now his own, and feels a pride in seeing it in a high state of improvement. Besides, as he knows that every addition to the produce will belong exclusively to himself, he is interested in sparing no toil to increase the total amount. He does not nicely calculate whether much of what he thus gains is not dearly purchased, for to labour he has been always accustomed, and if by fresh exer-

tions he can force his land and capital to produce
even but a little more, he is content to make them.
Thus we find from experience, that when a property
is too small fully to employ a man, who must therefore in great part depend for subsistence on day labour, he nevertheless finds time to cultivate his little
spot of ground. For this he toils late and rises early,
no sacrifice of ease is too great for him. Much may
be done in this way at odd moments, *à temps perdu*
as the French call it.

If the little proprietor have children, sons especially, they assist him in his work, and as he must
support them whether they toil or not, their labour
is all gain to him. He maintains them not because
they are his servants, but because they are his offspring. Therefore, though their exertions may not
be very productively applied, they must be far better
than nothing to the head of the family. Perhaps it
might not be worth his while to hire one day labourer, but if he have sons, he may well make them
work rather than support them in idleness. When
his own land through their means has been cultivated to the utmost, then, but not till then, will he
allow them to work for others.

For these reasons, a small farmer, especially if a
proprietor also, will bestow upon the land a much
greater quantity of labour than a rich master-capitalist, who looks to profits alone, could find it his interest to hire, and on this account will be able to
draw more from it than the latter, and even to make

fertile soil of that which the other would never un-dertake to reclaim. The Pays de Wäes, and the country around Bruges, I consider as an exemplifica-tion of this truth. In other parts of Belgium, as in Brabant and all the upper country extending from Brussels to Maestricht, Liege and Namur, where the soil is naturally fertile, and does not require the same minute attention and expenditure of labour as in East and West Flanders, farms are commonly much larger.

In mountainous countries also, where land is much divided, the patience and industry of the little pro-prietor are most remarkable. Thus, in the Alps of Savoy we see cultivated fields at an astonishing height above the valleys, and in situations to at-tain which, by the help of good limbs and a good staff, most travellers would think no contemptible feat. When we consider that the implements of hus-bandry are to be brought up to such elevated spots, and the crop to be transported to the bottom, we may form some notion of the exertions to which these little landowners submit.

It may then be fully granted that the plan of cul-tivation by small proprietors is that by which the greatest amount of produce may be drawn from the soil. But does it therefore follow that it is most conducive to the wealth of a country? The reason why the gross produce is so great under this system, is because so much labour has been bestowed upon the land. There can be no doubt, however, from the

principles bearing on all branches of industry, which
we arrived at when considering the doctrine of Profits,
as well as from the observations peculiarly applicable
to Agriculture, made under the head of Rent, that the
gross produce, though absolutely greater, will be less in
proportion to the quantity of labour expended, whether ordinary or of superintendence, than when land
is occupied by a comparatively small body of rich, intelligent, and enterprising master-capitalists. In other
words, labour is less productive in the former case
than in the latter. Therefore, in the one instance as
compared with the other, there is a *waste* of the
principal source of wealth.* If the gross produce of the
soil be greater, there will on the other hand be a deficiency in every thing else. This is the pith of the
question. Unquestionably, the amount of national
riches will be more considerable, where a smaller part
of the population is employed upon the land, but
with a larger proportional return to their exertions,
while the rest are left free to engage in commerce
and manufactures, which we may be sure they will
not, unless these two last branches of industry be
found at least as profitable as the former. There
may be less of agricultural produce in this case than
in the former, but this will be much more than balanced by an excess of every other kind of wealth.
Nay, even of agricultural products there *may* be
more, not raised at home indeed, but obtained from

* " La plus grande des économies," said Talleyrand ; " c'est l'écono-
mie des hommes."

abroad in exchange for manufactures. The error then lies in this, that it is overlooked that the large amount of gross produce obtained by petty cultivation, is purchased by a falling off in every thing else, so that upon the whole, the total return to the industry of the country is less than where labour is more advantageously applied. Petty cultivation, when pushed to its farthest extent, terminates in spade husbandry, and in it therefore the utmost consequences of a minute subdivision of land, must be seen. There is no doubt that a country cultivated in this way could be made to produce much more than under any other system of agriculture, and were food the only necessary of man, that therefore it might support a much larger population from the growth of its own soil.* But then, the wealth of this population would be reduced to a bare subsistence, the whole crop, or nearly all, would be consumed by those employed in raising it, and there would be little or nothing over to purchase home or foreign manufactures, the productions of art, or the works of genius, and no means of supporting a population engaged in such occupations. And even though persons might be found willing to addict themselves to the arts and sciences without expectation of pecuniary reward, yet none could be rich enough to have

---

* Of two fields of equal extent and fertility, cultivated, the one by the plough, the other by the spade, the latter will always give the more ample return. On some soils, clay for instance, the difference, I am told, is greater than on others, but on all it is considerable.

leisure to follow such pursuits. Thus, gradually an universal barbarism would overspread the land.

I have said that under a system of spade husbandry, a larger produce could be raised, and hence a more numerous population supported, *from the growth of the soil of any particular country*, than by any other plan of agriculture. But a nation greatly advanced in manufactures and commerce, may nevertheless nourish far more people than one exclusively agricultural whose land is cultivated by the spade. For the produce of the soil of any country is necessarily limited by the extent of territory, whereas, to the increase of manufactures no bounds are known. As long as these advance, and can be advantageously exchanged for the various articles of food raised in foreign parts, so long may the population go on and multiply. And we may be sure, that whenever food comes commonly to be imported from abroad, it is more advantageous for the nation to do so, than to force the lands at home to produce a greater quantity.

Thus it appears, that the reason why a country cultivated by the spade would be very populous, is simply because the great mass of the people would be employed in raising food and that alone. But it seems to me quite evident, that the same country, simply by a different distribution of its labour and capital, and without supposing the amount of either increased, might support a population quite as great, and more abundantly supplied with food, provided their wants, as in the above instance, were restricted chiefly to that most indispensable of all necessaries.

After all the good lands have been cultivated in the manner best suited to turn them to advantage, that is, to get the greatest return with the smallest expense of labour, if manufactures are resorted to solely as the means of procuring subsistence from foreign countries, a much greater quantity of food may thus be obtained than could be raised by the labour of the same number of persons employed in turning up with the spade an ungrateful soil at home. Thus, supposing the population to be the same, it would be much more amply fed; or it might increase, and yet be as well off as that supported by spade husbandry.

In a highly civilized community, however, where luxury and the arts have made great progress, only a part, perhaps a minority of the people, is engaged either in raising food, or in fabricating commodities to be sent abroad and exchanged for food; the rest, if not taken up with the service of the state, the liberal professions, or the cultivation of literature and science, are employed in producing the comforts and elegancies of life consumed at home, or in ministering to the mere follies and caprices of the great. No wonder, then, if the number of inhabitants should be less than it might be even under the disadvantageous system of spade husbandry, so very much smaller a proportion of them being occupied in increasing the supply of food either directly or indirectly. But if they be fewer, they are, on the other hand, incomparably richer, and both on that account, and because the mode of employing labour to the most advantage is better understood, and therefore the capabilities greater for a further accumulation of wealth, there will be more scope for a future extension of the population.

So much for the notion, because a minute subdivision of land is favourable to the amount of gross produce raised from the soil of any particular country, that, therefore, it is the system most conducive to the national riches. We have now seen that this is quite erroneous. I have only to add, that in France and Ireland a much larger proportion of the population is employed in agriculture than in England, owing, in great measure, to the subdivision of properties in the one case, and of farms only in the other. Are these countries then more wealthy than England? The contrary is notorious.

But Ireland, as is supposed, supports in one way or another a greater number of inhabitants in proportion to its extent, than even the southern division of Great Britain, the richest and best cultivated district in Europe. Allowing this to be the case, (which however seems scarcely to be true,) the reason is, that the vast majority of the people is employed in raising food alone, and that too a kind of which the crop affords a greater quantity of human subsistence than most others.*

One word more, and I have done with this subject. No one, I presume, will contend, that it is a good plan, so far as national wealth is concerned, to force barren moors and mountains to give a scanty produce, by means of a great expenditure of labour and capital. But the case is exactly the same, whether this labour and capital be applied in the above manner, or in painfully extracting a further return from lands already cultivated. In this way, the crop raised on an acre may indeed be very great, but still the sources of national wealth are as much wasted in the one instance as in the other. So false is the notion, that a system under which any given extent of surface may be made to grow the greatest possible quantity, is therefore advantageous to the general riches. The large return is looked to, but not the price given for it, " that original purchase-money which was paid for all things," namely, labour. If the latter be considerable, so likewise, no doubt, will be the former; but in comparing the one with the other, the produce may after all be scanty.

---

* M. de Stael says (Lettres sur l'Angleterre), " In England they reckon 3½ acres to each inhabitant; in Ireland, only 2⅖ on an average, and scarcely an acre in the most populous provinces."

By a reference to the population returns for 1831, however, I do not find this to be the case. Comparing the number of inhabitants with the extent respectively, the average appears to be nearly the same, whatever may be the differences in certain districts. But no part of Ireland can be nearly so populous as the country for twenty miles round Manchester.

Having dismissed the argument in support of a minute division of landed property and of farms as favourable to the wealth of a country, an argument derived from the circumstance of the gross produce being in such cases generally very great; we may now turn to another consideration which may be urged in the same view, to prove that great estates are adverse to national riches.

When discussing the subject of profits, I mentioned, that although great master-capitalists had proportionally much more facility for saving out of their gains than those who conducted business on a smaller scale; yet that their actual accumulations were far from being always in accordance with their capabilities, by reason of the taste for expense, which is apt often to increase even faster than the means of its gratification. Now, if this observation apply to those whose fortunes are the fruit of their own exertions, and who may well be supposed highly to value that which they have spent their lives in acquiring; much more will it hold good of great land-owners, who, from infancy, brought up in the lap of luxury, have not, by experience of the want of riches, formed a due estimation of the advantages of possessing them, are not attached to them by that most powerful tie, personal labour employed in their acquisition, have never been used to economy, of which the habit often lasts when no longer required, and instead of hearing it lauded as a virtue, have been rather taught to con-

sider it good in a shopkeeper, but unworthy of a gentleman. These are not persons very likely to save.
Nay, it is notorious, that so far from saving, no class
is so apt to run into debt as that of great landed proprietors. They not only live up to their revenue,
but frequently squander unproductively borrowed
capital, whether lent to them in money or in tradesmen's goods ; and thus instead of increasing the national wealth, they absolutely diminish it. On this
account it would appear, that great estates are unfavourable to the riches of a country.

Very different is the case of the small or even the
moderate proprietor of land. The former is the
most industrious and prudent of mortals. At the
same time that he toils more than any day labourer,
he has much more foresight and economy. The idea
of his being a proprietor, of having something secure
to rely on for his subsistence, gives him a dignity in
his own eyes, which preserves him from those excesses into which mere journeymen are apt to run.
Besides, the very possession of a little gives a desire
for more, as well as renders the acquisition of easier
attainment, according to the principle, that the richer
one is, the greater is the facility for a further increase
of wealth. Whereas, the poor day labourer having
nothing to begin with, finds his wages accumulate so
slowly, that he thinks it hardly worth while to save,
and therefore is the more readily led into temptation.
In France, the industry and prudence of the little

proprietor are quite notorious, while their great land owners are, I believe, as much in debt as our own.*

Thus the subdivision of the soil is eminently favourable to economy, and on that account to the increase of national wealth, while the concentration of the same just as certainly leads to extravagance.

No set of men are so apt to live beyond their income as those whose *wants* are greater than their *means*, be these last what they may. The same cause will also render them very dependent in a political point of view. Now, great land-owners, or even those who, in a country where vast estates are common, would be considered but as moderate proprietors, are especially in this case. They have a rank to maintain, a name to support, handed down perhaps from distant ages, a reputation for costly hospitality to keep up. Nothing is so expensive as family pride, for it demands not an occasional extravagance only, but a permanently large and ostentatious establishment. The *wants* then of landed gentlemen are numerous and costly, so that their rents, however large, barely if at all suffice for their indulgence. For this reason they are always in need, either for themselves or some member of their family, and, therefore, they naturally

* It appears by an official account furnished two years ago by the person styled *Directeur general de l'enregistrement,* that the value of all property under mortgage in France, amounted at that time to 11 *milliards,* 233 millions of francs, equal to more than 449 millions sterling. Now, the interest on this at 6 per cent., which is below the average, would amount to nearly 27 millions sterling, a sum not much inferior to what is annually paid for the national debt of Great Britain.

become dependent upon government for its patronage.

The more family pride prevails in any country, the more extravagant and the more dependent will be the landed gentry. This explains why proprietors in Scotland live in general much more expensively than those of equal fortunes in England, although the national tendency is rather the other way, and at the same time accounts for the want of public spirit, which was formerly attributed, with too much justice I fear, to the land-owners of the northern division of our island. Of all the classes of his Majesty's subjects, the most submissive to the ministry of the day, was the Scottish nobility; and why? They were proud, and poor in proportion to their pride.

Of course I do not mean to say that all great proprietors live beyond their income, or even spend the whole of it unproductively. Many of them undertake improvements of unquestionable advantage to the country.

It sometimes happens that a landlord assists a tenant in the expenses necessary for reclaiming land, draining, enclosing, or otherwise turning it to advantage. This is no uncommon practice in Scotland, and probably in other countries also; without supposing the Metayer system to prevail, as it does still in many parts of the continent.* As for the land in the im-

---

* Under the Metayer system of agriculture, the landlord furnishes his tenant with the capital necessary for working the farm, and the whole produce is divided, in general equally, between them.

mediate vicinity of his house, this, we may well suppose, he will spare no expense in improving to the utmost.

Many even of these ameliorations which are considered as ornamental more than profitable, are yet far from destitute of utility. There are various changes which it would not be worth a farmer's while to undertake, because the profit would either be too long in coming in, or might never be sufficient to remunerate him, but which a proprietor will often accomplish. And though his funds may not in this way be expended in the manner *most* advantageous to the country at large, still it is better than if they were employed altogether unproductively.

How many great proprietors spend a portion of their income in planting? Witness the enormous extent of mountainous ground in Scotland, covered with thriving woods within the last thirty years. Now, all this is certainly an addition to the wealth of the nation; and even though the owners may never derive a great profit from them in proportion to the expense, still, both they and the country in general will be richer, than if the sums spent in planting had been squandered in feasting and entertainments.

Thus much it seemed proper to say in justice to great landlords, though it by no means follows that the same, or even more improvements would not be made by smaller proprietors. These observations only go to prove that the former are not quite so useless to the country in an economical point of view as might by some be supposed. Splendid instances indeed there are of persons whose ample fortunes have been employed in a manner most beneficial to the agriculture of their native land, their vast possessions enabling them to make expensive experiments with a view to a general improvement of the systems of cultivation. The name of Mr. Coke is on this account justly celebrated, and not the less so from the rarity of such examples. Landlords who make this use of their great revenues are real benefactors to their country, and cannot be too highly commended. Would that such cases were more numerous!

However much we may be struck by a few such splendid instances, there can be no doubt that a great inequality of fortune, more especially when derived from land, is highly conducive to all sorts of unproductive consumption, whether for the purposes of luxury or ostentation; whereas a general equality of incomes is just as favourable to economy. Ostentation, above all things, runs away with a man's fortune, for where there is no proof of expence, the love of display cannot be gratified. Cost is the very element on which it feeds, and cheapness here, so far from being an advantage, is of all things most to be shunned. But ostentation as well as luxury is the child of inequality of fortune, for it is to prove superior riches that the expenses of ostentation are incurred. Where all were equal or nearly so, how could this passion be born and nourished? It is the genuine offspring of superior wealth, and is fostered by its parent.

I have formerly had occasion to refute the argument in favour of a great inequality of fortunes, drawn from the notion of its giving a spur to enterprise, and we now see, that it is positively injurious to the national riches by creating habits of extravagance. This taste for expense, which belongs more or less to all classes of men possessed of superior wealth, we have found to be in a peculiar degree the besetting sin of great landed proprietors. And we must always remember that *saving*, that is, *productive expenditure*, is quite as fertile a source of increase in national or individual wealth, as an improvement in the powers of labour and capital. This is the grand circumstance which counterbalances, in part at least, the obstacles which may arise to the progress of riches in any country, from a minute subdivision of land, leading to a less advantageous application of those powers. For, as has been observed, the little proprietor is quite as remarkable for industry and economy, as the great for extravagance.

Having now treated of the Circumstances, real or supposed, peculiar to agriculture, which tend to limit the effect of those General Causes which influence all occupations, and render large establishments commonly more advantageous to the national wealth than

a greater number of small ones ; it remains to be seen,
whether, on the other hand, there are any Circumstances proper to agriculture which go along with the
General Causes, and make the subdivision of landed
property and of farms, especially unfavourable to the
riches of a country.

In the first place, I may remark, that this subdivision of land constantly going on, must occasion a great
waste of that part of the wealth of a nation, which
consists in buildings, whether dwelling-houses, or offices
constructed either for luxury, or for carrying on the
business of cultivation.   The proprietor of a moderate
estate builds, we may suppose, for his own use, a comfortable mansion on his ground, which he surrounds
with stables, coach-houses, and other such tenements
suitable to a man of his fortune.   He dies, leaving five
or six children, among whom the land is to be divided.
What is then to become of his house and offices?
They must evidently be on too extensive a scale for
any of his descendants to occupy, for if they were in
proportion to the estate when undivided, they must
be quite out of character with only a fifth or sixth
part of the whole.   None of his children, then, can be
rich enough to keep up such buildings, and to maintain the number of servants required to have them
always in order.   The son to whom the paternal mansion is allotted, must therefore confine himself merely
to a corner of the dwelling-house, and thus the rest
will gradually fall into disrepair ; or he will pull it

down altogether, and build another more in accordance with his fortune.   In either case, there is a waste of the national wealth.

The same thing will happen whatever may have been the size of the estate originally, if it is to be subdivided.   It is not necessary to suppose the proprietor to have been a gentleman living from his rents alone, and occupying a spacious house, surrounded with all the luxuries that great riches can purchase. He may have been but a yeoman cultivating his own domain : still, the dwelling, stables and farm buildings suitable to a person of his means, and to the extent of land which he had in his own hands, would be all too great for one whose estate had been reduced perhaps by four-fifths.   Thus, in all cases, the subdivision of landed property must lead to the waste of an important part of the wealth of the nation, consisting in country houses and farm-offices of every description.

At the present day, we have an example of this on a great scale in France, where so many old substantial mansions are either falling into ruins, or are pulled down for the sake of the materials.*   If the division of land continue to go on as it has done for the last twenty years, there will soon be scarcely a considerable country house of any antiquity inhabited and in good repair, from one extremity of that kingdom to

* An association, well known under the name of the *Bande Noire,* and which will presently be taken notice of, greatly accelerates this destruction.

the other.   New mansions may indeed be raised, or old ones maintained by those who, having made fortunes by trade or manufactures, have purchased lands with a portion of their riches; but these also, for the reasons above stated, will not be likely to have a long duration.   The loss of wealth by the premature decay or destruction of that which otherwise might have lasted for ages, cannot but be very considerable.

Perhaps it may be said, that people aware of this, will probably build in a much less substantial manner, that country houses will be erected to last only for a short time, as in some parts of London for forty years. But even supposing this to follow, another evil would be unavoidable, the evil of having insecure and uncomfortable dwellings, dwellings where to dance is perilous, where thin walls protect neither from the cold of winter, nor the heats of summer.   It is evident also, that an isolated abode in the country cannot, with any regard to safety, be built in so slight a manner as a house in town, which receives support and defence from those adjacent.

Another objection which may be thought particularly to apply to small farms and small properties, is drawn from the ignorance and attachment to old routine, into which an agricultural population is at all times apt to fall, but which will become more fixed and incurable, where cultivation is committed to a numerous and poor set of people.   Undoubtedly there is truth in this remark.   The opportunities of instruction possessed by small agriculturists, derived either from books or personal observation of the usages of other countries or districts, must of course be limited as their means, even supposing their minds ready to receive such instruction. Improvements of all kinds, whether in the breed of cattle, the processes of cultivation, or the construction of rural implements, will be more slowly adopted by such a class of producers, than where land is occupied by a rich and more intelligent tenantry. In all the particulars just mentioned, it is certain that at the present day, agriculture is in a very backward state over by far the greater part of the kingdom of France. Cattle of all description, whether intended for food or labour, and the implements of husbandry, are lamentably bad.*

But it would not be fair to attribute this inferiority exclusively to the minute division of properties. It is one of the inheritances of the old times, when land was in general sufficiently concentrated in the hands of a few. Agriculture, of all things, is not improved in a day, but there can be no doubt that it is in a far better state now than before the Revolution. In a country not possessed of a body of farmers with large capitals, the breaking up of the extensive domains of

---

* " If we except some parts of French Flanders, of Alsace, of Normandy, &c. on almost all the lands owned or farmed by our little proprietors, the horses, mules, asses, oxen, cows, and sheep, are of a degenerate breed." Again, " In five-sixths of France, the instruments of husbandry are still of the rudest form. They are so badly combined, they are so ill adapted for draught, that their employment causes the loss of a half, two-thirds, and sometimes of three-fourths of the animal force exercised."—Dupin, " Petit Proprietaire."

the nobility, must have been of immense advantage to the cultivation of the country. For, as has been observed, there is no questioning the superiority of the system of small proprietors over that of small tenants. Still less then can it be doubted, how far preferable it is to the Metayer plan which formerly prevailed very generally in France, and still does in the southern part of that kingdom, to a very considerable degree.

Much too may be done for the enlightenment of the small proprietors by the institution of agricultural societies, such as are now formed or forming in different parts of France, which offer premiums for the best specimens in every department of rural industry ; and by the creation of model farms for the practical exemplification of all new improvements.

Of such a farm, an account is given us at full length by M. Dupin, in his little work " Le Petit Proprietaire." It is situated within six leagues of Nancy, in the valley of the Meurthe, at a place called Roville. It is composed of 190 hectares, and seems to embrace every thing necessary for a practical school of agriculture, even a work-shop for the construction of ploughs and other rural implements, and a distillery for potatoes.* We are told that " at Roville, owing to an improvement in the instruments of labour, and a more judicious employment of them, five horses and nine oxen perform as much work, nay more than from thirty to five and thirty beasts of draught formerly

---

* The hectare is a good deal more than two English acres.

employed in cultivating the same domain." The mean produce of a hectare of ground in the department of the Meurthe, is estimated at 28 francs 50 centimes, all expenses deducted, whereas that of the same extent of land in the farm of Roville, is valued at 59 francs, more than double of the general average.* In 1822 this farm began to be worked on its present plan. A greater division of labour has been introduced than has generally been thought practicable in agriculture. Thus there is, 1. The *chef des attelages*, or head-man who presides over the work performed by animals. 2. The *chef de main d'œuvre*, who directs the works executed by men. 3. The irrigator, who takes the charge of the waters in all the lower parts, superintends the operations which the improvement of the meadows requires, the hay crop, the drying of the arable lands in winter, &c. 4. The shepherd. 5. The *marcaire*, with the assistants under him, for taking care of the fatted animals, the cows and pigs." We can easily conceive the immense advantages which may be derived from such establishments.

But of all the objections that can be urged against

* The account of the farm is thus given:—

Total of receipts	.	.	47,733 francs.
Total of expenses	.	.	36,470
Excess of receipts	.	.	11,263

which, divided among 190 hectares, gives about 59 francs for each. This example, so far as it goes, tends to show how much a scientific cultivation on a great scale tends to increase the net produce, not only proportionally, but absolutely, agreeably to what was said on that head in the chapter on Rent.

a minute subdivision of landed property, the strongest unquestionably is derived from the tendency which this system may be supposed to have, to run into an extreme. What is good within certain limits, may, when carried beyond that point, be highly injurious to the prosperity of a nation. This, I think, is manifestly true with the case before us. It is unnecessary to enter here at large into the consequences of an extremely minute partition of land, having already dwelt upon them when discussing the consequences of spade husbandry, the last term in the series of progressive division. We then found, that were such a system of cultivation universally established, all or nearly all the produce of the soil would be consumed by those who raised it, that there would be little or no surplus for the purchase of home manufactures, or objects of foreign commerce, or for the maintenance of a population engaged in such branches of industry; none for the acquisition of works of art or genius, or for the subsistence of a class of men devoted to these glorious pursuits. In short, that the subdivision of land pushed to its ultimate term, led directly to barbarism.

Now, what is true of this system in its last stage, must apply to it, though in a less degree, before it reaches that point. Many and great evils will result from the minute partition of land, without supposing it carried so far as to replace the plough by the spade. If a farm be not too extensive to be superintended by one cultivator possessed of capital and intelligence, it is impossible to suppose that it could be managed as well and as economically when split into twenty separate tenements. This follows of course from the general principles common to all occupations already laid down. In the case of agriculture in particular, we may easily conceive what a waste of capital there must be, when farms become so small as not to give full employment even to one horse and plough. This is the very circumstance which would gradually lead to the substitution of the spade, for it would be far too expensive to keep a horse for the cultivation of a mere spot of ground. But, before farms become so very minute, the waste of capital or of labour might still be considerable. Thus, suppose an extent of land at present occupied by one individual, and which fully employs five and twenty horses. If this farm come to be divided into ten separate and equal establishments, it is evident that as two horses will not suffice for each, three must in every case be required ; so that a space formerly worked with twenty-five horses, cannot now be tilled without thirty. In order to avoid this expense, if the cultivators content themselves with two horses a-piece, it is clear that much must be done by the spade. In the one instance there is a waste of capital, in the other of labour.

One way, indeed, to obviate this inconvenience would be, that several small proprietors should keep a horse and plough between them. An association of this sort might, if generally practised, be highly advantageous, and something similar is in truth quite indispensable to the coexistence of plough husbandry, and the use of animal power, with the continued subdivision of land. It is easy, however, to foresee to how many disputes this joint-stock work must give rise.* Take, again, any of the more costly agricultural machines, a thrashing-mill for instance. For one or two, probably even half a dozen very small proprietors, the expense of such an instrument would be quite out of the question, for besides the original cost and repairs, there must be several horses to move it, wherever water power is not to be found. And how are even half a dozen people to be got to agree on the respective shares they are to take in such an undertaking as the building, repairing, and working of a thrashing-mill? This instance will give us some idea of the obstacles which a minute partition of land creates to the introduction of improvements in agricultural industry.

The evils of an excessive division of land being fully admitted, it may, however, be said, that the practice of leaving property in the soil equally shared

---

* A more feasible plan is that in which the petty cultivators hire from their more wealthy neighbours horses and ploughs for the occasion. This to my own knowledge is practised in Savoy, where land is much divided among small proprietors. The plough, oxen, and a man to guide, are all hired for so much a-day. Notwithstanding this expedient, spade husbandry is much used. Many, I suppose, cannot afford the expense even of hiring, and so rather give their own labour. Besides, the larger gross produce obtained by the spade is a main object with very small proprietors. The same expedient is adopted in Switzerland, but there also the spade is much employed.

among all the children of a family, does not necessarily lead to this too great subdivision, but that the
very experience of these evils suggests a cure, so that
the system corrects itself. In other words, that the
owners finding it contrary to their interests to break
up the farm, will keep it entire.*

There are various ways in which this is possible.
First, all the children, on the death of their father,
who is supposed to leave his estate equally amongst
them, may agree to live together, and to cultivate
the land in common. This it is evident, may be possible enough, so long as they remain single, but must
become more and more inconvenient, perhaps impossible, when they marry and have families. They
might, no doubt, still continue to labour in common,
though they occupied separate houses on the property. But the natural love that every man has
for possessing something exclusively belonging to
himself, must always be opposed to this system, but
especially when the members no longer live together,
and have wives and children of their own. A separate interest then springs up, which ill accords with
a community of property.

Secondly, one of the sons may take upon himself
the sole management of the common possession, en-

* In the fourth number of the Westminster Review, there is a very
able article on the subject now before us, in which the writer, arguing
against the privilege of primogeniture, fully allows the evils of a great
subdivision of farms, but collects all his force to prove that the equal
partition of landed property leads to no such result. On this account
I have been induced to dwell on the point in question longer perhaps
than to many may seem necessary.

gaging to pay annually to each of the others a due
portion of the total return, until he be able to give
them a principal in money equal to their shares in
land.   They, on the other hand, may be supposed to
go and seek their fortune where best they may.   But
independently of the difficulty of a man's making his
way in the world when he has so very little to begin
with, as must be the case with him whose income is
derived from a small bit of land, which is not supposed to be sold, and the value of which his brother
may perhaps never be able to pay him in capital;
we must bear in mind how very much opposed this
plan is, to all the habits and feelings of the little
proprietor.   He is naturally attached to the soil on
which he has been brought up, and to a country life
and pursuits; he detests the idea of removal to any
other spot, and still more of a change of occupation.*

All persons educated among the fields and woods
have these sentiments, more or less, inherent in them,
but the little proprietor above all others.   The notion of having a bit of land which he can call his own

---

* A remarkable instance of the attachment of country people to the
place of their birth, I remember to have heard mentioned by M. Say
in one of his public lectures at Paris.   He had been at considerable
trouble and expense in removing a number of labourers from the department of the Oise, where it seems they were badly off, to another
part of France, where he knew they could get employment on better
terms.   Well, in no long time they were all back again in their former
situation.   It is the poorest and most numerous class which is most
firmly rooted to the soil, chiefly from a total ignorance of any other
place than that in which they have been born and brought up.   It is
almost as great an effort for a poor labourer to change his parish, as for
a rich man to change his country.

binds him amazingly to the soil, and it must be a strong inducement indeed that can lead him to quit it, and embark his fortunes on the uncertain ocean of a world to him unknown.

However much a certain class of writers may sneer at the brutal ignorance, as it is called, of the rustic who would rather vegetate on his native spot of ground than endeavour to push his fortune elsewhere, who would prefer seeing the family estate disadvantageously cut up, to separating himself from it for ever, still it cannot be denied that men have feelings often sufficiently strong to make them act contrary to their *material* interests, even when these are evidently seen. Much more must this be the case, when the expediency, in an economical point of view, is perhaps not so clear to the individual concerned, as to more cool and enlightened observers. We must always remember that man has interests of various kinds, and though wealth be a principal object of desire, it is far from being the only one.*

* It were well had this very evident proposition been always attended to. But though allowed perhaps in words, it has in our days been often forgotten in argument. Thus, when it is said that man is exclusively governed by his interest, if by this word be meant every kind of interest material and immaterial, the statement may be quite correct. But this sense being too vague for the purpose of certain writers, they have contrived to forget it in the course of their investigations, and have substituted another and much more restricted signification of the term. When taken to mean merely that coarse, palpable interest which can be touched, tasted, and handled, then, though the conclusions drawn from such a definition may be perfectly logical, yet as the premises on which they are founded, namely, that *in this sense* man is exclusively governed by his interest, are decidedly erroneous, of course the deductions, if not entirely false, must at least be liable to great limi-

It may, however, be asked, Why must the little proprietor change his place of residence and his occupation? May he not let his land to his brother or any other person, and serve for hire as a day labourer, either on his own ground, or in the neighbourhood. Thus, his taste for a country life might be gratified, and yet the paternal estate kept entire. Let us then see whether his interest, merely as wealth is concerned, would really prompt him thus to act.

His land, it is said, might be let, and rent obtained for it, his little capital lent, and interest received for it, and his labour offered to others. But, in this way, it is evident, he would realise only three kinds of revenue instead of four. He would receive rent, interest, and wages, but no profits of enterprise. In order to gain them, he must superintend the cultivation of his own ground, and if so, it will surely be better for him to employ his own labour and that of his family upon it, than to hire others for the purpose. Therefore, in no way can his land, capital, and labour, bring him in so large an income on the whole, as by tilling with his own hands his little property. Nor is this all. Were he to let his little patch of land, not only would he lose the profits of enterprise,

tations. Epicurus considered Pleasure as the *summum bonum*, and in *his* sense of the word, perhaps, he was right. His disciples, however, chose to take it in its more usual and confined signification, and thus what in the hands of the master was really a system of philosophy, became in those of his followers a mere excuse for immorality and profaneness.

but also he would be deprived of that which affords a profitable occupation for all his extra hours. It is not always that a day labourer can find full employment. On such occasions his own land affords a sure resource against the waste of time, and usefully engages those hours or days which otherwise would be spent in idleness. It must therefore manifestly be the interest of the peasant to keep his small estate in his own hands. It has already been remarked how much work is really done in this way at odd moments. Besides, the feelings of security thence derived is a most urgent motive to this line of conduct. By having a property of his own in which he may usefully vest his labour, he is in a degree relieved from that sense of dependence and precariousness which is felt by those who rely solely on others for employment and subsistence. So strong indeed do I believe this motive to be, that even could it be proved that the peasant might probably make more in the course of the year by selling or letting his little patrimony, and serving others as a day labourer, and also, what is important, could he be made sensible of this, still he would prefer the feeling of independence and security arising from keeping it in his own hands, to the uncertain prospect of a larger income. Security is one of the first wants of man, and its attainment the principal object of all law and government.

In what has here been said, I am sufficiently borne out by the experience we have of France and other countries where the system of equal partition prevails. The exceedingly high price there paid for land by the peasantry, amply proves how much they hold to it. So far, indeed, is this partiality carried, that in Savoy, to my personal knowledge, it is very common for the country people to buy land on credit, and work the price out of the soil, paying it by instalments.

Thirdly, if, in order to pay off his brother's portions, the one who took upon himself the charge of the whole property should borrow money on mortgage, this would put him in a very dependent and disagreeable position, being all his life hampered with a debt, which he might never be able to discharge. Instead of having his brothers for creditors, he would have strangers, who, no doubt, would be more rigidly exacting of their dues.*

Rather than place himself in such a position, it would be better that the whole should be sold, and the price divided, which forms the fourth way in which each may have a share of the common inheritance, and yet the landed estate remain entire. But, besides that this requires the consent of all the parties, which must often be impossible to obtain, I may remark, that much the same motives will operate to prevent this arrangement, which we found to exist in the second case. If they are to remain where they were, and work as day-labourers, the arguments against

* In France, at the present day, the high interest of money borrowed on mortgage, before noticed, most effectually prevent this expedient against division of farms being much resorted to.

selling, as drawn from pecuniary considerations, and the feeling of security, are exactly similar to those against letting. The possession of a capital obtained by the sale might indeed enable them to become farmers on other people's land. But, in this way, they would realize but three sorts of revenue out of the four, for to rent they would not be entitled, and though their income might nevertheless be as great or greater, on account of the larger amount of gross profit derived from a capital more considerable, and perhaps its better application, yet they could not enjoy the same feeling of security and independence which are among the principal charms of landed property. To a change of place and of occupation, on the other hand, powerful motives are opposed, attachment to the spot of one's nativity, where careless childhood and buoyant youth have alike been passed, and love of country habits and country recreations. Can we suppose that a set of rustics, who all their lives have been employed in the labours of the field, and whose hours of leisure have been given up to village amusements, will change their habits in a moment when the head of the family dies, and quit the only sort of business with which they are familiar, to go and learn new trades, and mingle in societies to them indifferent or disagreeable? Surely it requires no very deep knowledge of human nature, to prove that such sudden transformations are of rare occurrence. Man is the creature of habit, especially as years advance, but an agricultural population most of all, as is shown by their great attachment to routine, and the difficulty of making them change any of their old established customs.

But even suppose the estate to be sold, still, it by no means follows that it is sold undivided. Nay, the contrary, is, to say the least, fully as probable. The reasons for this opinion may be seen above, under the head of rent. We there saw that when once landed property becomes an object of general desire to the rural population of any country, and is considered principally as a subject on which their labour and little stock may find constant employment, it will bear a much higher price than where it is looked upon chiefly as an advantageous investment for capital, in which last case, its value will depend upon the rate of interest. In proof of this, I instanced the price of land in France at the present day, where notwithstanding interest is higher than in England, forty years' purchase is not uncommonly paid for that species of property. And what renders the proof more complete is, that before the Revolution, and consequently before the breaking up of the large domains, not more than twenty years' purchase was usually given.

Partly from the above reasons, partly from the incessant division of fortunes diminishing the number of persons capable of bidding for any considerable extent of ground, it now constantly happens in France, that when an estate of any size is to be sold, it is found more advantageous to dispose of it in lots than undivided. M. Dupin informs us, that so great is the

competition for land among the peasantry, that companies as well as wealthy individuals sometimes buy
an estate for the express purpose of selling it again
in lots. He states that a man will work for twenty
years in order to purchase a piece of ground, for
which he pays a price out of all proportion with the
rent. The existence of these companies is a fact well
known. They are called the *Bande Noire*, being so
stigmatised by the nobles, because, when they purchase
an old domain, for the sake of disposing of it to the
peasantry at a much higher rate, they demolish the
ancient mansion and sell the materials. Associations
of this sort exist not only in France, but in other
countries where the system of equal partition prevails,
in Savoy for instance, where, since the French invasion that practice has been commonly introduced.
The difference between the price paid for land by
these companies, and that at which they sell it to the
people, is, I am told, astonishingly great.

Thus does experience support the truth of the statement I have made, that in a country where equality
of partition was universal, even if all the members of
a family should agree to sell the patrimonial acres,
from a consciousness that it was more for their interest so to do, than for each to cultivate his little share,
still, the property may not, after all, remain entire.

These are the different expedients which we may
suppose resorted to, in order to put a stop to the too
great subdivision of land, consequent upon equality of

partition among all the children of a family, and though one or other of them may occasionally be adopted, especially among the upper classes, yet so many are the obstacles to such expedients, that I cannot conceive they will ever become so general as effectually to check the undue splitting of farming establishments. At most, they will only retard in certain localities the natural tendency of things, but cannot prevent these from ultimately running their course.

But as land, whatever it may be in mathematics, is in real life certainly not divisible *ad infinitum*, this partition constantly progressing, must some time or other come to a stop. Now, what is to arrest it? I confess I see no cause sufficiently powerful, but what shall limit the increase of population. When land has become universally cut up to such a degree, that if again split into parts, a family could not possibly be supported on a fraction of it, then indeed will an effectual stop be put to its division. But some may say, what is to hinder the little proprietor from serving as a day-labourer for hire, if his time and strength are more than sufficient for the cultivation of his own patch of ground, and if he cannot support his family from it alone? But those who make this objection forget, that although this would be very possible, and is in reality practised, in countries where the system has not yet been pushed to its ultimate consequences, yet in a state of society, such as above supposed, no one would stand in need of labourers; for when land was once universally split up into small properties, each cultivated by its owner, every person would be in the same condition, having plenty of labour to dispose of, and demanding none. The value of labour would in such a case be reduced to little or nothing. The peculiar and essential tendency of the small proprietor system is to fix people to the soil, and to cause more persons to be occupied upon it than can find full and profitable employment for their capital and industry. The population of a country in which this system prevails, may not be so great as that of another where labour is better applied, and most likely it will not increase so rapidly from the smallness of the net produce. For, it is on the amount of the net produce that the future enlargement of the population must depend. But, unless the preventive check operate with peculiar force, it will have a strong tendency to become redundant, and each family sufficing for the cultivation of its own domain, there will be little room for any extra labourers. In such a state of society, these could not find subsistence ; in order to live, it would be necessary to have a bit of ground, and some little capital to work it. Hence, a great competition for land, and its high price, whether sold or let.*

It appears then that when once land had become exceedingly subdivided, the market price of labour would be reduced to little or nothing, and the occu-

---

* This principle has helped us to explain the high Irish rents. See Chapter on Rent.

piers of the soil would have no resource beyond the cultivation of their own little properties. When these came to be so small, that a family could not be supported on the produce of the separate portions, supposing division pushed still farther, then indeed the progress of population must be arrested, either by a decrease in marriages, or by the horrible check of famine and disease. And the population becoming stationary, of course the further division of land would cease. Here, then, we arrive at the natural limits of the system.

For some time, however, before this limit was attained, the condition of the little proprietor would be very miserable. The state of the small cultivator in a country where there are none but very small ones, must be far more precarious than that of a day labourer in other parts of the world. Depending entirely for subsistence on the produce of his little farm, if any accident befall the crop, which, from the mutability of the season, and from sudden storms, must be sometimes expected, he has no resource, for, as has been shewn, nobody stands in need of his labour, which is therefore worth nothing. Labour is useful to him, only because he has a spot of ground on which to apply it, in the market it is of little or no value. If his own crop fail for one year, how then is he to subsist till the revolution of the seasons brings round another? Unless he previously have accumulated something, starvation must stare him in the face. Surely the condition of a day labourer in most other countries is preferable to this. His labour is not bound down as it were to a spot, there to be exercised with advantage, or no where else; on the contrary, if he does not find employment in one quarter, he generally will in another. In reality, his life is more free, and his existence more secure than that of the petty proprietor, in a country where the subdivision of land has become universal. Of course, it is only on this latter supposition that the small proprietor is worse off than the day labourer, for until the splitting of territorial possessions has become so general as to render labour of little value in the market, he combines the advantages which belong to both conditions. But it is the ultimate consequences of any system which we must steadily bear in view, and not suffer our sight to be dazzled by temporary appearances, however brilliant. This observation I consider particularly to apply to the subject before us. Within certain limits, the division of landed property must be looked upon as highly desirable, as the source of great advantages, moral, political, and economical. But once establish the custom of equal partition among all the members of a family, and there is the greatest danger that these limits will be passed, and the system pushed on till it terminate in universal poverty and barbarism.

Even in more fortunate circumstances, the life of very small proprietors has its peculiar evils. We have already seen that they toil much more than any day labourer could be induced to do. Indeed, they are perhaps often inclined to over-work themselves.

Their life is also far from devoid of anxiety, for as they depend on the coming crop, not only for immediate subsistence, but likewise for the reimbursement of their little capital, a failure in the return would endanger all. In this respect they are subject to much greater care and watchfulness than he who has nothing to depend on but his daily labour. They are perpetually tormented with the fear of some disaster, and with thoughts of what can be done to prevent it, while at the period of harvest in particular, they can rest neither by day nor by night, till the crop is secured. From these evils at least, the common labourer is free.

The principle I have endeavoured to establish is this, that no causes seem sufficiently powerful to give an effectual check to the division of properties and farms but those which arrest the progress of population. The extent, then, to which the former is carried, will depend upon the latter, and the extreme consequences of the system may be long of being felt, or may even be completely obviated, where the preventive check, consisting in prudence and foresight, is so strong as to retard very much the increase of population, or to put a stop to it altogether. From this cause, no doubt, it happens that in certain countries where the system of equal partition has long prevailed, its evil consequences have not yet been fully felt. Such is the case in a great part of Switzerland, in many cantons of which scarcely a very poor person is to be seen, and no beggars, but an air of comfort and neatness universally prevails.* Gentry there are hardly any, a general equality prevails, and all have a competence. I know of no spectacle more agreeable than is presented to the traveller in that really happy country.

It must, however, be allowed that this is not a fair representation of every part of that little republic. In some cantons, the Valais for instance, poverty is sufficiently manifest, and disease its usual attendant; while in others, as Berne, a landed aristocracy is not unknown.† But, in the most favourable view of the case, however much we may be delighted with the aspect of a country where the small proprietor system has long prevailed, and allowing this system to have been one main cause of its prosperity, though free government and a pure religion must also be taken into account, yet we must hesitate before concluding that what is a source of happiness in a limited district, would be beneficial if universally adopted. It would indeed be rash to pronounce that plan in general desirable, the tendency of which certainly is to establish a general mediocrity not of fortune only, but of knowledge and intelligence, and to

---

* M. de Stael informs us that in the part of Switzerland more particularly known to him, the increase of population for forty years previous had been little perceptible. " Lettres sur l'Angleterre," lettre **v.**

† A singular usage prevails in the canton of Berne. It is there the custom, as I am told on good authority, to give the land to the *youngest.* This may help to explain the greater prevalence of aristocracy in that canton. It is but fair to remark, that both in internal prosperity, and in political influence, Berne has always been particularly distinguished among the confederate states.

prevent the growth of superiority in every department. I have said that in many parts of Switzerland gentry are almost unknown. Accordingly, little
farmers, graziers, and cow-feeders, compose the legislative assemblies of those districts. How far such
persons are fitted for the offices they discharge, we
may in part learn from the late squabbles and splitting of cantons already sufficiently small. But were
they even better calculated than they appear to be
for the business of legislation, surely the same talents
which may serve to regulate the petty affairs of a
Swiss canton, might be totally unequal to conduct
the various and complicated interests of an extensive
kingdom. But the constant division of land must
tend more and more to do away with that class of
persons, who, being freed from the necessity of bodily labour, have leisure to devote themselves to intellectual pursuits, whether with a view to take a
part in the government of their country, or to aid in
nourishing the torch of science, and transmitting it
from generation to generation. A small state surrounded by nations differently circumstanced, and
from whose literary stores it can freely borrow, is in
a very different condition from what it would be if
left to its own resources. But it is to the consequences of the practice under consideration, supposing it to be generally adopted, that we must chiefly
look.

Since we have found that the only effectual check
to the continued subdivision of land, arises from the

slow increase, and ultimately stationary condition of the population, it becomes a question of great interest, whether the small proprietor system be or be not favourable to a rapid augmentation of inhabitants. Many seem to take it for granted, that no plan is so likely to lead to this result as the one we are now considering. In this, I confess, I think them completely mistaken.

In what class of persons do we find the most improvidence? In that which possesses nothing, but is dependent entirely on daily labour for support. As soon as a man has something he can call his own, the desire of improving his condition gains strength by a nearer prospect of the possibility of success. Having something to lose, he is no longer careless, having the hope of more, he becomes prudent and economical. When, on the other hand, a man is possessed of little or nothing beyond his daily bread, and the clothes on his back, so distant is the view of an improved existence, and so difficult the first steps towards it, that it seems less worth while to resist the present temptation. Hence, in all countries, the lowest class of all is the most reckless and improvident; and the greater the necessity for restraint, the less is it practised. How infinitely more imprudent is the miserable Irish cotter than the well-fed and well lodged English labourer!

But nothing is so likely to quicken foresight and curb present indulgence, as the possession of a small bit of ground. This gives the dignity and feeling of independence which property of every kind has a tendency to inspire, but landed property especially. A man actuated by such sentiments is not likely to run into follies or extravagancies, above all, to form imprudent matrimonial connexions, which he well knows must entail poverty upon himself and his posterity.

So far as our experience extends, it fully corroborates the truth of the above conclusions. I have already alluded to the case of Switzerland, where the preventive check to population has been very powerfully felt. But an example of this kind, on a much greater scale, is offered to us by the extensive kingdom of France, in which, as we know, equality among all the children of a family is universally practised, and, for the most part, even enforced by law. Now, we know, from the results of the census taken every five years in that country, that the population has for some time past increased much more slowly than in the other great monarchies of Europe. The difference in this respect between it and Great Britain and Prussia is very striking indeed. Even in Austria the population augments much more quickly than in France.*

* According to M. Dupin, of all the great states of Europe, Prussia is that which has increased the most rapidly in population since the peace of 1815, and France the least. Prussia would double its inhabitants in 26 years, Great Britain in 42, Russia in 66, Austria in 69, and France in 105. " Forces Productives et Commerciales de la France." Paris, 1827, Liv. i. Ch. iv.

Perhaps the slow progress of population in the last country, may also in part be attributed to the slow increase of wealth, which, if true, would tend to prove how unfavourable is the system of division to the

The observations just made apply only where land is occupied by a number of small proprietors. The case is very different where it is held by a small tenantry. The petty tenant is neither a proprietor, nor has the feelings of one. He is always dependent more or less upon his landlord, which serves to keep down his spirit, and he knows that the ameliorations he may bestow upon the soil do not descend as a heritage to his children, but after a time, become beneficial only to his superior. He cannot, therefore, be supposed to have either the dignity, industry, or foresight of the little proprietor.

Accordingly, the most striking instances we know of an excessive subdivision of farming establishments, and of the evils resulting from it, are to be found in

advance of national opulence. The example of France as compared with England affords, so far as it goes, a corroboration of the truth of what has been said above ; " That the population of a country in which this system prevails may not be so great as that of one where labour is better applied, and most likely it will not increase so rapidly, from the smallness of the net produce." Another cause of this slow increase is the greater prevalence of the preventive check. Labour and capital are employed in most branches of industry, probably less productively in France than in England. The work of M. Dupin just quoted, bears ample testimony to this. On the other hand, notwithstanding the gay character of our neighbours, they are more prudent and less extravagant than we. Comparatively speaking, it may be said, that the English get rich by toil, the French by economy. For the inferiority of the French in production, three causes in particular have been assigned by the Commissioners of inquiry appointed at different times. First, the bad state of internal communications ; secondly, the high rate of interest resulting from the want of credit ; thirdly, the inferior skill of the workmen and masters as compared with the English. The two former causes apply to all branches of industry ; the last to some only, particularly the mechanical arts, for in the chemical, our neighbours are our equals in knowledge and address, and often, I believe, our superiors.

countries where the system of small tenantry prevails. We have only to turn to Ireland as an example of this.   Assuredly, that island could never have arrived at its present wretched condition, but for the plan of sub-letting, which has covered the land with mud cabins and potatoe gardens.   This system coming into operation among a people naturally reckless and improvident, accustomed to marry under twenty years of age, has there been pushed to its ultimate consequences, and its further progress is now checked only by the scourges of famine and pestilence.   By far the greater part of the excesses committed in that country are in reality owing to a squabble for land, without a portion of which there is no security against starvation.   Most of the cruelties exercised arise from vengeance for being dispossessed of the only means of gaining a livelihood, and have not robbery for their object.   No doubt, crimes are perpetrated on account of tithes also; but as compared with the other, this is but a trifling source of commotion.   To turn a tenant out of a farm is often as much as a man's life is worth.

I say that the holding a bit of land is the only way of gaining a subsistence, for exactly in agreement with what, from theory, we found would be the ultimate consequences of the system of division, there is such a superabundance of labour, that very little indeed can be got for it; so that those who wish to turn it to account, are obliged to take a journey to England for that purpose.

Before the introduction of large grazing farms, the

system of cultivation by small tenants was very prevalent in the Highlands of Scotland. But this class of persons was in general very poor and needy, always in arrear of rent, and therefore at the mercy of tho landlord. And as Mr. Malthus observes, in no part of Great Britain was the population so redundant as in that district of the island. This is the case in some places still, as on the banks of Loch Tay, where the small patches of corn and potatoes mark the minute subdivision of tenements.

The great check to imprudent marriages among country people is, the difficulty of getting a bit of ground for building a cottage to shelter the young couple, and from which something like a provision for a family may be expected. By the practice of splitting farms, the first obstacle to their union is removed, and an illusory prospect of secure subsistence held out, and where the character of those who occupy the soil has not been elevated by the feelings which property has a strong tendency to create, there we may well suppose that a redundant and miserable population will spread over the land.

It is now time to inquire what further proofs can be derived from experience, in support of the conclusions above arrived at from reasoning, that where it is the custom to leave landed property equally among all the children of a family, a great subdivision of the soil will really take place, in spite of the inconveniences which may be found to attend it; and that all the expedients which may be devised, in order to prevent this partition, will not be so commonly adopted as to make any material difference in the general result.   And here we must again have recourse to the example of France, as being the country with which we are best acquainted, and the only one where we have an opportunity of seeing the system tried on an extensive scale.

In 1827, not forty years had elapsed since the famous law was passed enforcing the equal division of all kinds of property among the sons and daughters of a family.   And though by the present law, a father has always the power to dispose as he pleases of a certain portion of his fortune, varying according to the number of his children, but in all cases sufficient to allow of his making one son twice as rich as any of his brothers, yet so completely has the spirit of the legislative enactment passed into the minds of the people, that this permission is very very rarely acted upon.   Were the compulsory disposition abolished to-morrow, there would probably be no change in the practice, popular feeling and custom would be found as powerful as law.   But whether the system of equality be the effect of the one or the other, whether voluntary or compulsory, can make no difference in its *economical* results.   Now, let us see what has been the influence of this system on the division of the soil. In 1827, not forty years, as I have observed, since the law was passed, the number of landed proprietors in France had increased to four millions, as we learn

from M. C. Dupin, an excellent authority on all such matters. We shall have some idea of the enormous difference between France and England in this respect, when we know that the number of landed estates in the latter kingdom is but thirty-two thousand.* If we take, then, the very moderate computation of four individuals, on the average, to a family, we shall have sixteen millions of individuals in France having a direct interest in the soil as proprietors, or as the wives and children of such. Now, this is exactly one half of the whole population of the kingdom. If we supposed families to average five individuals each, then the number of persons in the above condition would be twenty millions, or nearly two-thirds of all the inhabitants. " Since the Revolution," says M. Dupin, in his larger work, " almost four-firths of the agricultural population have become proprietors, and enjoy, as heads of families, a landed revenue of more than 64 francs," equal to about two pounds eleven shillings. Such was the state of landed property after scarcely forty years' trial of the system of equality.†
And we know, for a certainty, that during the fifteen

---

* As by England, foreigners almost always mean Great Britain, I suppose that, in the above statement of M. Dupin, Scotland is comprehended. Be this as it may, the difference is immense. See the " Petit Proprietaire."

† It is proper to remark, that, strictly speaking, the practice of equal division did not first begin in France at the Revolution, but existed previously in some parts, especially in those districts where the Roman law prevailed; *pays de droit ecrit*. Thus, we find Arthur Young already deploring the consequences of the splitting of properties. The fact is corroborated by M. de Staël. " Lettres sur l'Angleterre," Lettre IV.

years from 1815 to 1830, subdivision has gone on at
a very rapid rate.   This is a fact ascertained by an
actual survey of the property of the country at different times during that period.   It is proved, moreover,
by the continued decrease in the number of persons
qualified to elect the members of the Chamber of
Deputies.   Under the government subverted by the
Revolution of July, this privilege was confined to
those paying 300 francs, or twelve pounds sterling,
direct taxes.   By direct taxes, is meant not only the
land-tax, whi h, however, is by far the most important of all the public burdens, but also the taxes on
doors and windows, on furniture and the person, besides the *patente* paid by people in business, which
varies with the extent of their dealings.   But, as I
have said, the land-tax is by far the most considerable
of all the taxes, whether direct or indirect, and
amounted, according to the budget for 1828, to 211
millions of francs, or nearly $8\frac{1}{2}$ millions sterling, being more than a fifth of the whole public revenue.
The total of the direct taxes for the same year was
289 millions of francs.   Now, when the Bourbons
first returned, the body of electors was about 130,000,
which number, however, in fifteen years, had declined
to 80,000, chiefly in consequence of the splitting of
landed property.   In 1815, there were 130,000 proprietors, whether of land or of houses, having estates
sufficiently large to permit of their paying twelve
pounds of direct taxes to government; in 1830, no
more than 80,000 were found rich enough to be as-

sessed to that amount.   This surely is very startling.
But, to continue.   Soon after the last Revolution, the
common qualification for elector was lowered from
300 francs to 200, from twelve to eight pounds; and
for some particular classes of persons whose capacity
was supposed to be proved by their literary station,
or by the exercise of some one of the learned professions, this was still farther reduced to four pounds.
But with all this, the number of electors in France is
still no more than 180,000.   Supposing none of these
to pay less than eight pounds, (which is not likely to
be the case, for a few, as I have observed, may exercise that function on being rated at four pounds only,)
it then follows, that, of the four million of small landed
proprietors existing in that country, as well as of the
proprietors of houses, there are not above 180,000
whose possessions are sufficiently ample to permit of
their contributing so much as eight pounds directly to
government, although, in 1835, the land-tax amounted to 250 millions of francs, or 10 millions sterling,
fully a fourth of the whole State revenue, and the
total of direct taxes to 359 millions of francs.*

In the year 1829, I was present at a lecture, on
this very subject of the division of landed property
in France, delivered by M. Comte, son-in-law of the
late celebrated political economist M. Say, and him-

---

* It was stated the other day in one of the best French newspapers,
Journal des Debats :   " There are bits of land which figure on the rolls
of direct taxes for 5 centimes (one halfpenny,) and which, consequently, are worth about 20 francs (16 shillings).   Many are rated at 10 and
15 centimes, and are, therefore, worth 40 or 60 francs."

self the author of several much esteemed publications. The lecturer, like all other Frenchmen of the present school, was evidently attached to the system of equality; but still, it was clear, that the facts which he had collected were so very remarkable, as in some degree to stagger his preconceived opinion. Some of these facts I shall now mention. In 1825, the number of *immoveable* properties in France was stated in the official documents at ten millions. But we must not consider the number of proprietors equal by any means to this, and that for two reasons. First, the same individual has in some instances more possessions than one, quite separate from each other; secondly, the real number of properties is less than it appears to be, from the same being sometimes counted twice over. This depends upon the peculiar manner in which the assessment for the land-tax is made. A sum is first fixed for each *department* by the annual law of Finance, then this amount is divided among the *arrondissements* by the council general of the department, again the sum allotted to each arrondissement is subdivided among the *communes* or parishes, by the council of the arrondissement; lastly, the portion of each *commune* is distributed among the separate properties by persons appointed for that purpose. In this way, it is the *communes* in the last instance which are charged with the assessment, and as the number of properties in each *commune* is reckoned separately, if an estate happen to lie partly in one, partly in another, it will be rated in both

for the part belonging to each respectively; and thus
in summing up the whole number of properties in
the kingdom, there will sometimes appear to be two,
where in reality there is but one. Now, as the *communes* are very numerous, we can easily conceive that
this double reckoning must frequently happen. We
must also bear in mind, that the above estimation of
properties includes houses as well as land. Thus
much I thought it necessary to say, in order that the
reader might not suppose, that, in 1825, any thing
like 10 millions of landed proprietors existed in
France. Indeed we learn from M. Dupin, that about
this time there were four millions of these. But to
proceed. In 1825, then, there were in France ten
millions of *estimated* properties. Of these there were
but 17,000 paying, in that year, one thousand francs
(forty pounds) of direct taxes and upwards. De-
scending in the scale, the number of properties becomes more and more considerable, as we lower the
sum at which they are assessed, until we arrive at
those which contribute to the State only 20 francs,
(16 shillings) and under. Of these there were no
fewer than $7\frac{1}{2}$ millions. But this is not all. In
comparing the returns for 1826 with those for 1825,
we find a most astonishing increase in the number of
properties in that one year. They had altogether
increased by more than 200,000, but those paying
1000 francs and upwards, had *diminished* by no less
than a *fourth*. Continuing to descend in the scale,

the number had diminished, but less and less in proportion as the assessment lowered, until arriving at
those contributing from 20 to 30 francs, when first
an increase was found. But in the last class, paying
20 francs and under, the enlargement of numbers
was very great, not less than upwards of half a million; so that whereas, in 1825, there were of this description but $7\frac{1}{2}$ million of properties, in 1826 there
were more than 8 millions. These facts require no
comment.*

In addition to the above, I may mention, that
whereas M. Dupin stated, as we have seen, in a work
published in 1827, the number of actual proprietors
of the soil to be four millions; only two years after,
he observed in the Chamber of Deputies that there
were four millions and a half of families possessed of
land. The remarks of the same writer fully confirm
the truth of what has been before said, that the splitting up of territorial possessions is favoured not only
directly by the law and custom of equality among all
the children of a family, but also by a circumstance,
which no doubt may be traced to the same custom
as its origin, namely, that an estate sells better when
cut up into lots than when kept entire. The immediate cause of this is the great competition for land

---

* By an account published in 1835, I perceive that, according to the
latest survey, the number of *cotes* (quotas) for the direct taxes, which
expresses the *estimated* number of properties, whether in land or
houses, has risen to 10,814,000. In 1826, it was 10,296,000, and in
the preceding year, less by upwards of 200,000.

on the part of the peasantry, the reasons for which, in a former part of this Essay, I have already endeavoured to explain.

But other proofs from experience still remain behind.

So far as my own observation has extended, in those countries where the system of equal partition prevails, the peasants always cultivate with their own hands that portion of ground which falls to their share, rarely, if ever, disposing of it in any other way; unless it were too large for them fully to turn to account, in which case they might let a part. However minute may be the family inheritance, it must still be subdivided among the sons at least, if not the daughters. In whatever country I have travelled where the above system is practised, the constant answer to my inquiries, as to what became of the family estate after the death of the father, has been, that each takes his share to occupy and cultivate himself. In France, Savoy and Switzerland, I never got any other statement. Among the upper classes, I am aware that the case is often different. Family arrangements are frequently made, by which the patrimony in land is preserved entire. But with the peasantry, who form the great number, the reverse almost always occurs.

Indeed, the very aspect of the land in those countries where the system of equal partition has long prevailed, and in particular the substitution of spade for plough husbandry, is sufficient to prove its minute subdivision.

A great deal of territory in Flanders, Savoy, and Switzerland is cultivated in this primitive manner. M. De Stael, who resided in the *Canton de Vaud*, where the plan of equality has long been established, in arguing against the privilege of primogeniture, does not deny that the district around Coppet, the place of his abode, was split up into very minute properties. " Around me," says he, " the lands are divided to such a degree, that the greater number of properties are less than an acre."* This precisely agrees with my own experience of Switzerland. I have often spoken to these petty proprietors, who have pointed out to me the extent of their domains, sometimes but a small fraction of an acre.

Let us now see what is the actual condition of that immense body of persons who in France are owners of the soil. The picture which M. Dupin

* " Lettres sur l'Angleterre," Lettre V. The French *arpent* is very nearly the same as the English acre. M. de Stael, after having made the above assertion, goes on to say, that in spite of this, no country in Europe presents such a picture of prosperity. " Far from the population being redundant, labour is there higher than in any other continental state." In 1835, the price of common labour about Lausanne was ten batz a-day, equal nearly to fifteenpence, which, as provisions are reasonable, must be considered good wages. The best wheaten bread is three-halfpence the pound, and meat fourpence-halfpenny. Groceries also are cheap, since little or no duty is paid. We are surprised to find colonial produce lower in the heart of the continent than in the sea-port towns of England and France. I have already mentioned, on the authority of M. de Stael, that the population of that part of Switzerland had for forty years been nearly stationary.

draws of their comforts is not very brilliant. " In going from Paris to Caen through the department of the Eure, (a division of ancient Normandy,) we are equally surprised and afflicted to find, in a rich and fertile country, in the midst of a superb district, habitations of the most miserable description, covered with thatch, and constructed in a rude manner with wood and mud, such in short as are still to be seen in *three-fourths* of the kingdom."

" In Picardy, the progress of agriculture, the increase of manure, resulting from an augmentation in the number of cattle, and from a better employment of some mineral substances for that purpose, have allowed a great quantity of land to be cultivated for wheat, which formerly was sown with rye. By these means, the little agriculturist has come to be better off in the most improved parts of France, but he is still very badly fed in the rest of the kingdom." " Petit Proprietaire."

Again, " Near two-thirds of the inhabitants of France are almost entirely deprived of animal food, and more than a third is fed solely on oats, buckwheat, chesnuts, Indian corn, or potatoes." Forces Productives de la France, ch. iv.

In travelling through the department of the North or French Flanders, the richest and best cultivated of all the departments of that extensive country, the information I received perfectly agreed with this account. It was quite evident to me that the small proprietor is not nearly so well fed there, as our

agricultural day labourers are in England. Beer is
a luxury too expensive for him, and since that district
produces neither wine nor cyder, water is his only
beverage. His diet is almost exclusively vegetable,
meat being a rare indulgence. If any, it is pork. M.
Dupin tells us that nearly four millions of pigs are
slaughtered yearly in France. " It is," says he, " the
food of the little agriculturist." Now, should we suppose this aliment to be confined entirely to the rural
population, which is far from being the case, for a
great deal of it is consumed in the towns, and dressed
up in various ways by the pork-dealers; yet even on
this assumption, not more than one of these animals,
on an average, would fall to the share of each landed
proprietor's family in the course of a whole year.
For, as we have seen, the number of these families is
four million and upwards.

These facts and statements do not give us a high
idea of the comforts of the very numerous body of
French landed proprietors. But while they serve to
show that the subdivision of the soil has not been
sufficient to put the mass of the rural population in
easy circumstances, we must not therefore conclude
that their poverty is owing to that cause. If they
are poor now, they were much more so before the
Revolution, as we learn from the testimony of travellers who visited France prior to that event, particularly of Arthur Young. The breaking up of the
great estates which then took place, cannot but have
very much improved the condition of the great body

of the people, for a time at least. It is therefore quite natural that they should at present be better off than formerly, whether the system of division be on the long run good or bad. Considering how recent still is the splitting of the vast possessions of the aristocracy, we ought then rather to wonder that the condition of the people is not more comfortable than we find it to be.

During the course of a summer spent in Savoy, I had frequent opportunities of studying the effects of the system now under consideration. The French law of succession was introduced into that country at an early period of the Revolutionary war, and though since the peace of 1815, the old code, namely, the Roman, has been revived, yet the practice of dividing equally has still continued. At least this is the case as regards the sons, for now the daughters get only a legitimate portion, which is but a fraction of the third or of the half. With the exception, then, of what goes to the daughters, which exactly corresponds with the allowance of the Roman law as finally determined by Justinian, the rest is shared equally among the sons.* It would appear that previous to the French invasion, though the law was the same as now, yet the practice was different, for the division of land dates only from that event. Already it has

---

* By the Roman law, if a father left four children or fewer, the legitimate portion to be divided among them was one-third, if five or more, one-half. Thus, in every case the father could dispose of half his property as he pleased, and often of two-thirds. At an earlier period of the Roman annals the legitimate portion was only a fourth.

been carried very far. All accounts agree in stating
that a great increase of population has taken place
within the last forty years.* Nor is the condition of
the inhabitants by any means enviable. Their food
is exclusively vegetable, consisting of bread composed
chiefly of rye, for of wheat the peasantry eat very
little, Indian corn, potatoes, and all sorts of garden
productions, especially turnips. But their two
greatest wants are fodder for the working cattle, and
fuel. It is impossible to conceive any thing more
miserable than the expedients they are obliged to
have recourse to for the former, such as the leaves
obtained by lopping trees and pruning hedges. This
is part of their winter provision. We cannot therefore be surprised to learn in how wretched a condition are the poor beasts at the opening of spring.
They are often so weak as to be unable to stand.
Nor do the people suffer less from a want of fuel. In
winter they are obliged to crowd together into the
stables to keep themselves warm. Formerly the
country was covered with woods, but these within
the last forty years have been in a great degree destroyed. So urgent are the wants of these little proprietors, that they cannot afford to let a wood grow
to any height, but are perpetually cutting it, so that
it never comes to any thing. This is highly charac-

---

* One fact which struck me as a proof that a great increase had
lately taken place in the population was, that in the finest part of Savoy extending northward from Chambery, very few old persons were
to be seen. This, in a country certainly not unhealthy, seemed to show
that they were the remaining representatives of a less numerous people.

teristic of the poor, to whom the present is all in all. On many of the mountains are seen the beginnings of fine forests, but as the young plants are lopped every three years or so, very little good is ever got from them. In Switzerland, the system of division has gone hand in hand with free government and general education, while in Savoy these last advantages have hitherto been wanting. This may serve to explain the different states of these two countries, although that system prevails in both. It is proper, however, to observe, that the Savoyard peasantry, though poor, are decidedly moral, while their manners are courteous, equally removed from rudeness and servility.

I have thus taken a survey of the circumstances peculiar to agriculture, which may be supposed either to limit or to extend the influence of those general causes which act upon all occupations, and make it commonly more advantageous to the amount of national wealth, that production should be carried on by a comparatively small number of rich master-capitalists, than by many small ones. The conclusion we are forced to draw from the whole discussion is, that although agriculture cannot with advantage be conducted on so extensive a scale as manufactures or commerce, yet the general causes before mentioned, are, in the case before us, fortified by others peculiar to itself, which render a minute subdivision of farming establishments particularly unfavourable to the riches of a country. And we found that a subdivision of farms must follow that of landed properties. We were thus led to investigate the probable effects of that system, according to which land is left equally among all the children of a family. Here we took occasion to notice the habits of the little proprietor, which are as favourable to accumulation as those of the great to extravagance. But we found, though cultivation by small proprietors is certainly preferable in all respects to that by a small tenantry, yet it cannot be considered so conducive to the wealth of a nation, as that carried on by a body of rich and enterprising master-capitalists. Still, this of itself might not be a sufficient reason for rejecting the system of equality, for the happiness resulting to the great mass of the rural population from this partition of property among them, might far outweigh the inconvenience of a smaller absolute amount of riches. And this is the conclusion at which, as in the case of moveable property, I should certainly be inclined to rest, could I see any effectual check upon a too great subdivision of the soil. For such a check we have looked in vain. Nothing is likely to stop it but the population becoming stationary. However much, then, we may be delighted with the idea of a country in which property in land is widely diffused, where a great portion of the rural inhabitants enjoy the blessings which flow from the possession of a small domain, competence, dignity and independence of character, foresight, prudence, and a spirit of economy; yet when the system of equal division has once been fairly introduced, as there is the greatest danger of its being pushed so far as to terminate in universal poverty and barbarism; we are forced (though reluctantly) to decide against the expediency of a plan which is likely to lead ultimately to such disastrous consequences. Whatever may be the evils of a too great concentration of landed property, they are small in comparison with those which result from its excessive division.

I am therefore of opinion that in this case an exception ought to be made to the general rule. Perfect liberty of testation should in all cases be allowed, but where a person dies without a will, every kind of property ought by law to be divided equally among the sons and daughters of the deceased, except land. Here the legislature is bound to interfere, and without restraining the right of bequest, to prevent the evils to be dreaded from an excessive partition of the soil, by giving its sanction to the custom of preserving estates entire. This sanction would be quite sufficient to render the practice general, and it would not be at all necessary to have recourse to entails of any description, whether perpetual or temporary, these expedients for concentrating property being liable to insuperable objections. Because a great subdivision of land is bad, must we therefore run into the opposite extreme? As in case then of a person dying intestate, the legislature is to select one of his descendants as heir to his landed possessions, of course the eldest of the family will naturally be fixed upon.

But, at the same time, the law ought to oblige him to pay to each of his brothers and sisters a suitable portion in money, varying of course with the value of the property.

The practice of leaving the land to the eldest son is to be defended on the very same grounds on which the right of property itself rests, general expediency. If this expediency be clearly made out, there is no more injustice in the one case than in the other. A poor man who is obliged to toil all day to gain a scanty subsistence for himself and family, may think his lot very hard indeed, when compared with that of the great lord, who though he perhaps does nothing but saunter about, or shoot partridges, yet fares sumptuously every day. Still, the instant the right of exclusive property of any kind is introduced, from that moment inequality springs up, and though it may be moderated, can never be entirely prevented. There will always then be the possibility of a frequent comparison between the poor and industrious man, and the rich and idle one, but no rational person on that account thinks of objecting to the institution of property.

In like manner, though it may appear very shocking that one out of a family should alone inherit the territorial possessions of the father, yet if, upon the whole, this custom be more conducive to the common prosperity of the country than the contrary system, the younger brothers and sisters have no right to complain. Besides, by the plan which I have recommended, a father has it always in his power to will the division of his lands if he thinks it can be done without inconvenience. A great concentration of estates is by no means to be wished for,—both this and the opposite extreme are to be avoided, and the only mode by which I conceive a medium attainable, is that just now proposed.

CHAPTER IX.

POLITICAL CONSEQUENCES OF THE SAME.

THE above view of the advantages and disadvantages of a division of landed property, has been almost exclusively an economical one, which, strictly speaking, was alone suited to the nature of a work like the present. I have not at all entered into the Moral and Political consequences of the system, which branch of the subject is quite distinct from the other, and of itself opens a vast field for speculation. But I cannot quit altogether this most interesting and important question, without offering a few observations upon these points also, although not belonging to the science of political economy.

In considering the political expediency of a subdivision of landed property, what first strikes us is, that this must mainly depend upon the nature of the government of the country. The same degree of partition which may be excellent, nay indispensable, in a republic, would probably be fatal to a monarchy. By a republic I of course mean a really democratical government, for the term has often been applied where there was little popular in the institutions, excepting the absence of royalty, or at least where an aristocracy had a great share of power.

Nothing I think is more certain than that a purely popular government cannot exist without a considerable equality of fortunes, especially of territorial possessions, and it seems scarcely less doubtful that no monarchy can be secure without a landed aristocracy. The nature of the government then which we wish to introduce or support, must determine whether the system we are contemplating be politically expedient or otherwise. This only let us carefully bear in mind, that we cannot reconcile contradictions, and that if we desire the end, we must also adopt the means necessary for that end.

A monarchy, for instance, surrounded with republican institutions, is a political monster which must soon devour itself. This is the great fault which the first National Assembly of France committed. The great majority of that body wished for a monarchy, and I have no doubt they sincerely wished it; but they took good care to render it impossible, by creating institutions of too popular a nature, to exist along with royalty. Most of these soon passed away, swept off by the revolutionary torrent, but not so the law of succession.*   This is the grand event of the first

---

* This law has undergone several modifications. By a law passed in April 1791, the *Assemblée Constituante* decreed the equal division of all the property of a person dying intestate among his descendants, without distinction of sex or primogeniture, but did not interfere with the liberty of testation. This was reserved for the National Convention, which, by a law passed in the second year of the Republican era,

Revolution,—it has outlived imperial despotism and Bourbon subtlety and violence,—has changed the aspect of France from one end to the other,—and has by degrees so deeply fixed itself in the affections of the people, that to attempt now to alter it would seem little short of insanity. But there can be no doubt that so long as it does exist, the monarchy can never be very secure.

Here, then, is the position in which that kingdom is now placed in consequence of the above law: Royalty has no adequate support, and yet a republic is impossible. It is perhaps hardly necessary to mention the reasons for this last assertion, but, in short, they are these :—First, the ancient habits of the people, formed under a monarchy, and totally opposed to self-government; secondly, the character of the people, gay, fond of pleasure, easily excited, fickle, and destitute of perseverance, quite different from that steady, commercial, calculating disposition which is most essential to check the natural inconstancy and rashness of purely popular governments; thirdly, the

(Décret du 17 Nivose an. 2.) permitted a proprietor to dispose of no more than a tenth of his substance, if he left heirs in the direct line, and a sixth if he left only collaterals. All the rest was to be divided equally among the children, or failing these, among the other heirs. Besides, the disposable portion could not be left to one child in preference to others, but only to strangers; if it went to the lawful heirs, *it* likewise was to be divided equally. By the Code Napoleon, which is now the law of the land, if a father leave one child, he may dispose as he pleases of one half of his property, if two, of a third, if three or more, of a fourth; all the rest must be divided equally between them, as is the case with the whole, if he die intestate.

national taste for military glory; lastly, the political state of the other countries of Europe, the sovereigns of which would never quietly suffer a great republic in their immediate neighbourhood. The wars which would unavoidably arise, would speedily put an end to the democratical government, whether successful on its part or not: on the latter supposition, through foreign interference or internal tumult; on the former, through the ambition of a victorious general.

While, then, the law of succession has rendered monarchy insecure, it has not of itself been sufficient to make a republic possible. Hence, a great uncertainty cannot but hang over the future destinies of France, which past experience is not calculated to dispel. The frequent changes of government in that country within the last forty years, from the extreme of licence to the extreme of despotism, and the perpetual disturbances ever since the present dynasty came to the throne, are sufficiently known to all. Such are the evils to be apprehended from wishing an end, and yet rejecting the means indispensable to its existence and duration.

The example of France ought to be a warning to all nations engaged in the paths of Reform, to abstain from pushing change so far as to endanger that form of government which it is intended to support. If the object be to alter the form of government entirely, it is then a different question, and to be argued on its own grounds. The case I allude to is that, in which it is the wish of the majority to preserve this form entire, but to remedy the evils of the system, as far as may be.

It is the especial duty of all public men who have this in view, to see clearly where their measures lead, and to remember that there are many changes in themselves good abstractedly, that is without reference to the existing state of things, which yet may compromise the safety of those institutions which they are as far as any from desiring to see subverted. Thus, supposing it allowed that the equal division of landed property among all the children of a family, is of itself the best possible system *where the circumstances permit*, yet it by no means follows, on that account, that we ought to wish for its adoption. If the government of the country be monarchical, and if we feel convinced that this form is best adapted on the whole to the state of society in which we are placed, or even that the dangers attendant on a change are too great to be risked, we must make up our minds to bear the inconveniences which attach to this as well as to all other human institutions. For, it is not Monarchy or Aristocracy only that has its unavoidable evils; Democracy has others peculiar to itself, which no less constantly attend it. What it is above all things necessary to be convinced of, is, that there are certain advantages which naturally exclude each other, so that it is impossible to enjoy both in perfection at the same time. A well guarded monarchy cannot enjoy the same equality as a truly popular state, nor evince the astonishing energy of really democratical governments; while, on the other hand, we should in vain expect the same stability in a republic, as under regal and aristocratical sway. We must then decide which system we on the whole prefer; and having made our election, we are bound to adhere to the object of our choice, notwithstanding the evils which necessarily attend it, and however much these may be checked by the bringing in of an opposing principle, we must well remember that consistently with the safety of what we wish to support, they never can be altogether prevented.

If a system have any force and vitality at all, it cannot but be liable to some excess, and therefore some evil. These can be completely obviated, only by reducing it to absolute imbecility. It is the same in the case of an individual: a man without passions could do no evil, for the same reason that he could do no good. In like manner, if, at the present day, the old aristocracy of France cannot injure, neither can it serve the body politic; it is reduced to a state of nothingness.

These observations naturally suggest themselves in connection with the subject of succession to property in general, particularly landed property, for of all political questions that can be agitated, this is beyond comparison the most important. It is the very keystone of the arch of the State. For where the property is, there, sooner or later, will the power be also.

These are natural allies, which but rarely, and for a short period, are ever separated.

The desire of power is a natural consequence of the possession of superior wealth. Such is the constitution of human nature, that the satisfaction of one want only gives rise to another, by rendering possible the acquisition of its object; for, we never ardently wish for what we know to be unattainable. Thus, the man satiated with riches, begins to feel a love for other distinctions which wealth places within his reach,— the merchant, for instance, whose coffers overflow with gold, pants for the honour of aristocratical acquaintance and connections.

But of all distinctions, none is so capable of firing the desires of the opulent, as power. No body of men, then, whose wealth is superior to that of their countrymen in general, will ever be contented with only an equal share of political authority. Rule they will, by fair means or by foul;—if not by influence and secret corruption, force will either establish their sway, or ruin at once their power and their fortunes.

Now, where land is usually transmitted in unbroken masses from father to son, not only is that inequality of wealth maintained which serves to create inequality of power, but each generation of proprietors derives strength from those which went before. It has not to commence its work anew, but finds the ground ready prepared, the seed sown, the crop ripening. An unity of purpose and of efforts is preserved through a succession of ages, which cannot but fortify amazingly the authority of the landed aristocracy.

The circumstance, too, of each family being fixed to a spot is an immense advantage ; as they are always operating in the same sphere, their influence must be far greater than if occasionally they were trying their strength in one place, occasionally in another. How paramount formerly was the authority of a Scottish proprietor over the people on his estate, and how strong is it still wherever land has been long in the hands of the same race.

This unity of design and efforts, not only among all the territorial aristocracy of the present day, but also among their ancestors from generation to generation, tending invariably to one end, the strengthening of their power, is the main source of the force possessed by a rich body of hereditary land-owners ; and hence, of the stability of any government which they may choose to support. In every thing, small or great, to know exactly the end you wish to attain, and steadily to march towards it, is a principal cause of success.

But where the perpetual subdivision of land has destroyed all those family influences, which, springing originally from the possession of superior wealth, are afterwards strengthened by habit and association, there is no longer any body of proprietors knit together by the feeling of a common interest, the love of ascendancy, and strenuously uniting in the defence of existing institutions, with which their own power must stand or fall. But it may be said that the immense increase in the number of proprietors of the soil, which results from the practice of equality in succession, tends greatly to strengthen the government, by enlisting in its support a much larger class of persons, who may be supposed particularly attached to order, and fearful of any change which might endanger their little possessions, to them so dear. It must, however, be remembered, that the feeling common to this numerous body of small land-owners would be that of attachment to good government in general, rather than strong affection for any one in particular.

The benefit which any individual of this class derives from good government, such as security for person and property, is more of a negative than a positive kind, and is especially of a nature, the prodigious advantage of which is never fully recognized until lost. Should any plausible scheme be proposed, either by ambitious or well-meaning men, which may promise, under a new form of government, equal security, with fewer public burthens, what is to prevent the body of small landed proprietors from favouring a change? Nothing but the dread of some unforeseen evil, not a passionate feeling of preference for existing institutions. But the instant the mind of man is free from any predominant and definite desire, there is no end to scheming and irresolution. The intellect becomes like a ship without a rudder, driven this way and that at the mercy of each successive wave. Man requires, above all things, a strong desire to give unity and consistency to his actions. That

absence of all antecedent preference for any particular system, which prevents prejudice, and is therefore the state of mind best suited to one philosophis-
ing in his closet, will not do in the real business of
life. The very habit of weighing all the probable advantages and disadvantages of any proposed step, is exceedingly contrary to that rapidity and energy which
action requires. Now, if even in the case of an individual who has no one to consult but himself, the
inconvenience of this too dispassionate and deliber-
ative character is greatly felt in practice, what must
it be when we have to unite the conflicting opinions of
many, " the incurable diversity of which, on all subjects short of demonstration," is so notorious ?*

The general love of good government, then, which
is common to all possessed of some property, is no
preservative against change, and the dangers which
accompany it, until these persons become convinced
not only that the existing institutions are, upon the
whole, good, but that they are the best possible.
But how can they ever be sure of that unless they
try others ? And when can all the possible combi-
nations be gone through, which the fertile ingenuity
of man is able to devise ? So little is a general love
for good government capable of fixing people to any
one in particular.

When, however, the country has been long con-
vulsed and fatigued by a succession of changes, a

* Paley.

feeling will be apt to arise, which will give some stability to government, and replace to a certain extent that passionate attachment to existing institutions, which, amidst so much vacillation, can have no time to grow up. This feeling will be, not a strong love for what is, but a dread of the unknown consequences of change, of the evils of which the nation has already seen so much. Thus, a conservative spirit will be created, particularly among the proprietors of land, which, however, may very probably not continue much beyond the present generation. A new race will soon spring up, who, no doubt, may hear of the ills their country has suffered from perpetual changes of government, but will not have witnessed them, and the impression produced will be in proportion to the difference between oral and ocular experience.

But, even should we suppose the numerous body of small proprietors to be sufficiently attached to the government of their country, and not at all desirous of new experiments, yet they cannot have the same ardent love for existing institutions, which animates an aristocracy, who derives from them not only security for person and property, in common with the rest of the community, but in addition to these general advantages, all the sweets of ascendancy—distinction, power, and emolument. Now, to give stability to any government, it is not enough that the great mass of persons of property, or even a numerical majority of the nation should be well disposed towards it; but the question is, is this feeling so strong as to permit of their exposing themselves in its defence to fatigue, danger, and death? That is the real point to be considered.

This remark serves to explain how it comes to pass, that an active minority may frequently effectuate a change in government in opposition to the wishes of the great mass of the people. As far as wishes go, they are all on the side of the powers that be; but when it becomes necessary to make sacrifices of personal ease, fortune and safety, then political sympathies may not be sufficiently energetic to bear them out. And the same lukewarmness which prevented them exerting themselves in defence of the old government, while it existed, will make them submit quietly to the new, or to any other which may in time succeed.

Very different is the case when land is held by a rich and powerful Aristocracy, who, in defending the existing state of things, maintain not only the cause of order in general, but the privileges of their own class in particular. This double motive is sufficiently strong to subdue the natural indolence of man, and to rouse his energies in active opposition to all innovation which may threaten, even remotely, that system with which his wealth and authority are inseparably connected. The very smallness of the body is highly favourable to its efforts, by rendering combination much more easy. When, on the contrary, land is divided amongst a countless host of little owners, individual spirit is paralysed by the difficulty of union.

These, then, are the causes which render the great subdivision of fortunes, particularly of land, unfavourable to the stability of government. They may be reduced to two; first, the want of an especial interest in existing institutions, so strong as firmly to fix the affections of any considerable body of persons. The mass may be well disposed, but it is too inert to be of essential service in time of need.* Secondly, the difficulty of union among proprietors, from their great number, their limited circumstances, which do not permit of many of them meeting frequently, and from the want of any smaller body, accustomed to influence those below them on common occasions, and therefore ready to direct, and sure to be obeyed on any extraordinary emergency.

Now, whatever the nature of the changes may be which threaten the existing government, whether they tend to extend or limit the degree of liberty at present enjoyed, the catastrophe will be greatly facilitated by this subdivision of property, and consequent absence of an aristocratical body. This is an important circumstance to bear in mind. It is not alone the assertors of popular rights who will find the system of equality favourable to their views, but also the

* The law of Solon against neuters, which, by many, has been thought so extraordinary, was evidently aimed at that host of inert and lukewarm citizens, who, in times of civil commotion, suffer things to take their course, and so prepare the triumph of a passionate minority.

crafty demagogue or fortunate general who seeks to rise on the ruins of his country's freedom. The same inertness and want of union which allow the former to bring about a revolution under popular colours, even though opposed to the wishes of the majority, will also enable the latter on another occasion to hoist the standard of civil or military despotism.

But despotism itself is not likely to be much more stable than any other more popular government, so long as the state of property remains the same.

The civil authority of Robespierre lasted but a moment, and all the military renown of Bonaparte could never have secured the throne, even of his immediate successor, although foreign powers had not interfered. Where the people have been once thoroughly imbued with notions of liberty, they never will submit for any length of time to absolute sway. They may give into it for a season when wearied out by a series of popular changes and commotions; but as soon as the remembrance of these begin to fade, and a new generation springs up, who have not witnessed them, down will fall the temporary fabric. Thus the government will vacillate between the opposite extremes of popular licence and despotism without ever being able to fix itself between the two.

The truth of these reasonings is exemplified in the history of all the republics of the ancients which really were democratical, such as Athens, Syracuse, and many other Grecian states, in the Italian republics of the middle ages, in the commonwealth of England, and the revolutionary governments of France.

America cannot be considered as an exception, for its constitution is not yet fifty years old, and it is placed in circumstances quite peculiar. Two of these, it may here be sufficient to mention, which are essential; first, it can have no land wars of any consequence, for it has no neighbours; it is therefore free from one of the grand dangers to which republics are exposed—military rule. Secondly, as yet it has no body of poor, an extent of virgin territory, fertile as boundless, rendering that impossible. It is therefore removed from the other rock on which democratical governments have split, the turbulence of the needy part of the population.

In countries, on the other hand, where the mass of the people has never heard of popular rights, much less enjoyed the exercise of them, though the monarch has nothing to fear from the resistance of the democracy, yet if his throne be unsupported by a body of rich proprietors, it will be perpetually in danger from the ambition of the leaders of the army, or the turbulence of a pampered and discontented soldiery. The want of a landed aristocracy has been a main cause of the instability of all eastern governments, of the throne of the Cæsars, as of that of the Mohammeds, and thus explains the so long stationary or declining condition of many of the fairest provinces of the earth. Where a successful general, or a band of Prætorian cohorts, Turkish guards, or Janissaries, could at any time change the destinies of an empire, what room could there be for progress in wealth, security and civilization?*

Perhaps in no country in the world is the power of the monarch so completely unlimited as in Persia. The people, as in all other eastern governments, have no influence; and of aristocracy, there is scarcely a vestige left. The consequences of this state of things is truly appalling. In addition to the other evils of unlimited sway, (the perpetual insecurity of person and property, the terror consequent thereon, the constant exactions of the Shah himself, and of all those placed in authority under him,) Persia has been from time to time exposed to all the horrors of a disputed succession; its provinces have been ravaged by war from one end of the kingdom to the other, and such of the higher classes as have not perished in the struggle have many of them been cut off by the watchful jealousy of the conqueror. Each of these wars has only tended to render the authority of the successful Shah still more unlimited than that of his

* Talking of the Turkish guards who, called in to protect, soon learned to govern the feeble caliphs of Bagdad, Gibbon observes : " As often as the Turks were inflamed by fear, or rage, or avarice, these caliphs were dragged by the feet, exposed naked to the scorching sun, beaten with iron clubs, and compelled to purchase, by the abdication of their dignity, a short reprieve of inevitable fate." " So uniform are the mischiefs of military despotism, that I seem to repeat the story of the prætorians of Rome." This was a sad falling off from the times of the renowned caliph Harun al Rashid. See " *Decline and Fall*," vol. x. chap. lii.

predecessors, by deciminating and impoverishing these ranks, which alone could present the slightest bar to the gratification of his will.* These perpetual wars may be traced to the want of any efficient aristocracy, (for the mass of the people are politically nothing) who, by rallying round one standard, might put a stop to those disputes, so fatal to the interests of all, but to theirs especially.†

If, on the other hand, we take a review of those governments which have been most remarkable in the history of the world for duration and power, we shall find invariably whatever difference there may have been in their outward forms, that in one essential point they all agree, the presence in their composition of at least a considerable mixture of aristocracy.

Of these the most remarkable instances are, Rome in the ancient world—Great Britain in the modern. It is surprising that the first has not been more dwelt upon, as affording an astonishing example of the effects resulting from the union of democratical energy with aristocratic stability. The whole internal history of the Roman republic presents a view of one long struggle between these opposing powers, which

---

* " What blood have I not shed," said Aga Mohammed Shah, " that this boy (his nephew and successor) may reign in peace !"

† See Narrative of a Journey in Khorasan in the year 1821-2, by James B. Fraser.

An instance of a disputed succession has lately occurred in Persia. The *fifty* sons of the late Fatih Ali Shah have been fighting for his throne.

must therefore have been pretty equally balanced. On the one hand were the popular assemblies, and popular elections, the tribunes of the people, and latterly one at least of the consuls. On the other, the senate and the patrician body, at first both of the consuls and most other magistrates, which afterwards, however, were chosen from both orders. I have no doubt, that the unexampled power and duration of this wonderful state was principally owing to the happy mixture of these two elements in its composition. In modern times, the example of England is scarcely less remarkable. Have all the abuses practised by its aristocracy prevented it from arriving at a pitch of power and prosperity unrivalled by any country of the same extent, since the fall of the Roman empire? And where in modern times shall we find an example of a kingdom which, for *so long a period*, has enjoyed the happy union of Liberty with Order?*

I may also mention Venice as it existed during

---

* For a long time past, this struggle between the aristocracy and democracy has been going on in Great Britain, just as in ancient Rome, without at all interfering with the internal prosperity or foreign grandeur of the state. Of late years, the contest has become particularly warm, and the democratical element has made great conquests over its antagonist. Witness the Reform bill, &c. In the very able article on " Government" in the Supplement to the Encyclopædia Britannica, an attempt is made to prove that two opposing powers never can co-exist in any government. This is the most extraordinary instance I know, of an endeavour to disprove a *fact* by reasoning. I say a *fact*, for who can seriously deny the presence in the English constitution of a democratical as well as an aristocratical element? It is asked by the writer, how can one power be prevented from swallowing up the

nearly fourteen hundred years, and Russia as it still
is, as striking instances of the power and duration of
aristocratical governments.   Since in the former of
these, during its later periods at least, the influence
of the democracy had sunk to nothing, and as in the
latter it has not yet risen into importance, these
states, while they afford us remarkable examples of
the advantages of aristocracies, give us no less convincing proofs of their injustice and oppression.   But
they nevertheless serve to establish the point which
at present I am concerned to make out, that stability
is the peculiar and inseparable character of such governments.   This is one main cause why Russia is a
neighbour so much to be dreaded by the rest of Europe.

other ?   Even allowing that this is likely to be the case *ultimately*, yet
in the mean time, they may exist together for a very long-period, for
centuries even, not indeed in perfect amity, perhaps always at war with
each other openly or secretly, but the struggle may, from various circumstances, be lengthened out amazingly, without any recourse to
arms on either side.   This is likely to be the last stage of the contest.
   In proof of this, I need only refer to the histories of Rome and Great
Britain.   The whole internal history of the Roman Republic is, as I
have said, nothing but an account of the struggle between the aristocracy and democracy.   This never ended till both were crushed by the
ambition of the military leaders.   And be it well remarked, that down
to the time of Tiberius Gracchus, the contest was a bloodless one.
Besides the increase of needy citizens, and the consequent virulence of
civil dissentions, the extension of conquests, and hence the great armies required to be kept on foot, at a distance from home, and for a
length of time sufficient to sink the citizen in the soldier, was a main
cause of the ruin of the liberties of Rome.   Nothing can resist a devoted army and a victorious commander, but the sanctity which surrounds an ancient dynasty of kings, supported by the *material* aid of a
powerful aristocracy.   But for the above cause, it is impossible to say,
how much longer the mixed government of Rome might have lasted.

Though some of the Muscovite Czars have met with violent deaths, yet these events have not in the least disturbed the tranquillity of the state. Every thing has gone on just as before, only one Emperor the more has been enclosed in the tombs of his ancestors. In our own days, the stability of the government has been put to a still more remarkable test. The heir to the crown, a prince in the prime of life, and remarkable for any thing rather than softness of character, we have seen set aside for his younger brother, without even an attempt at a struggle; for in the military insurrection at St. Petersburgh, so promptly quelled, Constantine took no part. Is it possible to produce a more striking instance of the stability of governments supported by aristocracies? For, though the sovereign of Russia styles himself autocrat, and is nominally despotic, since the constitution provides no check to his authority, yet is his power in reality limited, as well as upheld within these limits, by a rich and most influential nobility. Compare this instance of Russia with that of Persia given above, both of them countries in which the power of the sovereign is nominally unrestrained, but in the latter of which only it is really so, (though in neither the people have any influence), and how enormous is the difference! In the one, notwithstanding serfdom, wealth and population increase rapidly, and all the other elements of civilization are developing themselves, slowly perhaps, but surely, favoured by the undisturbed tranquillity which, for many generations, that extensive monarchy has not ceased to enjoy.   In the other, war, rapine, and desolation prevail.

Both theory and experience, then, prove that aristocracy and *that alone* can give stability, and therefore that *some portion* of it, at all events, is an indispensable ingredient in every government which can hope for permanence ; whether the people has risen into sufficient importance to influence state affairs, or whether it has not.

But the law or custom of equal division of land among the children of a family, completely annihilates aristocracy.   Are we not then forced to conclude against such a practice ?

CHAPTER X.

MORAL CONSEQUENCES.

HAVING now treated of the Economical and Political Consequences of an equal division of landed property among all the children of a family, it only remains for me to compare the Moral Effects of this and of the opposite system.

In the first place I may remark, that one of the most common arguments against the plan of equality is, that whereas by the right of primogeniture, only one member of the family is doomed to idleness, if, on the contrary, all got an equal share of the paternal inheritance, none would be obliged to work. Better one idle man than many.

This objection, I must confess, seems to me exceedingly superficial and short-sighted. In truth, whatever might be the immediate consequences of the system of equality, supposing it now first introduced, it appears to me that its more permanent and ultimate effects would be exactly the reverse of what is above asserted. The evils of the custom will be precisely of an opposite nature, arising from the want of any class of men freed from the necessity of earning a subsistence.

Supposing the rights of primogeniture abolished for the first time in any country, it might certainly happen that the younger sons of wealthy families, who, under the former system must have attempted to push their fortunes, now finding that they have enough to live upon, would be content without seeking to increase their incomes. But this, if an evil at all, which is by no means clear, (for if a man has no occasion to labour for his livelihood, why should he?) is not likely to be of long continuance; for if the members of the present generation do not improve their fortunes, it is evident, that when these come to be subdivided equally among their children, each of them will be poorer than his father, and will therefore find a necessity for entering into some gainful employment. If people do nothing to increase their fortunes, there is little danger but that in one, or at most two generations, their descendants will become sufficiently needy to induce them to exert themselves. Truly that is a singular objection which, if good for any thing, would prove that the system argued against would make every body so rich as to free from the obligation of toiling!

Unfortunately, so golden an expedient has not yet been hit upon. Man, we are told, was condemned upon the fall, " to eat bread in the sweat of his face," and assuredly the primeval curse has not yet departed from him, nor is likely to do so by any plans which we can devise.

The real evils of the system of equality are, as I

have said, of a nature exactly the reverse of those supposed in the above objection. Its tendency is to throw a level over all men, to prevent the rising up of any class exempted by their easy circumstances from the necessity of earning a support, and to destroy all *leisure*, that most indispensable condition of improvement in knowledge and civilization. The importance of such a class to any community cannot be over-rated, for upon it all progress depends.

Whether we consider the interest which every country has in enlightened legislation, in the advancement of the arts and sciences, in the elegancies and refinements of life and manners, and above all, in the prevalence of a high religious and moral feeling throughout society, we shall be alike forced to admit how great is the value to the nation at large, of a body of persons, who, being freed from the drudgery of gain, have time to cultivate their mental faculties.

Bonaparte called the English a nation of shopkeepers. He might with far greater justice have applied this term to the Americans. In the United States, the shop is every thing. The passion for money-making is predominant and universal. The image of Mammon is worshipped with undivided adoration from the rocks of Maine to the swamps of Louisiana. For the pursuit of wealth, the arts and sciences, literature, refinement of mind and manners, even gaiety and amusements are alike neglected. Now, however well suited such a system may be for cultivating and peopling an extensive and fertile territory, still, it cannot be considered as the model of all that is most delightful and most improved in the condition of society.

Such, however, is the state of things which the custom of equal division, after it has existed for some time, has a tendency to produce. Gradually the number of persons whose fortunes afford them leisure for intellectual pursuits, becomes fewer and fewer. This follows directly from the whole of the preceding disquisition. We have seen an instance of this fact on a grand scale in the extensive kingdom of France, where the body of rich proprietors, whether of lands or houses, decreases so rapidly.*

Some of the inconveniences which flow from the want of a class of gentry, have been already mentioned, when alluding to the state of Switzerland, and

---

* Where manufactures and commerce flourish, the effects of the system of equal partition of landed property may in part be counteracted; for as great fortunes are not unfrequently made in the above branches, land will be purchased in masses, and therefore there will be some concentration as well as division. At all events, there will be some *leisure*, for the sons of rich manufacturers and merchants will have their time at command. But we must remember, that when land has once become an object of desire to the peasantry, as happens wherever the system of partition has long prevailed, then the high price to be paid for it will discourage rich capitalists from thus vesting their funds. Besides, the small surplus which remains on the little culture plan, after feeding all the persons employed, must greatly tend to discourage manufactures and commerce, as has been shown in the chapter on Rent. One circumstance which essentially distinguishes agriculture from the other great branches of industry is, that large fortunes are never made by it. Therefore if land do not change hands, and be purchased by opulent manufacturers and merchants, it must go on subdividing. This is one reason why equal partition, which we fully allow to be desirable in the case of moveable property, may be injurious when applied to land.

need not therefore be here repeated. But in addition to what has there been said as to the difficulty of finding proper persons for exercising the important business of legislation, when, from the subdivision of landed property, the above class has nearly disappeared, how, I would ask, without a resident gentry, are all the other subordinate offices to be filled, no less necessary to the well-being of every civilized community? Where are we to look for persons fit to exercise the duties of justices of the peace, members of provincial assemblies, (such as the councils of *Departments* and *Arrondissements* in France,) members of country municipalities, trustees for roads, which, above all things, require a local superintendance, lastly, of jurymen? Can we really suppose that all these functions can be equally well performed by a set of people who, for the most part of their time, are occupied in the business of cultivating their little properties, and who therefore can have little leisure for reading, reflection, or communing with others?

In France, since the Revolution of July, different laws have been passed of a liberal nature, for the purpose of extending the elective system to the various local subdivisions of the kingdom. Since the period of the *Assemblée Constituante*, the territory has been split, first into *Departments*, these into so many *Arrondissements*, and the last again into *Communes*. Now, the object of the laws just alluded to, was to give to each of these divisions a council for managing its local affairs, elected by a certain body of the people. The intention of the laws was excellent, but hitherto in many Communes it has not been found possible to put them in execution, from the want of suitable men. A very short time ago, it was openly asserted in the Chamber of Deputies, and the statement was received with symptoms of assent, that in two-thirds of the *Communes* of the kingdom, there was great difficulty in finding any person having the common acquirements of reading and writing, and at the same time willing to exercise the duties of mayor or assistant. For, in France, the office of mayor is one of the very few unpaid. And though we should suppose this to be an exaggeration, yet what a state of things must that be in which such an assertion could be hazarded? No doubt the progress of primary education may expel this dense ignorance, and afford in country situations, individuals better qualified than at present, for public employments, if not better inclined. Yet, had the class of gentry been more numerous, a want of proper persons could never have been felt; nor are the evils resulting from the absence of such a class, ever likely to be altogether obviated.

I have heard very enlightened Frenchmen complain of the evils experienced in many localities, in consequence of the ignorance and general inferiority of that order of men who fulfil the duties of justices of the peace, and occupy the benches of the lower judicial tribunals. The justices of the peace are so very

numerous a body, that, where there is no gentry willing to discharge the business gratuitously, it is impossible for any government to afford to pay the office
so highly as to induce people of talent and education
to depend upon it for their livelihood. Hence, the
duties must be performed by a very inferior sort of
persons. The pay, not only of justices of the peace,
is miserably small in France, but that of the members
of the lower tribunals also, who are likewise very
numerous, for they decide many of those causes which
in England come before the magistrates assembled in
Quarter Sessions. It would be well for those who object to the unpaid magistracy of Great Britain, first
to obtain some information as to the consequences of
an opposite system.

One argument against making an eldest son, as
it is called, is derived from the imbecility which is
said to attach to those born to superior wealth ; and,
in proof of this, the old nobility of France and Spain
have been adduced. But when it is asserted that
leisure is indispensable to knowledge, no one supposes
this alone to be sufficient. If it be shown to be a
necessary condition, it is enough. The contact of the
democracy with the aristocracy forces the latter to
improve their leisure, otherwise they would lose their
influence. In a society where the people have some
power, so many are the motives to exertion, so various is the field of activity, from the Quarter Sessions
or a County Meeting up to the National Senate, that
the higher orders are strongly impelled to turn their

time to account. In a word, primogeniture gives leisure; and popular opinion, desire of distinction, fear of losing caste, all insure that in general it will not be thrown away. No argument then can be derived from the experience of despotic kingdoms, against the utility of the practice in more popular states. The nobles of Spain and France sank into insignificance because they had no sphere of activity, but in many respects, they were perhaps quite on a par with the rest of their countrymen. Their inferiority was in reference to their station, rather than to other classes. In Great Britain, besides the numerous body of gentry, are not the members of the House of Lords at least as accomplished individuals as any in the country? Now, most of these were born to fortune.

We come now to a very grave objection which may be made to the privilege attached to primogeniture, namely, that it sows dissention among the members of a family, between brothers and sisters, as well as between father and son. Were this objection well founded, it would go far to decide the question against the privilege; for could that be good, of which the effects were so contrary to morality?

Let us first consider how it influences the feelings of the children one towards another.

Were the custom of enriching one member of a family at the expense of the others introduced for the first time into any country, I can easily conceive that its effects would be to stir up jealousy against the favoured individual. What more unjust, if all the remote consequences of an opposite practice be kept out of view, than that the mere circumstance of being born a year or two sooner, should make such a difference in the prospects of the eldest, and those of his brethren ? This is a reflection which cannot but occur to the mind, where Custom has not produced that acquiescence in the many, which in the few is owing to deep meditation. But the fact is, that custom does produce that acquiescence, when once the practice has become fairly established. It is then thought quite natural that the landed estate should go undivided to the eldest, and the younger members of the family no more think of complaining of such an usage, than that they are not all born kings and emperors. They see that the system is universal, or at least most common, and is favoured by the laws of the state, therefore it is not the consequences of a parent's partiality. It must then have arisen from some views of general utility. If they reflect at all upon the subject, these are the ideas which are likely to spring up, and to prevent any feeling of jealousy towards their more favoured brother.

That such is really the truth, I think sufficiently proved by the example of Great Britain, where one certainly does not often hear of the ill-will of younger brothers towards their elder. In fact, I believe dissentions to be much more common among the former. This is quite natural. All acknowledged superiority does away with jealousy, which can exist only where there is doubt, and therefore room for competition. From its very nature, this is a passion which can exist only between equals, or those who think themselves so; where inequality is allowed and undisputed, it cannot spring up. There is then much more probability of jealousy among the younger members of a family, than between them and the elder, who is considered to occupy a station apart, and to whom the rest have from their infancy been accustomed to pay a certain deference.

Let us now see how the relation between parent and children is influenced by the privilege of the eldest. To the notion of any bad feeling being created by it from the younger members of the family towards the father, a sufficient answer has been given in discussing the former part of the objection. For the same reason that no jealousy is felt towards the favoured individual by his brothers and sisters, no resentment is roused against the parent. The custom is observed to be general, and is encouraged by the laws of the state, it is not therefore the result of blind favouritism, but of some supposed public utility. But where there is no ground for suspecting undue partiality, there is no cause for bitterness of spirit, either against him who gives, or him who receives the benefit.

We may therefore safely conclude, that the practice we are now considering has no effect in stirring up hostile feelings on the part of the younger children towards their parent.

But how stands the case between the eldest son and the father? Here, I confess, we touch one of the weakest parts of the subject of primogeniture. It must be allowed that the tendency of this system is to create jealousy between the present possessor of a domain and his heir apparent, from the same cause that often alienates a monarch from his son and successor. The difference is so great between the actual condition of the eldest son, and the station which he will be called upon to fill on the death of his father, between the dependence in which he now lives, and the brilliant prospect of wealth and distinction which lies before him, that something like a wish *may* sometimes arise for the removal of that obstacle which alone intervenes between his present state and his future destinies. Such is the tendency of the human mind to look forward, and to gild even an unpromising future with the rays of hope, while it longs to leap at once the gulph of time which divides it from the objects of desire, that we may well believe, where the view is really so inviting, it will be no easy task to divert the eyes from that smiling land which lies before them. Impatience of the present, is the natural consequence of dwelling on the future; and from impatience to irritability against the obstacle which opposes our wishes, there is but one step.

The father, on the other hand, *who himself was once an eldest son*, cannot but be well acquainted with the feelings peculiar to one, is consequently ready to suspect such wishes and such impatience, even where they do not really exist, and is therefore apt, by the coldness of his demeanour, to lessen affection and give

origin to such thoughts, where as yet they had not
sprung up. Thus gradually an estrangement begins
between the parties, which may frequently increase
till it terminate in open rupture.

That such is really the tendency of the privilege of
primogeniture, is unfortunately confirmed by what we
witness in England at the present day, where nothing is more common than to see the eldest sons of
the aristocracy on cool terms, if not at absolute variance with their fathers. In the whole moral condition of society in that country, I know of nothing
more deplorable than this.

But the privilege attached to the eldest is not the
only cause of this unhappy state of things. It is
greatly assisted by another cause, the mode of education generally adopted in England. The sons of the
aristocracy are usually sent from home at a tender
age, to schools where they are boarded for the greater
part of the year, and they visit their relations for a
few weeks only, twice or thrice during that period.
When first a boy is sent to school, he looks forward
to the time of his return for the holidays with intense
pleasure, but as years advance, continued absence
gradually weans his affections from the paternal roof,
and loosens the ties of infancy and childhood. As
the boy ripens into the youth, he acquires a love for
being his own master, a feeling so natural to all,
and the freedom from control which is felt at school,
(except where the general regulations of the place interfere,) fosters this premature attachment to inde-

pendence and self-will. The father's house is no
longer a happy beacon, which, amidst all the drudgery
of learning, sheds a light upon his path, but is looked
upon rather as a sort of gentle prison, of which the
parent is governor. The young man, accustomed to
do what he pleases at school, and who has even enjoyed the luxury of tyrannizing over his youngers,
feels the constraint of home insupportable. Thus,
the affections of the son are estranged from the father, and he becomes an alien in the halls of his ancestors. The same system of external education which
was begun at school, is continued at the university,
with this difference only, that the vacations are longer.
But by this time, the hatred of constraint has already
taken such hold of the mind, and the liberty enjoyed
at college so encourages this antipathy, that the character will still be stamped much more abroad than
at home, which will be always associated with unplea-
sant ideas of control.

When filial attachment is thus destroyed, it is not
wonderful that those ideas of future grandeur, and
that impatient longing for the period of liberty,
wealth, and distinction, which the rights of primogeniture have a tendency to create, should gradually
rise up in the mind.

That such are the consequences of the English system of education co-operating with the rights of primogeniture, and not of the latter cause alone, I think
evident from the example of Scotland, where the pri-

vileges of the eldest are allowed even to a greater extent than in England, but where sons are brought up in quite a different manner.

In the northern division of Great Britain, there are no such establishments as large boarding-schools for boys, but they are sent to places of education during the day only, and return home before night, generally to dinner. The system followed at the universities is the same as at school. Thus the tie which unites children to the paternal roof is never broken, the constraint which has always been experienced is never felt, and filial affection, continuing up to years of manhood, stifles those ambitious views which might otherwise be engendered in the mind of the eldest by the prospect before him, and prevents the growth of that most horrible of all desires, impatience for a parent's death. Thus it happens that disputes between a father and his eldest son are just as rare in Scotland, as in England they are of frequent occurrence.*

The example of the northern division of the kingdom, seems to me to prove that the jealousies and dissensions between a father and his heir, which the privilege of primogeniture has certainly a tendency

---

* Nothing to my mind more clearly proves the sort of terms on which fathers and sons so often live in England than the use of the phrase *governor*, so much applied to the former by the latter. This word exactly defines the kind of relation which is felt to subsist between them. Never in my life did I hear such an epithet, or any one analogous, given in Scotland by a child to a parent.

to create, may, by a proper system of education, be greatly diminished, if not entirely prevented.*

But besides the system of education, there is still another circumstance of much importance to be attended to, and which may serve in great part to explain the misunderstandings apt to spring up between a father and his eldest son, where the rights of primogeniture are generally acknowledged, and that is, that along with the practice of leaving the landed property to the first-born, is very frequently associated the institution of entails. Now, this makes a wide difference in the case. The system which I was led to recommend, by no means embraced the permission of en-

* This, as well as some unfavourable effects upon the general tone of moral sentiment caused by the recognition of the rights of primogeniture, has not escaped the notice of an able writer, and very keen observer of manners, Monsieur de Stael. In his *Lettres sur l'Angleterre*, he attributes to this cause the degree of sympathy shown in favour of heirs-apparent, and the consequent want of feeling manifested towards the old, who, it seems to be thought, cannot be too soon pushed aside, to make way for the rising sun. It would appear that every year added to the life of the aged, is considered as so much deducted from the legitimate rights and pleasures of the young. Men are at all times sufficiently prone to regard youth with partiality, for with it is associated both the idea of joy in the present, and hope in the future. But when, as in the case before us, that future is really splendid, the idea is apt to present itself, What a pity it should be so long delayed! The next feeling akin to this, is a wish for the removal of the only obstacle which retards the fulfilment of those brilliant prospects. " If the *old gentleman* were but out of the way," is a desire not only secretly felt, but often even openly expressed.

M. de Stael, in general a great admirer of England, has remarked that the death of a father or of an elder brother whose estate is expected, is on the stage of that country made a subject for jokes, which are not only tolerated, but even applauded, but which among the French would revolt the least delicate audience. This corruption of moral sentiment he attributes to the cause now under consideration.

tailing property, but otherwise gave the father unre-
stricted liberty of disposing of his land as he pleased,
provided only, that in case of his dying intestate,
the estate should descend to the eldest son, with
suitable burdens on it for the younger children.
Where the rights of primogeniture are general, but
optional on the part of the father, the heir knows
that he must behave himself, otherwise he may be
placed on a level with his brothers and sisters, or
even entirely disinherited. This is a check which
tends to prevent any outrageous conduct on his part.
But where the property is entailed upon him, he
knows that his parent has no power of keeping him
out of it, be his demeanour what it may. Thus, all
authority on the part of the father is done away with,
and the most powerful check to filial disobedience removed. Among the many evils of entails, this is not
the least.

These are the principal moral and political arguments which have occurred to me for and against the
equality of succession to landed property ; and if from
economical considerations we were before constrained
to come to a decision unfavourable to the practice, it
must, I think, be allowed that this decision is powerfully supported by views of political expediency ; and
that the moral objections brought in opposition to it,
are by no means of sufficient weight to invalidate this
conclusion.

The excessive dislike felt in some countries to the
principle of inequality in succession, is owing probably

not so much to the principle in itself, as to the extremes to which it has been pushed. From it has arisen the introduction of entails, the total impoverishment of all the younger children of a family for the sake of making one great, and the concentration of all the land in the kingdom in the hands of a very small number of persons. Far be it from me to defend any such abuses of the principle in question.

According to the old adage, " Corruptio optimi pessima," and so it is with the case before us.

It is the principle alone that I am concerned to establish, not its extravagant application.

Just as the abuses of the Roman Catholic religion have prejudiced the minds of too many in France against any religion at all, so has the excess to which the privileges of primogeniture were carried under the old government, given a complete detestation for the custom in general. The hardships, moreover, of the laws of succession, were aggravated by their great diversity throughout that kingdom. No uniform system prevailed, so that the younger members of a family in one province saw themselves much worse off than those perhaps in another adjoining. The customs in regard to the sort of possessions which conferred a privilege on the eldest, in some places the lands of the nobility alone giving this right, in others, all lands indiscriminately, were no more uniform than the portions of the inheritance reserved for the younger sons or daughters. In almost all places where custom was the only law, the most insignificant dowry was considered sufficient to exclude a daughter from all share in the succession. In certain parts it was necessary that this dowry should have been conferred by the father, in others, it was required to have been bestowed by the father and mother, or by the father in the lifetime of the mother; in others again, if given either by the father, mother, grandfather or grand-mother, it was enough. In Normandy, the daughters could demand no part of the heritage of their father and mother, either from their brothers or their child-ren, except in case of marriage. According to the customs of Anjou, Touraine, and Maine, the daughter portioned with a chaplet of roses, could ask for no-thing more.*

In a country where such customs as these formerly prevailed, it is no wonder that all inequality should now be looked upon with hatred. But we have no occasion to revert to France under the old govern-ment, for instances of the rights of primogeniture pushed to the extreme. Our own country will furnish us with sufficient examples, especially the northern division of the kingdom. It is there alone, where perpetual entails are found. Nothing can exceed the cruel effects of such institutions in par-ticular cases. When the owner of an estate en-tailed on the male line happens to die, leaving

---

* Speech of M. Chabot (de l'Allier) on the law relative to succes-sions, delivered before the Tribunes and Legislative Body; 26 Germi-nal, an. xi. (April 15, 1803.)

daughters only, the property goes away, perhaps to a distant relation, and the children of the former possessor, accustomed from their infancy to all the indulgences of wealth, are in a moment thrown destitute upon the world. If entails are at all to be preserved, surely it ought not to be allowed thus barbarously to disinherit the daughters of a house. At all events, they ought to come in, failing the brothers. In other respects, the strictness of Scottish entails has of late years been somewhat relaxed, by the permission now granted to the present holder, to settle one-third of the rent as a jointure on his widow, and three years' entire rent as the total portion of the younger children.*　But to however great an excess the rights of primogeniture may have been pushed, we ought always to remember that it is highly unphilosophical to object to a principle altogether, merely from the extravagant application made of it in certain ages and countries.　There is nothing in the nature of things to prevent the recognition of the principle in question, and at the same time its limitation within reasonable bounds.

Having thus brought to a conclusion the series of arguments by which it seems to me to be proved, that in the case of landed property an exception ought to be made to the general principle of equality in suc-

* That is in the case of there being three children, or more.　If there be but one child, one year's rent only can be left; if two, two years' rent.

cession, it now only remains for me to say a few words
on the policy of a compulsory division.

If the preceding reasonings have been sufficient to
prove that the system of equal partition applied to
land is bad, even when the result of the free-will of
heads of families ; of course we must object to their
being prevented by law from making a different settlement. But the plan of compulsory division has
disadvantages peculiar to itself, some of which it may
not be out of place here briefly to enumerate.

In the first place, this system may with justice be
objected to, as a most unnecessary intermeddling with
the private concerns of families. Liberty ought in all
cases to be the general rule, restriction the exception.
In most civilized countries, accordingly, it has been
looked upon as a salutary practice to allow proprietors perfect freedom to dispose of at least a great
part of their possessions, the law wisely supposing
them to be the best judges how they should be
left. Vain would be the idea that the law by one
unchangeable rule could suit the numerous varieties
of individual circumstances, better than the persons
themselves interested. Unless some very strong case
could be made out in favour of an exception, the general rule of liberty should here be maintained. The
first objection then to compulsory division is, that it
goes against general principle. If again we enter
more particularly into the consequences of this system,
we cannot but be struck with the evils which are apt
to result from interfering with the power of a father

in the disposal of his property. The authority of a parent must be considerably lessened where the children know that, be their conduct what it may, their interests in the inheritance cannot thereby be affected. The law having determined that the family possessions shall all be equally divided amongst them, where better motives do not secure good behaviour, these will not be strengthened by views of pecuniary advantage. A son naturally unruly may therefore fly in his father's face, without the latter having any effectual means of bringing him to order.

The law of compulsory division, then, has the same tendency to loosen the paternal authority in reference to all the members of his family, which the very opposite practice of entails has in regard to the eldest alone. Nor is this all. The system in question is no less injurious to the interests of the children in general, than to the authority of the head of the house. Not to mention that the dutiful and disobedient are thus put upon a level, and that the father has no means of recompensing the exemplary conduct of the former, by assigning to him a larger share in the inheritance; how highly unjust is it that all the family should suffer from the disorder and extravagance of one. The son who, during his parent's life-time, has squandered all he could get, and has incurred debts which the father was obliged to pay, thus lessening the common inheritance, finds himself afterwards as well off as his brothers and sisters who have always led a regular life. At least the portion of the former ought to be diminished by reason of his excesses ; but under the system of compulsory division, instead of the burthen being borne by the culprit alone, it is equally supported by the innocent and the guilty.

The law of compulsory division may be consider- ed as a permanent satire against parents ; it evidently takes for granted that they are too tyrannical, too ca- pricious, or too much interested in the grandeur of their name, to do equal justice to all their children. But upon what experience of human nature is this opinion founded ?   Evidently upon a very limited one indeed,—upon what has been found to take place in those countries where the law, instead of establish- ing equality as the general rule, and inequality as the exception, has adopted a policy altogether the re- verse.   Now, the effect of laws in modifying the mo- ral sentiments of a nation is too palpable to be dis- puted.   Where it was decreed by the highest autho- rity in the state, that the first-born had a right to all, and the younger to nothing, it is not astonishing that family pride, thus encouraged by the ruling powers, should, in many instances, have overcome the natural feelings of paternity.   But, to argue against the equity of fathers in general, from the ex- perience of such a condition of society as this, in which the genuine sentiments of human nature were perverted by unjust legislation, is surely to found conclusions upon a very narrow basis.   Be- sides, the hardships often felt under such a system, particularly by the daughters of a house, were most frequently such as the parent had no power of preventing. The land had been entailed, perhaps by a remote ancestor, who very probably might have had some way of providing for his own younger children, and could not be supposed to feel very warmly for the interests of those yet unborn, who might belong to his descendants.

Desire of perpetuating the grandeur of a family may easily overcome any scruples on this head, even where it might not be sufficient to stifle the love for one's own immediate offspring. But effectually to prevent all evil from this source, it is sufficient to prohibit entails, at least those which are perpetual.

In countries where the law of compulsory division has been adopted, as in France, for instance, during the Revolution, the principal object has unquestionably been to annihilate the aristocracy, and to produce an approximation towards a general equality of fortunes. Now, granting, for the sake of argument, an equal division of all kinds of property among the members of a family, to be desirable, still, it by no means follows that it is necessary to encroach upon the liberty of testation, in order to secure that object.

The very circumstance of the passing of the law seems, in a good measure, to prove its inutility, for, in a country where the opinion of the people, as expressed by their representatives, was so much in favour of equality, what occasion could there be for enforcing it? Why not allow that opinion to manifest itself freely, encouraging it by such means only

as do not interfere with the liberty of individual will?
The legislature should never resort to direct compulsion, when, by indirect ways, it can arrive at the
same end. By simply decreeing, that all the property of every man dying *intestate* should be divided
equally among his children, the same general result
would be obtained, and yet the exceptions required
in particular cases provided for. It is in the highest
degree improbable, that a law of this sort could long
subsist, without influencing the sentiments of those at
first opposed to it, in favour of the practice it was intended to encourage. Besides, the number of persons
who die without making a will is very great. So
that, were it even granted that an equal partition of
land, as of other property, is a consummation to be
wished for, still, the law of compulsion would be quite
unnecessary, and for that reason alone ought to be
rejected. This, it is true, is only a negative argument against it. But we have before seen that it is
liable to positive and weighty objections.

Having already had occasion more than once to
refer to the subject of entails, I shall conclude this
long inquiry into the best mode of succession to landed property, by some observations on these institutions. These may be considered as the extreme application of the principle of inequality, as the law of
compulsory division is of that of equality. The following are the principal evils which belong to them.

In the first place, it may be objected to entails,

in an economical point of view, that they prevent a proprietor from making those improvements on his estate which otherwise he would be induced to effectuate, for the owner of land so tied up can neither sell any portion of his domains with a view to ameliorate the rest, nor borrow money for that or any other purpose.

This inconvenience has been felt with particular severity in those countries where no body of farmers existed, possessed of considerable capitals, whose stock might to a great degree supply the place of those funds which the landlord was unable to procure. This was one principal cause of the very backward state of agriculture in France before the Revolution. Many of the great possessions of the nobles were left half uncultivated. The change produced by breaking up these vast and waste properties was the main source of the force displayed by France in the revolutionary wars—a force which arose partly from material, partly from moral causes. The great and rapid extension given to the cultivation of the soil afforded the means of making these extraordinary exertions, and the interest which the new and numerous body of proprietors had in supporting that cause to which they were indebted for their territorial possessions, afforded a powerful motive for upholding the new order of things.

If this evil consequence of entails has been less felt in Great Britain, it is because the middle classes, from which farmers are derived, have long been both numerous and wealthy in that country. Besides, in England, perpetual entails have not been allowed.

The second objection which may be brought against entails is, that it is very unjust to the great body of the community, thus to favour the monopoly of land by a few great families, and so to deprive all the rest of the nation of the security, independence, and pleasure attached to the possession of a landed property, and a country life. Of the natural partiality of man for this mode of existence, no better proof seems to be wanted than what occurs in those countries where land is frequently sold in small portions.

I have before mentioned the very high price paid for the possession of the soil in France, and stated that a man will often toil for many years in order to accumulate enough to buy a small piece of ground, for which he pays a sum out of all proportion with the rent. And though, for the reasons previously detailed, the small proprietor finds it less disadvantageous to give so enormous a price, than one who looks to the rent alone, yet without supposing a partiality for land on account of the security, independence, and pleasure supposed to be derived from its possession, we could not fully account for its being so eagerly demanded. In every country, in fact, the revenue derived from land is somewhat less in proportion to the sums paid for it, than what can be obtained from any other investment of capital.

Thirdly, entails are highly objectionable on this ground, that they serve to defraud creditors, reliev-

ing the family of the debtor from the legitimate consequences of extravagance, and putting the yoke
on the neck of those by whom it ought not to be
borne.

When the owner of an entailed estate dies, whatever debts he may have incurred are that instant
cancelled, and the heir enters on the possessions of
his ancestors free from all incumbrance. It is quite
unnecessary to dwell on the injustice of such a system as this. But some will say, why do people trust
the holders of land thus tied up? They cannot but
be aware how the law stands, and if they give credit,
they do so at their own peril, and with their eyes
open to the possible consequences. In answer to this,
it may be said, in regard to tradesmen not giving
credit, particularly in countries where entails are general, that they had much better shut up shop at
once, for if they refuse to sell to the great on their
own terms, they may be very certain that they shall
not sell to them at all. By refusing to deal with
even one member of the aristocracy they are liable
to see themselves deserted by the whole body, for
the nobility and gentry have a fellow feeling for
one another. What then would be the consequence
of their sturdily refusing credit to all! The ruin
of their business would be the inevitable result, and
the elevation of some fortunate rival who had
been found more complacent to the wishes of the
rich and powerful. The error of the objection lies
in this, that unless the refusal of credit became ge-

neral, it never could be practised at all, for otherwise, if there be danger in trusting, there is certain ruin in the opposite conduct. And again, that it is utterly impossible such a denial should ever become general, so long as there are needy tradesmen who, having little to lose, will run any risks for the sake of getting into employment. This reasoning is abundantly confirmed by experience. So great is the competition in all the ordinary branches of trade, that notwithstanding the danger that may be incurred by selling on credit to those whose heirs are not bound to discharge their debts, it very rarely happens that trust is refused, except in some notorious instances. The fear of being supplanted in business overcomes that of not being paid.

The above objections are all made with a reference to the general advantage of the community.

The following are derived from a consideration of the particular interests of those families in whose favour entails are established. But having already touched upon some of these evils, it will be the less necessary to dwell long upon this part of the subject. Where entails are strict, the injustice exercised towards all the younger children of a family, to the daughters especially, for the sake of making *one* great, must be evident to all. I say to the daughters especially, for the sons may, even without any fortune to begin with, perhaps succeed in making their way in the world, favoured by the interest of their elder brother and high relations. But what is to become of the delicate scions of a lordly house? Nursed from their infancy in the lap of luxury, unaccustomed to want of any kind, and therefore totally unfit for exertion to ward it off, (even though pride should permit them to demean the family name by industrious occupations) when the father dies, how hard must be their lot! They must now exchange wealth, ease, and distinction, for poverty, dependence, and the prospect of perpetual celibacy.

In France under the old government, the system of entails was found in all its purity. As there was little or no provision for the younger sons and daughters, they were thrust, the latter especially, into convents and monasteries, as the best security against want, or the disgrace of the family dignity. Where entails are not so strict as to prevent some settlement being made on the junior members of the house, perhaps the sons have not much reason to complain of those institutions, which secure to them in their pursuits the advantage of high aristocratical interest, and but for which they might perhaps have been born in a very inferior station. The fate of the daughters is much more severe.

But of all the evils which entails bring upon individuals, none can be compared with the sudden poverty to which a family of girls is at once reduced, when the father dies without leaving a son, and the estate being settled *in the male line*, goes away perhaps to a distant relation. To this I have before alluded. The permission of such institutions as these,

by which the interests of women are sacrificed to the
vain-glory of a name, is a disgrace to the legislature
of any civilized community. So long as the property
remains in the same family, the daughters have at all
events the protection of a brother's roof in case of
need, but when it goes to other relations, what resource is left for those who never before knew indigence and woe?

There is another family evil belonging to entails,
and which has already been mentioned, namely, that
the authority of the father over his eldest son is
thereby greatly weakened; and while all effectual
control over the turbulence of the one is removed,
the degree of restriction to which the heir is subjected only induces him to look eagerly forward to
that bright period when a weary expectancy shall
give place to possession.* On the other hand, the
father is effectually prevented from rewarding the
filial piety of the rest of his children, of a daughter
perhaps, whose anxious and unwearied attentions
have soothed and prolonged his declining years. If
he have amassed no moveable property, he may die
with the certainty that the comfort and prop of his
age shall be left in a state of destitution.

If all these effects of entails have not been felt to
the fullest extent in every country where they have
prevailed, it has been either because the system has

---

* I once heard the owner of an entailed estate assign this as a reason for sending his eldest son out to India. "An heir," said he, "who
remains at home has nothing to do but to wish for his father's death!"

not been strictly acted up to, or because other causes have served to modify its results. Thus, in England, the proper consequences of these institutions have not been so palpably visible as in France or Scotland, partly because there entails were never perpetual, partly because the English aristocracy have more frequently condescended, through the means of matrimonial alliances, to fill their empty chests, and portion a numerous offspring by supplies drawn from plebeian coffers. In Scotland, however, where they have not, as in old France, the resource of monasteries, the chief portion of the younger sons has long consisted in the family interest, by which they are sent to seek their fortunes in all the corners of the globe, while the daughters most frequently remain, for ever single, at home.

When, on the other hand, the legislature attempts to remedy some of the evils of entails, not by giving permission to sell a part of the property, but by allowing it to be burdened to a certain extent, it is then the eldest of the family who begins to feel the smarting of the sore. He comes into possession of an extensive estate with a large nominal income, but of which in reality he may not enjoy one-half. The rest, we may suppose, goes to pay a widow's jointure, the portions of the younger children, and other burdens.* Still, he has to support the name and state of a man whose fortune is estimated not by what he ac-

* Entailed estates in Scotland may now be burdened to a certain extent on account of improvements.

tually enjoys, but by what he is supposed to possess, not by the revenue he has to spend, but by what his property is calculated to yield. Thus his wants are constantly beyond his means—a situation certainly by no means enviable, and which offers a perpetual temptation to run in debt.

So truly is the evil of this position felt since the relaxation of the principle of Scottish entails, that many of the actual proprietors of land in that country, are themselves most anxious for the liberty of selling at least a part of their estates.

In answer to these numerous objections against entails, the only arguments which I have ever heard adduced in their favour, are derived from one or other of these two considerations. First, from a view to the interests of families ; secondly, from some supposed advantages to the community at large.

Entails, it is said, tend to perpetuate the dignity and welfare of families, and by preserving the aristocracy from ruin, maintain the stability of governments.

In answer to the first of these arguments, it may be said, that were it even granted that entails *do* contribute to the welfare of certain families, and not to the grandeur of one only in each, which, from the observations made above, is, to say the least, very doubtful, still, this would be an extremely weak ground for supporting these institutions. If from the reasonings now detailed, it appear that they are detrimental to the public at large, they cannot for an

instant be defended on the score of partial advantage
to a few families.   But it is not to a few families
only, say their advocates, that entails are beneficial,
for by the force which they lend to government, they
help to maintain order throughout society.   To this
it may with truth be answered, that entails are not
necessary for that purpose.   The acknowledgment of
the rights of primogeniture is amply sufficient, without such institutions, for preserving as much concentration of property as is required for that end.
And thus I am naturally led to the last objection
which may be made to entails, which is of a political
kind: that they give too great an extension to the
power of the aristocracy, and so tend to perpetuate
all those abuses which ever flow from the uncontrolled dominion of the Few over the Many.

CHAPTER XI.

GENERAL SUMMARY.

HAVING now concluded that important division of the science of Political Economy which treats of the Primary Distribution of Wealth, it may be well before dismissing the subject to take a summary view of the doctrine above laid down.

We have seen, in the first place, that there are four classes of persons who in one way or another concur in the business of production, and who therefore are entitled each to a share in the common result. These are Labourers, Masters, Capitalists, and Landlords, the last of whom is in many cases out of the question, often even in agricultural industry.

Now, it is evident, that the greater the productiveness of labour, capital, and land, the more will there be to be distributed between these different descriptions of persons, who receive amongst them the whole of the produce. Again, the degree of productiveness being given, the amount of each share must depend upon the proportion in which the division is effected. The welfare of all then rests upon these two circumstances. 1. The total amount of the produce; 2. The ratio in which it is shared.

The former of these depends upon the degree of productiveness of labour, capital, and land ; the latter upon the following causes.

If we consider the four classes above mentioned, as regards the part they take in raising wealth, we shall find that they may be reduced to two, of which the one operates more with the mind, the other more with the body, or by means of extraneous matter. The former we may call the Intellectual, the latter the Material class. The labour of the master as such, is chiefly that of the head; it is for him to lay the plan of production, while he must depend upon the concurrence of the others for the agents or instruments by which alone it can be put in execution. In his character of master, he is not essentially an owner either of land or capital, nor yet a common labourer who toils with his hands. He is an intelligent being, having capital at his command. Now, as on the one hand, his intelligence can go little way by itself towards increasing the sum of human comforts, and as on the other, the owners of the material sources of wealth have need of a directing head who may turn them to the best advantage, it comes to pass, that two classes of men, so radically different, have a mutual occasion for each other. The one body is composed of masters only, the other of labourers, capitalists, and proprietors of land united. From this contrast in their character and position, arises a difference in their interests. The object of the members of the second class, is to *let* their labour, capital, or land to those who will engage to pay for the use of them, that is to the masters. The last, on the other hand, are desirous of *hiring* these instruments of production, expecting, after paying all charges, to have over a sufficient remuneration for their own trouble and risk. The one class, then, wishing to *let* these instruments, and the other to *hire* them, we may naturally suppose that the former is anxious to receive as much as it can for the loan, while the latter strives to give as little as possible.

The competition between these two opposing classes determines the share of each. Not that all the three divisions of the second make common cause, and combine against the masters, but the struggle is carried on separately between these last, and each of the three sections of their antagonists.

From the above it follows, that the amount received by the labourer, capitalist, and landlord, can always be easily ascertained, because it is specified in the agreement, whereas the sum realized by the master being never stated, is generally known with difficulty, and by indirect means. Even the individual himself does not always know exactly his own gains.

Now, it has been remarked, that the master is never reduced to the necessity of demanding the use of the land of some proprietor, for the sake of turning his talents to account, since, if the country be newly settled, much of the soil will belong to no one, and may be occupied by the first comer; or it may be purchased either with his own funds or borrowed capital; and, lastly, all the numerous branches of commerce and manufactures are open to him. From this, it follows, that even in old countries, the owners of land have it not in their power to reduce the profits of farmers much below that rate which is usual in other occupations; still less, below what is commonly made by agriculturists cultivating their own possessions. In the early stages of society, where much of the territory is still unclaimed, there can, it is evident, be no room for competition between proprietors and masters, for the latter can assume the former character whenever they please. So long as this state lasts, the share of the latter must depend entirely on the competition between him on the one side, and capitalists and labourers on the other. As yet the class of landlords or receivers of rent does not exist. For the present, then, they may be left out of the question, and our attention exclusively directed to the three others.

The competition above referred to between the different classes, expresses a fact which depends upon the simple principle of each wishing to get for himself as much as possible of the gross produce. Now, the question is, what limits this possibility?

First, as concerns the labourers, we have seen that the proportion of the whole which falls to their share, will depend *proximately* on the ratio existing between the quantity of labour offered, and the amount of funds, that is, the circulating capital, destined for paying that labour. Now, the quantity of labour is made up of two elements; the number of persons desirous of being employed, and the number of hours during the day, and of days during the year, usually dedicated to work.

Ultimately, however, this share will depend, on the one hand, upon the degree of productiveness of the labour and capital employed in raising the necessaries of life ; on the other, upon the mode of living rendered necessary by the nature of the climate, or considered by opinion as necessary to the existence of the labourer. The former of these ultimate causes affects not only the *amount* received by the labourer, in other words, his real wages; but, as was shown under the head of Gross Profits, modifies also the *proportion* of the whole produce which falls to his share. This one observation, however, must be attended to, that an improved productiveness which increases real wages tends to diminish the proportion received by the labourer, so that the former may rise, while the latter is stationary or even less than before.

Secondly, the share of the capitalist depends upon the following causes.

1. Upon the proportion existing between the capital offered on loan, and that demanded to be borrowed.

2. Upon the greater or less surplus called Gross Profit which the masters expect to have over, to be divided between them and the capitalists, after paying the whole cost of production. Now, it is evident, that supposing this cause in no way to affect the amount of funds either offered or demanded on loan, still it must influence greatly the degree of pertinacity among

the borrowers, disposing them more or less readily to submit to the terms of the lenders. Where much is made by capital, much can be afforded for its use. But it is probable that the cause we are now considering acts also remotely on the rate of interest, by increasing or diminishing the number of borrowers, or the amount of capital demanded; for where gross profits are high, more persons are tempted to enter into business upon borrowed funds, and those already so engaged, are induced to enlarge their dealings. When, on the contrary, profits are low, a contrary effect takes place. We have seen, moreover, that the influence of this cause alone would be felt, were it not that, on the one hand, great sums are often *borrowed* by government and individuals without any view to productive employment; while, on the other, the proportion of capital to be *lent* has a constant tendency to increase with the riches of the country.

Since interest, or the revenue of the capitalist, depends so much upon the rate of gross profits, it becomes essential to know by what this is regulated. Accordingly, it has been shown at considerable length, that the causes by which this is determined are of two kinds. 1. The degree of productiveness of the labour and capital employed in raising the necessaries of life, and the various elements of fixed capital. 2. The rate of real wages.

Thirdly, the share of the master depends, partly on the rate of gross profit, and consequently on the causes by which it is regulated; partly on the rate of interest or net profit, and therefore on the causes by which this also is determined. He is, as we have seen, the great distributor of the wealth of the society, the agent through whom the other classes receive their portion of the gross produce. And when once the custom is established of paying these portions in money, it is he also who immediately supplies the consumers with all the various objects of which they may stand in need.

These are the causes which determine the ratio in which the total return shall be divided between labourers, capitalists, and masters, previous to the creation of rent in land, and which still continue to operate after that event. The only difference now is, that in consequence of the advanced price of some articles of raw produce, the owners of certain lands can demand, and the masters or farmers are able to pay, a portion of the whole to the proprietor of the soil. For, since the produce of these lands remains the same, while its price or value has augmented in consequence of a new demand which cannot be met with as great facility as formerly, it follows that the master can now pay both his labourers and capitalist at as high a rate as before, though with a smaller share of the gross return. If the articles which have risen in value be a part of the customary food of the working class, their share, so far as these are concerned, will no doubt be the same as previously; for the advanced value of that which they must consume can be of no advantage to them. But a smaller part of the gross produce will now suffice for obtaining by purchase all those other commodities which they were in the habit of procuring by exchange, whether different kinds of food, clothes, furniture, or fuel. Therefore, with a less share upon the whole of the gross produce, the labourer will be quite as well off as formerly. No change, moreover, is supposed to take place in the interest of capital, which being the same sum as before, must now form a less proportion of the total return which has risen in value. But, since the shares of both these classes, labourers and capitalists, are diminished, it follows that a larger proportion of the whole will be retained by the master or farmer. Besides the ordinary profits of enterprise, there will in consequence be a sum over, which, if he continue to cultivate his own grounds, he may not distinguish from his other gains by a peculiar appellation, but which, if he let them to another, he will insist on receiving under the name of rent. Thus arises a new order of persons in the society, who, without any trouble or risk on their part, derive an income from their lands, just as capitalists live upon the interest of their funds without the necessity of personal superintendence. We likewise perceive that the creation of this new revenue, which, whether it be paid away or not under that name, essentially constitutes rent, cannot take place without diminishing the proportion of the total return formerly received by the other classes, though real wages, the rate of interest, and the ordinary profits of enterprise are thereby in no wise affected. Were that proportion not diminished, one or all would in reality be increased.

When the rise in price takes place, were the distribution to go on as before, each of the three sets of persons would be benefited ; but as they cannot long continue to gain more than their fellows in other situations and employments, the owner of land is able to draw all the advantage to himself, and by retaining a part of the produce, to disturb the proportion in which it was formerly divided. It is then perfectly correct to say that the creation of rent is the *immediate* cause of the change in the ancient order of distribution, though the rise in price be a more *remote* one.

It seems scarcely necessary to add, however, that rent can influence distribution only where it actually exists. But as no branches of industry except agriculture afford this revenue, and as even very many lands are exempt from it, it follows that in all these cases, its creation can in no way affect the proportion in which the gross produce is divided between labourers, capitalists, and masters.

It has been shown that rent originates on the most fertile or most favourably situated lands, from a permanent increase in the price of certain articles of produce, owing to the impossibility of meeting the increasing demand for them, without a proportionally greater expenditure of labour and capital. Now, this impossibility can arise from nothing but the limited quantity of the best soils, or of those most advantageously placed. This then is one fundamental cause of rent. But however limited this quantity might be, were it not universally appropriated, no one would ever consent to pay for the use of any portion thereof. The existence of rent, then, as an independent revenue, not only necessarily supposes the institution of property in land, but also that all the best soils have already been taken possession of. Therefore, the second cause essential to its creation is, the universal appropriation of the most highly favoured lands.

Nor is it absolutely necessary to suppose that all these are cultivated; for, if one or more great proprietors should have a fancy for keeping a large part of their domains under wood to enjoy the delights of the chace, or should dedicate a portion of them to garden and pleasure ground, the price of corn &c. might rise sufficiently to create a rent upon the estates of those who were inclined to make a more profitable use of their possessions, even before all the best land in the country was turned to account. I mention this case merely to show, that the universal appropriation of the superior soils is essential to the origin of this branch of income, while that they should be all cultivated, is not so strictly necessary.

Having determined to what rent owes its origin, the next question is, what are the limits to its rise? We have seen that it is prevented from getting beyond a certain point, by the existence of other lands less fertile or less favourably situated, no doubt, than those first occupied, but capable, at the same time, of raising some produce. The supply thus obtained prevents for a time the further rise in price, and puts a stop to the increase of rent. Were it not for these inferior soils, when once all those fit for cultivation had been made the most of, there could be no limit to the augmentation in the price of raw produce, and consequently in rent, except what arose from a stationary or declining population.* But as lands even of very low fertility can be made to yield something, and as they may in time be very materially improved, not to mention the additional returns to be drawn from those already cultivated, it must be long before a nation can arrive at that state in which its territory could produce no more. Then, and then only, would the increase of rent be really unlimited, except by the cause above stated.

As rent owes its origin to the limited quantity of the best land, so it is indebted for its rise after a certain period, to the limited quantity of that of second-rate quality; and again, after another lapse of time, it owes its further increase to the restricted extent of that of third-rate fertility, and so on. Thus, land of each different quality limits the rise of rent on all those above it, while being itself not unbounded, these limits are necessarily temporary.

It has also been pointed out, that while rent in its origin is the *effect* of the high price of certain articles the growth of the soil; being once created, it acts in

---

* This of course supposes a foreign supply to be out of the question.

its turn as a *cause* of an increase in the price of other
raw products, such as grass, cattle, and wood; and
that owing to this rise, even poor and totally uncultivated lands may give some rent to the proprietor.
It has likewise, I think, been proved that these would
afford some revenue of this description, before it
could be advisable to convert with this view any arable ground into pasture or forest, and therefore that
waste lands would be the first to yield a rent from
this species of produce. Hence the preference shown
by great proprietors in poor districts, such as the hill
country of Scotland, to grass over corn. On indifferent soils and in cold climates, the one gives a rent
long before the other.

One observation more it may not be useless to repeat before concluding this subject. Were there but
one species of commodity produced by the industry
of man, or were exchange unknown, then the condition of each class of persons concerned in distribution, would entirely depend upon the productiveness
of capital and labour in that employment in which
they were engaged, and on the ratio in which the total produce was divided. But when a separation of
trades takes place, and exchange is introduced, then
the easy or difficult circumstances of these different
sets of people, depend quite as much on the degree
of productiveness of labour and capital in other occupations, as in their own, often indeed much more so.
For, in the case of articles of primary necessity, we
have seen that this productiveness affects distribu-

tion universally. And even though the *proportion*, and therefore the *quantity*, belonging to each class, should not be influenced by the condition of other branches of industry, yet its power of purchasing would thereby be materially affected. The state of things in any one employment remaining the same, and the ratio of division undergoing no change, it is clear that the greater the productiveness of labour and capital in all other departments, the greater will be the sum of almost all the elements of wealth which the shares of the labourers, masters, capitalists, and landlords engaged in that one employment, will respectively enable them to command. Every class, then, is interested in the universal productiveness of industry, as much as in the increase of its own share of the common stock, at the expense of its competitors.

CHAPTER XII.

ON THE NATIONAL REVENUE.

THE term Revenue is one of such constant use in all works of political economy, and so frequently occurs in the course of the present Essay, that clearly to understand its meaning becomes of first-rate importance. At the same time, it is a term which could not well be explained in the commencement, because a thorough knowledge of the whole theory of distribution is required for that purpose.

This point is of the greater moment, since, by some of the best writers, the word Revenue has been employed very vaguely, and even confounded with the annual gross produce of industry.* How then are we to distinguish it from the latter?

I may remark, in the first instance, that revenue itself being usually divided into gross and net, it will be advisable first to determine in what the former of these consists. Wherever the contrary is not specified, gross revenue must always be understood.

---

* M. Storch must be classed amongst this number. In his excellent " Cours d'Economie Politique," he runs into this mistake. " En un mot," says he; " le revenu d'une nation est egal à sa production annuelle," and so on. Ch. xiv. liv. iii.

Revenue may be defined to be, that portion of the annual gross produce of any country, which either is actually employed in satisfying *immediately* the physical wants of its inhabitants during the course of the year, or which may be so employed, without at all impairing the sources of national wealth. And as it ministers to the necessities of men *immediately*, so, if it assist production at all, it is but *remotely*.

To revenue then belong, in the first place, the rents of the Landlord, the Net-profits or Interest of the Capitalist, and the Profits of Enterprise appertaining to the Master. In respect to all these there can be no doubt. It is quite evident that whatever be the portion of the annual Gross Produce which is divided into these different fractions, the whole of that portion either is really consumed by its respective owners, or at least may be so, solely to satisfy the wants of nature, and without any view to a future production, but at the same time without at all interfering with the previously existing sources of public wealth. All that is produced in the course of a year destined to make up Rent or Gross Profit, may be consumed in any way the possessors of these incomes think fit, without in the least impairing the quantity or quality of the land, labour, or capital of the society. So far then the case is clear.

But what are we to say of Wages? Are they also a part of the National Revenue?

Were we to suppose that wages, instead of being advanced, as they generally are, by the master, were not paid until the completion of the product, the present instance would not appear more doubtful than the preceding. The labourer receiving a part of the finished commodity as the reward of his exertions, might, it is clear, consume this in kind, or what amounts to the same thing, exchange it for other necessaries of life for the use of himself and family, without at all encroaching upon the sources of public riches. Neither land, capital, nor labour, would thereby be at all impaired or diminished. The first is of course quite out of the question; and for the second, we must remember what has been observed in the beginning of this Essay, that when we talk of capital as one of the sources of national wealth in conjunction with labour, fixed capital alone can be meant, that is, all commonly included under the more general term, except what is advanced as wages, which is called circulating.

This is a distinction of the greatest consequence.

The capital which alone is *immediately* a source or agent of national wealth, consists in all those elements formerly enumerated, such as the seed of the agriculturist and the raw materials of manufactures, implements and machines of every description, buildings used for productive purposes, cattle, whether working or otherwise, substances collected for the amelioration of land, and for the necessary renewal and repairs of all the above objects. All this is called fixed capital, in opposition to that which is advanced as wages, and

termed circulating. And it may very properly be so
styled, not so much on account of its being more durable, as because when employed in production it remains constantly in the hands of its owner, or at least
of him who turns it to account; while the other, in
order to serve its possessor, must pass away altogether from himself, and become the property of others.
The former, while being employed, leads *immediately*
to production, but in the mean time actually benefits
no one; the latter conduces only *remotely* to the creation of wealth, though in proportion as consumed, it
ministers to all the physical wants of the labouring
population.* Therefore, the whole of it may be applied by them to their daily necessities, without at all
impairing the sources of national wealth. On the
contrary, since thus alone can the strength of the labourers be maintained, and their numbers kept up,
the springs of public riches are thereby remotely fed.

Now, were we to take the case at first supposed, of
the labourers not being paid until the completion of
the product, and receiving their share of the whole
result in *kind*, it is clear that no circulating capital
could be required. This observation is alone sufficient
to show that this species of capital is not an *immediate* agent in production, nor even essential to it at all;
but as I have said, merely a convenience rendered ne-

---

* The one is *immediately* productive, but does not *immediately* satisfy physical wants; the other *immediately* satisfies physical wants,
but is not *immediately* productive.

cessary by the deplorable poverty of the mass of the people.*

The following cases will render this still more evident. Let us suppose two districts, of which the one being in the possession of a comparatively small number of persons, is let out into farms of considerable extent, and cultivated by labourers employed by the tenant, while the other is divided among many very small proprietors, each of whom, assisted merely by the members of his own family, is able to make the most of his little estate. In the first case, it is clear, that the farmer will have occasion for circulating capital, in order to pay the wages of his day-labourers, supposing them to be remunerated in the usual manner. But, in the second instance, there will be no necessity whatever for a similar fund. Necessity there could not be, for each proprietor having no more land than he can fitly turn to account with the aid of his own family, would have no occasion for hiring labourers to assist. Now, as he and the members of his house receive no pay from others, they must of course subsist on their own resources until the completion of their present work, that is, on something derived from a former production. All that is essentially required for the maintenance of the existing quantity of labour, is, that the physical wants of the working people be amply supplied; and assuredly there can be no reason why the creation of wealth should

* See Chapter II. on Production.

not go on as well when they are their own paymas-
ters, and live during one year on what they raised
during the preceding, as when they must depend for
subsistence on the funds advanced to them by a
wealthy capitalist.   Now, the case here brought forward is not merely an imaginary though possible one,
invented for the sake of illustration, but is really found
to exist in many countries.   Various are the regions
of Europe in which much of the land is in the hands
of proprietors so small as to require no assistance in
cultivating their little estates, beyond the members of
their own families.   France, Savoy, Switzerland, and
Belgium, abound with such lowly lords of the soil.

Thus we see, that whether wages be paid in *kind*,
and not until the completion of the work, (which,
while the simplest way of viewing the case, is also that
which goes to the bottom of the transaction between
labourers and their employers,) or whether they be
advanced by degrees out of a fund called circulating
capital, can make no real difference.   In either mode,
they may be applied *immediately* to satisfy the physical wants of men, without in the least impairing the
sources of national wealth ; for if they assist production, it is but *remotely*, by means of that very support
which they afford to the working classes.   Therefore,
wages completely agree with the characters by which
Revenue has been above defined, and consequently
must be classed along with rent and gross profits under this denomination.

From the above, it follows, that if the usual classification be retained, by which the whole wealth of the society, or simply its annual reproduction, is divided into capital and revenue, we must be careful to state that fixed capital alone is meant. For, as we have just seen, that styled circulating is in reality the revenue of the labourers, and may with truth be considered as their share in the common result of industry, advanced to them in another form. The total riches of a nation, or merely its annual gross produce, may then either of them be divided into fixed capital and revenue.

Thus we have found, that revenue differs from the annual gross produce, simply by the absence of all those objects which go to keep up fixed capital, and have therefore solved the question with which we set out. All except this may be consumed in satisfying the immediate wants of the population during the course of a year, without in the least intrenching on the different sources of national prosperity.

From all now said, the distinction between capital (that is fixed capital) and revenue is clearly established. The former is composed of all those material objects which are *immediately* productive, but only *remotely* satisfy the physical wants of men; the latter is made up of those which *immediately* minister to those wants, and if productive at all, are so only *remotely*.

Having now traced the distinction between gross produce and revenue, which is but a part of the former, it remains to be seen whether the latter may not itself be subdivided, as it usually has been, into gross and net, and if so, wherein consists the real difference between them. Revenue, we have seen, is employed in ministering to the physical wants of men. Now, since in order that production may go on, it is necessary that people live, it follows, that *some portion* of revenue is indispensable to the future progress of wealth. So far then, revenue, though not an *immediate* agent in production, is *remotely* essential to its continuance.

Now, the question is, how much revenue is necessary to be created, in order that the present sources of riches may not be impaired, and the national prosperity in consequence decline? This we may call Necessary Revenue.*

In order to come to a conclusion on this subject, let us examine the different parts of which revenue is made up.

First, as to the rent of the landlord, we may, without hesitation, pronounce, that it forms no part of necessary revenue. The reason of this is, that it is never essential that land should afford a rent in order to secure its cultivation. If it gives a sufficient profit, after paying all expenses, it is enough. There are various ways in which land of this description may be turned to account. First, it may be cultivated by the proprietor himself either by his own or

---

* This phrase is borrowed from M. Storch.

borrowed capital, the usual return to which, without any surplus as rent, will be quite a sufficient inducement not to let the soil be idle. Secondly, it may be placed by the owner under the care of an upper servant, receiving fixed wages as a recompense for his trouble in superintending the farm.* In this case also, of course, the capital is supplied by the proprietor. This last is a mode much employed in countries where estates are large, and of course in the possession of gentry, who, while they let to tenants the greater part of their domains, prefer keeping in their own power the lands more immediately contiguous to their habitations. But being themselves, from their habits of life, extremely unfit for the profession of farmers, they are obliged to trust mainly to some experienced person for the proper management of the business of agriculture. Now, it must be remarked, that it would be the interest of the proprietor to cultivate his estate in one or other of these ways, not only though it should afford no rent properly so called, but even though it should give less than the ordinary rate of gross profits. Having the land, it will be of advantage to him to turn it to account, provided it will yield but a little more than the net profits or interest of capital. If it will return nothing beyond, as well live on the income of that capital lent to another, but if it can be made to pro-

---

* This sort of person is called bailiff or land-stewart in England—grieve in Scotland.

duce more, that surplus, small though it be, may be sufficient to induce him to cultivate.

Thirdly, the land may be let along with other ground to a tenant, who, while he pays his rent entirely from the better soils, will nevertheless find it his interest to till the inferior, if they be likely to yield a fair profit. This is a circumstance which happens continually, and gives rise to the erroneous idea of rent being paid by lands of very low fertility. The proprietor receiving a certain sum for the whole, concludes, perhaps naturally enough, that he derives a revenue from all, whereas, it is possibly to a small part only that he is indebted for his income. The farmer, on the other hand, must have a certain extent of ground in order to employ his capital, and will consent to pay a high rent for the good, only on condition of having a certain quantity of the more indifferent thrown in along with it, to be improved and cultivated at pleasure. And even a tenant will find it advantageous to turn his capital on land, though it should not give quite the ordinary rate of gross profits, for, being engaged in the business of farming, he cannot superintend the employment of that capital in any other branch of industry, and will therefore be glad to derive from it, applied to agriculture, a revenue but slightly superior to its interest. This of course will especially be the case where leases are of long duration. From all this it follows, that rent is never essential to the cultivation of land, which will be turned to productive account, whether it be paid or not.   Therefore rent can form no part of what I have called Necessary revenue.

It is not, however, the same with the gross profits of capital and enterprise.   If no profit were made upon capital, there could be no inducement whatever to employ it in production, and moreover, the owners would be obliged to have recourse to it for satisfying their physical wants.   Therefore, both from choice and necessity, it would be consumed without a return.   It follows, that some gross profit is absolutely essential in order that production should go on at all, except so far as labour could act alone. Even if profit be very low, there will be a strong inducement to capitalists to emigrate to foreign countries, or at least to vest their funds in foreign securities, not to dwell upon those who, from the smallness of the annual return, may be led to spend their stock unproductively.   Therefore, in order to prevent the diminution of the national capital, it is necessary that gross profit fall not below a certain rate. What that rate may be, it is of course impossible to say.   It may vary in different countries, and at different periods in the same, according to the facility for secure foreign investments, and the prudence or improvidence of the people.   Suffice it to observe, that in any place, at a certain period, there is a point below which gross profits cannot fall without endangering one of the main sources of national wealth. Now, whatever may be the lowest rate required to obviate that evil, constitutes a portion of the Necessary revenue of the society, according to the definition above laid down.

In regard to the net profits of capital, the case seems to be different. Though gross profits were to fall so low, that it could answer the purposes neither of the master to borrow capital for productive employment, nor of the owner to lend it, the former not finding it worth his while to incur risk and trouble for so small a remuneration, and the latter not being able to live on interest alone, yet it by no means follows that stock would be squandered without any return. The only difference would be, that capitalists would be obliged to undertake the management of their own funds, and the class of *rentiers* would cease. But so far as national wealth is concerned, this is a matter of perfect indifference; provided the capital of the country be productively employed, it signifies little by whom, whether by the owners themselves, or by those who borrow it for like purposes. The only diversity is, that when a revenue can be derived from capital, independently of personal superintendence, gross profits are capable of subdivision into net profits and those of enterprise, and may become the property of different individuals; whereas, on the contrary supposition, these two incomes being always united in the same person, would be perfectly undistinguishable.

It therefore does not seem essential to the keeping up of the public wealth, that capital should be capable of affording a revenue to its owner separate from that of its employer. We must, however, bear in mind, that in proportion as it becomes more necessary for the former to superintend the direction of his own funds, the greater is the temptation to remove his substance to other lands where a higher interest may enable him to live at ease. Should gross profits fall so low as not to exceed the interest obtained in adjoining countries, this temptation to remove funds in large quantities would probably become irresistible. Therefore, again, it appears, that a certain rate of gross profit is essential to the keeping up of the national capital without diminution, and is therefore a part of the necessary revenue of the society; though it does not seem equally indispensable that it should be so elevated as to afford separate incomes to the owner and the employer.

The only branch of revenue which still remains to be considered is that of wages. Now, as it is with the capitalist, so with the labourer. If no profit were made by the one, there could neither be any motive to employ his funds in production, nor the power of doing so long. In like manner, if the other earned nothing for his pains he could have no inducement to labour, and no means of sustaining his strength; nor even his existence. The capitalist may support himself for a time on his funds, though they yield no increase, but if the labourer gain nothing, he must soon perish. Some amount of wages then is most strictly essential to the keeping up of this primary source of wealth. Neither is it enough that the revenue which goes for this purpose, be sufficient to preserve the existing race. It must also enable them to bring up to the age of manhood a number of strong and healthy children, so as fully to sustain the actual force of the population. Unless it do this, one of the principal springs of public riches must be enfeebled, for the quantity of labour must decline more and more.

Now, the amount of wages necessary for this end cannot be exactly stated, any more than the rate of profit essential to prevent the diminution of the national capital. It will vary exceedingly from two causes in particular; 1. The nature of the climate. 2. The state of opinion.

Whatever reason physiologists may assign for the fact, it seems to be indisputable, that natives of cold regions require much more nourishment than those of warmer countries. The difference even between England and Southern Italy seems great in this respect, and I have no doubt that the quantity of food consumed by a Sussex clown or London drayman would appear monstrous to the frugal Neapolitan, accustomed to support existence on a little ice and macaroni. In climates more opposed, the contrast is still greater. Thus we are told by Captain Ross, that an Esquimau is in the habit of eating twenty pounds a-day of flesh, seal oil, or salmon, without inconvenience, while, as he observes, he is neither more strong nor active than the spirited Arab who satisfies the wants of nature with a simple repast of barley-meal.* Even the Canadian boatmen consume, as we are told, eight or ten pounds of meat daily. The Northern Germans have long been celebrated for the quantity of food they contrive to devour, and no one, I would venture to say, accustomed to more frugal living, ever witnessed a dinner among that people, without having his ideas greatly enlarged as to the wonderful capacity of the human stomach. If we now turn to India and other tropical regions, how extraordinary is the contrast!

From the above, and many other similar facts, it seems pretty clearly established, that the natives of cold countries consume, and therefore probably require, more food than the inhabitants of milder districts. Besides this, they have many pressing wants of another kind, but little, if at all, felt by the latter, such as that of fuel, clothes, and warm habitations. The people of fine climates being much in the open air, home and home comforts are to them comparatively unimportant, whereas to those who, for the most part of the year, inhale a cold and humid atmosphere, they are all in all. It is not easy under the sky of England, completely to enter into that idea of happiness which the Roman poet considers as true felicity.

> " Prostrati in gramine molli
> Propter aquæ rivum, sub ramis arboris altæ
> Non magnis opibus jocunde corpora curant."†

---

* See Captain Ross's second voyage to the Polar regions.

† Lucretius, Lib. ii.

Secondly, Though opinion cannot alter the nature of things, and render that essential to existence which is not strictly so, still, since the belief of what is necessary influences men as much as the reality, it follows, that in the present case there is little difference between them. If the labourers suppose certain comforts to be indispensable, they will make it a point to obtain them, and if fully determined, they are sure in general to succeed. But for this purpose they must not scruple to submit to sacrifices, for these are the unavoidable condition of their triumph. In this case moral restraint is the price to be paid. If their present allowance be not such as they consider essential to their comfort, they must forbear to marry. Thus the labouring population will decline for a time, until the rate of wages has in consequence risen sufficiently to enable them to command those articles which they consider indispensable.

We see, then, that whether from positive necessity or from opinion, a certain rate of wages is required to prevent the quantity of labour from being diminished, and the progress of national wealth arrested in one of its principal sources. But as opinion is mutable on most subjects, so on this it differs widely in different countries. In some, the mass of the people are not content unless they possess a very considerable share of the good things of life, while in others, as in Ireland, marriage is undertaken without a scruple, if there be but a plot of potatoes to support the family, and a mud cabin to receive the happy couple.

We must then satisfy ourselves with saying, that in every country there is a standard, below which wages cannot fall without causing a decline in the numbers of the people, and consequently in the quantity of labour employed in production, though this standard is far from being the same in all parts of the globe.

Having now analyzed Revenue, and found that of the different parts of which it is made up, a certain rate of gross profit and of wages is essential to the sustaining of the national wealth without diminution, while rent and net profits are not indispensable to that end, it follows that the two former alone constitute Necessary revenue, according to the definition above given. The rate required for that purpose, and which as we have seen varies much in different ages and countries, may, for the sake of convenience, be called Necessary profits and Necessary wages,* provided it be clearly understood *not* that these must always be realised, for as regards wages this notion has formerly been refuted,† but simply that unless they be, the public riches cannot but decline. Now, if we subtract the amount of necessary revenue from gross, the remainder will constitute the Net revenue of the society. It will therefore comprehend the whole of the rent of land and of the net profits of ca-

* These phrases are taken from M. Storch.
† See chapter on Wages.

pital, and may include a *part* of the profits of enterprise, as well as of the wages of labour. For, if the
profits of enterprise be of themselves superior to what
I have called necessary profits, *i.e.* if they alone would,
at their present rate, be more than sufficient to en-
sure the undiminished employment of capital in production, then that surplus will form a portion of net
revenue. In like manner, all that the labourers receive above what is necessary for keeping up the existing numbers and strength of the population, must
come under the same category.

These then are the elements of which the net revenue of the society is composed ; the whole of rent
and net profits of capital, wherever they exist, and
possibly a part of the profits of enterprise and of the
wages of labour.

It is here requisite, however, to take notice of a
possible case, in order to show that the sum of all
the net revenues possessed by the different classes,
and which, so far as those classes are separately concerned, really belong to that head, still does not of
necessity give a fair estimate of the net revenue of
the nation at large. Thus, were we to suppose that
the reward of the labourers was in any country so
low as not only to deprive them of all share in the
net income of the society, but even to prevent them
from fully sustaining their race, it follows that, in order to have a just idea of the real net revenue of the
nation, it would be necessary to deduct from the
amount of income possessed by the higher classes as

much as if added to that already earned by the lower, would make up at least necessary wages. If, after making this deduction, some net revenue should still remain to the former, that surplus alone would deserve, in a national point of view, to be comprehended under that head. For, if the landlords, capitalists, and masters were to spend unproductively the whole of what might fairly be considered as their Net income, there can be no doubt that the public wealth would decline. But the essential notion attached to this term is, that portion of the annual return, which, if employed productively, will certainly augment the national riches, and, if otherwise, will at least not impair them. Therefore, it clearly appears, that in such a case, the whole net income of the different classes, would not fairly represent that of the country.

The above case has proved that the sum of the net-revenues of the different classes is not of necessity a true criterion of that of the community. But there are other causes which sometimes render the net incomes of individuals a very unfair measure of that of the whole nation. As soon as exchange is introduced, the value of commodities becomes to individuals, or even classes, of quite as much importance as their quantity. A sudden fall in the price of any article may be the source of ruin to many, while it increases the fortunes of others. If the fall be very great, the purchasers of the commodity in question may find their own net revenues augmented at the expense of the necessary revenue of the producers, perhaps even of their capital.*   In such a case, the net incomes of individuals afford an unfair estimate of that of the community, for if the revenues of one set of people be particularly high, it is only because those of another are unusually low, or reduced to nothing.   In order, therefore, to determine the proper net revenue of the society, we must deduct from the gains of the former as much as would be required to leave to the latter at least their necessary revenue.   In like manner, an extraordinary rise in the price of any commodity, independent of any increase in its cost of production, augments the net incomes of one set of persons at the expense of others, though, as these generally have it in their option to consume less of the article in question, an event of this sort is rarely so ruinous to the fortunes of any as the opposite occurrence, a great and sudden fall.   It does not therefore often happen that the necessary revenue of any considerable number of people is, on that account, materially, if at all, encroached upon.

The tendency of all monopolies is exactly the same. Their effect is permanently to raise the price of some article of consumption above what in a state of freedom would be sufficient to secure its continued supply, and therefore they divert just so much of the revenue of the rest of the society, in order to fill the

---

* If the fall be great, the incomes of all classes interested in the production may suffer, whether landlords, capitalists, masters, or labourers.

coffers of the favoured few. Although, to say the very least, monopolies can never increase the wealth of a nation, for what they give to one they take from another; still, if they do not actually encroach upon the necessary revenue of any class, the profits thence derived must be considered a part of the net income of the society. No doubt this would be quite as great upon the whole, nay, in all probability much greater, if all restrictions were done away with; but that is not the present question. We simply wish to know, supposing monopolies to exist, whether the extraordinary profits derived from them are to be classed or not as a part of the net revenue of the country. And we see that this will depend upon the degree in which they trench upon the incomes of the rest of the community. Should they be so oppressive as seriously to encroach upon the necessary revenue of other classes, a deduction must be made from them on this account, otherwise the whole will belong to the national net revenue.

Net revenue, then, we find, is that portion of the annual gross produce from which alone any increase of the national wealth can take place, for, as we have seen, all the rest is necessary merely to keep it up to its present amount. For the same reason, it is the only part of the yearly return which may be spent in any way its owner pleases, without diminishing the general prosperity. Having also shown the difference between it and gross revenue, and unfolded the ele-

ments of which it is made up, little more remains to
be said upon this subject.

Before concluding the chapter, however, it may be
well to notice certain consequences which naturally
flow from the principles above laid down.

In the first place, it is clear, from the definition just
given of net revenue, that this is the only fund from
which government can freely draw those taxes necessary for the public administration, without encroaching on the present sources of national wealth. If
these burthens swallow up the whole of the net revenue of the society, an effectual stop, no doubt, will
be put to the further progress of riches; but if they
do not go beyond this point, there will be no absolute declension thereof. The moment, however, this
fund becomes no longer sufficient to satisfy the increasing exigencies of the state, necessary revenue
and capital will be broken in upon, and the public
prosperity must consequently be seriously endangered.

From this, it follows, that so far as the Treasury is
concerned, the net revenue of the community is alone
of importance. And since a nation is formidable to
its neighbours, and occupies a distinguished rank in
the political world, solely in proportion to the income
of which its government can dispose, at least so far as
wealth is power, we must conclude, that an imposing
position in respect to foreign states, is due entirely to
the amount of net revenue possessed by the communi-

ty at large. The degree of consequence of any country in the eyes of others, will depend then not upon its gross but net produce, which is but a different term for net revenue.*

Hence it may very well happen, that of two countries, the one which is superior to the other in extent of territory, in population, and in gross produce, may nevertheless be inferior in political power and importance to its rival. This will be the case, should the net produce of the latter be greater than that of the former. How then is it possible that a smaller total return should afford a larger net revenue? This will depend upon the respective wisdom and skill with which the various sources of production are turned to account in the two countries. In the one perhaps, all monopolies and restrictions are done away with, large capitals accumulated in the hands of individuals enable them to introduce a very minute division of labour, to purchase the most expensive machines, and in other ways greatly facilitate production in agriculture, manufactures, and commerce; the intercourse between the various parts of the kingdom being freed from all duties on transit, is at the same time rendered easy and economical by excellent highways, and numerous canals and railroads, and by the wisdom of the government, a free trade is proclaimed with all nations. By all these means

---

* Gross Produce, as we have seen above, is not the same thing as Gross Revenue, for it includes this last as well as something more, but Net Produce and Net Revenue are identical.

are the sources of wealth rendered more fruitful, and consequently the net revenue increased, so as to bear a far higher proportion to the whole produce, than in a country placed in opposite circumstances. Although, then, the gross produce may be greater in the latter, as it must be, if its territory and population be both very superior, yet not only the ratio of the net return to the total result may be more considerable in the former case, but even its absolute amount. For, if industry labour under many disadvantages, the net revenue of the society may be reduced to very little indeed.

In proof of this, I may refer to the discussions which grew out of our inquiry into the doctrine of rent. We there saw that no system of agriculture is so calculated to increase the gross produce of the soil, as that of cultivation by very small proprietors, each employed on his own little estate, and especially if the spade and rake be substituted for the plough and harrow. The reason of which we found to be, that on no other plan could any thing like the same quantity of labour be bestowed on the land. But as this labour is assisted only by the very simplest implements, and every sort of expensive machinery is out of the question, the result is, that in proportion to the toil, the return is after all but scanty. The net revenue of a country cultivated in this manner would consequently be small, though its territory might be very extended, and its population numerous, and therefore from what has been said above, its political importance would be less than these might seem to warrant.

It appears, then, that political power, and therefore security to a certain extent against foreign invasion, are among the happy consequences of a large net revenue. Nor is this all. Since that is the fund from which alone any savings can be made, and fresh capital accumulated, it follows that the larger its amount, the greater will be the facility for those savings, and the more rapid the increase of national wealth. Therefore, a country possessing an ample net produce, cannot be long without a large gross produce also, procured in some way or another. I say procured in some way or another, for those changes which tend to favour the net revenue of the society, may frequently diminish, not for a time only, but even permanently, the produce of certain branches of industry.

Thus, the most improved system of farming, carried on by persons possessed of large capitals, will not succeed in raising from the soil the same amount as can be obtained by little proprietors, each cultivating his own patch of ground. Still, the large net income resulting from the former mode of proceeding, by facilitating the augmentation of capital, will lead to the increase of manufacturing and commercial industry, and thus ultimately give rise, in all probability, to a more abundant gross produce, than could have been realised in the same lapse of time, had the other system of husbandry been persisted in. This produce, it is true, will be, in the first instance at least, of a very different sort. It will comprise more of fabricated, and less of agricultural riches. But as much of the former will be sent abroad to be exchanged for corn, raw materials, &c., it will follow that by the time commerce has done its work, that is, when the production is fully completed, there will be less disparity between the two kinds of wealth existing in the country, than might at first be imagined.

Whatever, then, tends to favour the increase of net revenue, leads also *in the long run* to an ample gross produce both agricultural and manufactured, though a great part of the former may not be of native growth.

It is in vain, however, to deny that the tendency in certain classes, in master-capitalists and great landlords for instance, to sacrifice every thing for the increase of net revenue, is attended with very serious inconveniences. No change, such as the conversion of circulating capital into fixed, can be brought about for the sake of raising rent or profit, without diminishing, for a time at least, the annual produce, lessening the quantity of labour set in motion throughout the community, and consequently injuring the working classes. Changes of this description, in rural industry, have a peculiar tendency to render redundant a part of the existing agricultural population, and therefore to thin their numbers from distress, in some cases for a long period, in others probably for ever. Thus many people who, under a

different system, would have found employment in the
country, are compelled to live in towns, and addict
themselves to other branches of industry. Now, independently of the suffering connected with a total
change of occupation, there is good reason to believe
that an increase of the manufacturing population at
the expence of the agricultural is, beyond a certain
point, by no means to be wished. A variety of ills,
moral, political, and economical, seems inseparable
from an over-growth of the former.

Besides all this, there are certain changes of system in agriculture, which, while they certainly lessen
greatly the total produce of the soil, do not necessarily augment the *sum* even of its net revenue. Of
this kind is the conversion of corn land into grass. Because rent is raised by such an alteration, it does not
follow that the *total* net revenue derived from land
is thereby increased. For, if while the former species of income is augmented, less capital can now be
vested in rural occupations than formerly, a less
amount of profit will be realized. Consequently, rent
and profit together may make up a sum not greater
than before, perhaps even less. It will be said, no
doubt, that the capital thus set free from agriculture,
will find some other investment. This I do not mean
to deny. Still, it must be allowed, that it is deprived
of at least one profitable employment, and that too
upon the whole, probably the most favourable to the
happiness of the people. Besides, part is so mixed,

up with the soil as to become inseparable from it, and the rest is likely to suffer considerable diminution in value, in that change of shape which it must undergo in passing from one branch of industry to another. If that capital belong to the farmer, however, and not to the landlord, it may be the interest of the latter to adopt the new system at the expiration of the lease. Whatever the loss may be, it cannot in this case affect him. At all events, supposing that less capital than formerly can now be vested in rural occupations, not only the class of agricultural labourers, but that of farmers also, will suffer from the change. The same funds, which previously sufficed for a moderate extent of ground, will now stock a much larger. Therefore farms will be less numerous, and part of the existing tenantry thrown completely out of employment.*

The conversion of corn land into hay and pasture fields will then have a peculiar tendency to swell the population of towns at the expense of the country, because, in that case, not the agricultural labourers only, but capital also, with its owners, will be sent

* This difference between the interests of landlord and tenant, in respect to the system of agriculture, is so well understood in some parts of Scotland, that a clause is often inserted in the lease to prevent the latter from ploughing up more than a certain portion of land. A remarkable instance in point recurs just now to my memory. A tenant on an estate with which I am well acquainted, who had often tried to evade this agreement, having at length collected secretly all the horses and ploughs he could find, commenced his operations at night-fall, and before break of day, had turned up every foot of grass in his possession.

from the one to the other. This effect will likewise
be permanent.

There is every reason to suppose, that the above
change will go on throughout Great Britain more
and more. It is an easy affair to bring corn from
abroad, to transport hay, fresh meat, and milk, difficult and costly, if not impossible. Therefore, as society advances, the latter will gradually take the
place of the former. Now, we have seen under the
head of Rent, that the system of large landed properties, so prevalent in Great Britain, favours exceedingly the same change, and consequently tends to
diminish the number of people employed upon the
soil, and to promote the aggrandizement of cities.

A manufacturing population consumes much more
animal food than an agricultural. The vicissitudes
to which they are so liable, instead of making them
provident, as might be wished, tend on the contrary
to dissipation and extravagance. When wages are
good, as they know not how long they may continue so,
it seems less worth while to save, and they determine
to enjoy at least the passing hour. Besides, the very
hardness of the labour, together with its wearisome
uniformity, make some compensation the more necessary. Man cannot live altogether without pleasure,
and the more painful and laborious his ordinary condition, the more will he feel the necessity at times
for some extraordinary excitement. Intense exertion
and none at all lead to the same result ; excess, in
the one case to expel ennui ; in the other, to recruit

for a moment exhausted nature, and solace a toilsome and monotonous existence.*

Hence the disgusting scenes of drunkenness so frequent in manufacturing towns, and the costly repasts which the workmen are accustomed to indulge in so long as their wages permit. From the prevalence of these luxurious habits, much more meat is consumed by the labouring population in towns than in the country. Besides, the latter cannot so easily obtain exactly that small quantity which they may require, and just at the moment they wish. And if the peasantry be themselves proprietors or petty tenants, there is no doubt that they will support themselves, as far as they can, on the produce of their little farms, which, for the reasons before stated, will be chiefly of a vegetable nature.

Thus does the increase of the manufacturing population create a further demand for butcher's meat, and so favour still more the conversion of corn land into pasture. Not to mention, that the rapid fortunes made by master manufacturers, and the great addi-

---

* Colliers, whose life is one of the hardest and most disagreeable that can be imagined, being spent in great part under ground amid foul air and dirty water, are notoriously improvident. Rarely, if ever, do they save, although their wages are high; they live, when they can, sumptuously, and run into all kinds of excesses. I have visited cotton mills where the best spinners earned L.10 a month, and a family could commonly gain L.150 a year; yet such was the extreme improvidence of the workmen, that when a letter came to any of them at the end of the week, just before pay day, they were obliged to borrow of the master a sixpence for the postage, and whenever the mills stopped for repairs or from any other cause, they went about begging. The French are more temperate both in toil and in pleasure than the English.

tion thence arising to the numbers and wealth of the middle classes, greatly promote the same change, by augmenting exceedingly the consumption of all kinds of agricultural productions, particularly of hay and butcher's meat, which, as formerly shewn, are likely to rise in price much more than corn.

What is the practical conclusion to be deduced from all this? Simply the following : that in a country such as Great Britain, where the current runs so strong in favour of an increase of the manufacturing population rather than of the agricultural, it ought not to be the policy of the Legislature still farther to promote this tendency. Were it not for the extreme concentration of landed property, there is little doubt that the disproportion between them would be far less than it is. Now, the evils, whether economical or political, to be apprehended from an overgrown manufacturing population, are very serious. The larger this class becomes, the greater is the proportion of it employed in fabricating commodities for foreign markets, and who consequently must depend for their support partly upon the ready sale of these articles abroad, partly on the uninterrupted importation of food from distant shores. And not to dwell upon the last of these events, but supposing it allowed that there can be no danger of want of supplies, provided there be the means of paying for them, still, these means are liable to be cut off by various accidents. War, prohibitory tariffs, above all, the competition of rival states, and the growth of manufactures in those regions which now import them, all tend to render the foreign much more uncertain than the home market. And when to these disturbing causes, are added changes of fashion, which render the demand for manufactures so liable to vacillation even within the country itself, we shall then have something like an adequate idea of the extensive fluctuation to which those branches of industry are exposed, which are set in motion chiefly for other nations.

Mr. Malthus has remarked, that it cannot be considered a natural, that is, a permanent state of things, for cotton to be grown in the Carolinas, shipped for Liverpool, and again exported to America in its finished condition. The time must come when the United States will fabricate for themselves. The same observation may be applied to other nations. It is quite clear, that unless there be some extraordinary natural advantages peculiar to Great Britain, it cannot have any right to suppose that it shall always supply the greater part of the world with manufactures at a cheaper rate than that at which they can be raised in the respective countries. Much less is it entitled to imagine that *no* other people can ever come into competition with it, and furnish neighbouring or distant lands on as cheap terms as itself. At least, this remark is true, unless, as just observed, Great Britain possess some unrivalled natural facilities for manufacturing industry. The abundance and cheapness of coal is perhaps the only remarkable gift whereby it is distinguished among the nations of the earth. As for the excellent subdivision of labour, and the great improvements in machinery, which tend so much to the cheapness of commodities, there is nothing in all this which may not be adopted by foreign states. Indeed, the rapid advances made in France and other continental countries since the termination of the last war, sufficiently prove this. In the former, in particular, all cotton goods have fallen amazingly in price within the last twenty years. Besides, it is impossible to know what mines of coal remain yet to be discovered on the continent. There is good reason to believe that this substance exists in very many parts where it has not yet been worked, and requires only capital to bring it to light. In Belgium and the south of France, quantities are even now obtained, and in North America it is already made use of, and is said to be abundant. Water-power also may be employed in many places to great advantage, and with manifest economy. The greater part of the manufactories of Rouen are thus moved.

These circumstances founded on the permanent nature of things, joined to the unavoidable accidents of war and prohibitory legislation, sufficiently prove how uncertain is that fabric of prosperity, built upon a vast manufacturing industry destined to supply foreign nations. And when reverses do come, as come they must, the misery thence arising will be incalculable. Thousands, perhaps millions, may be almost totally deprived of employment and subsistence, or be left to depend upon the precarious charity of their fellow-countrymen, a consummation of human wretchedness from which the mind recoils with horror. Nor is the evil less in a political point of view. The existence of an immense population brought together within a small compass, and therefore ready to be worked upon by designing men, liable moreover to the most extreme vicissitudes of fortune, and prevented by continuity of toil from ever becoming deeply instructed, cannot but be a permanent source of danger to any government, and to popular institutions especially. Republican forms in such a state of society would manifestly be out of the question, for nothing but a powerful standing army could ever secure the public tranquillity. Already more than once, has the deeply founded state of England, strong with all that can support a government, strong in its monarchy, its aristocracy, and its military force, trembled at the intelligence of riots in the manufacturing districts. What, then, in similar conjunctures, would become of a feebler rule? Have we not within these two years, seen a single city of France, a city of weavers, almost a match for the government, and able to prolong the contest for more than a week? A government, too, protected by one of the largest armies in Christendom? The fear of such events must tend to induce the upper and middle classes to give up some of the securities against arbitrary power, for the sake of maintaining public order. Of this, examples have already occurred in our own country.

These remarks point out some of the evils to be apprehended from an overgrown manufacturing population. From this, as well as from what has gone before, the consequence which I deduce is, that in a country such as Great Britain, where, partly from the extreme concentration of landed property, partly from the natural progress of society, the above population has so strong a tendency to increase as compared with the agricultural, and even, as we have seen, at its expense, it becomes the duty of government, at all events not to encourage this unavoidable movement.

If, indeed, in order to check this progression, a system of restrictions on the importation of corn or other vegetable food were now for the first time proposed, I should certainly be very slow in agreeing to such an expedient. But when these regulations have already existed for a length of time, so that the condition of a great number of individuals has become dependent upon their continuance, the case is very different. The abolition of the restrictions would then have the effect of depriving of employment a part of the agricultural population, and of sending them to swell the crowds in manufacturing towns. At least this would be the result, supposing the restrictions removed to be really of importance. It is impossible to evade this dilemma. If an abolition of the corn laws would *not* considerably lower the price of bread, (as some would have us believe), it is then perfectly evident that at least they are harmless. Unless this consequence were to follow from doing

away with them, it is a matter of very little importance to the nation, whether they be allowed or not
any longer to cumber the statute book.   The amount
of good would be limited to the sweeping away a
useless law, and that would be all.   But for so trifling
a benefit it seems scarcely worth while making so
great a clamour.   The strenuous advocates for abolition must then, to be consistent, agree that such an
event would make a material difference in the price
of bread, &c.   But this could not happen without
throwing out of cultivation a great deal of inferior
land on which corn was before grown, and therefore
must render redundant the population so employed.
It is then a very great mistake to suppose, as many
have done, that the corn laws concern only landlords,
and that they alone are interested in their continuance.
The labourers would be more affected by their abolition than any other class; for least of all can they
endure any diminution of income.   No doubt, the
common answer to this will be, they can go and seek
employment elsewhere.   But *where* are they to go?
In agriculture there can be little chance of their
finding occupation, for the reasons just assigned.
They must therefore repair to large towns, and try,
as best they may, to fit those hands which formerly
guided the plough, to drive the shuttle or push a
spinning-jenny.   The degree of misery which, in
the mean time, would affect these redundant labourers, it is unnecessary to dilate upon; and in
the end, the disproportion between the agricul-

tural and manufacturing population would be still farther increased, a consummation by no means to be wished. Nor is this all. The change we are now considering would press very hard upon those tenants and little proprietors, who had sunk capital in the improvement of inferior soils paying no rent. No considerable fall in the price of grain could happen without trenching seriously upon the profits of that capital, since at no time is the land supposed to have afforded the other species of revenue. And as the funds in question cannot be withdrawn from the ground, with which they have become identified, there is no way in which the tenant or small proprietor can escape his loss. If he do not consent to abandon altogether the capital thus vested, he must continue to cultivate the land by fresh outlays, though at a manifest disadvantage.

But without insisting any longer upon this point, let us suppose that the farmer finding it impossible any longer to support himself by agriculture, is both anxious and able to realize his capital, and transport it elsewhere. Now, not to dwell upon the losses he is likely to sustain from the fall in the price of all those articles which compose that capital, of which corn is a principal one, a fall occasioned in part by the number of sales by persons similarly situated with himself, in part by the abolition of all restrictions on importation, what after all is to become of him? No doubt, he also is to turn manufacturer, a bitter change, even if possible, to one bred up under the canopy of heaven, and accustomed from his infancy to rural pursuits only. His chances also of success must be very doubtful. For a long time, at least, his situation cannot be very enviable. He will be something like the farmer of Tilsbury Vale, mentioned by the poet Wordsworth, who, when transplanted to London, used to be chiefly occupied in watching the clouds as they passed over the street, and whose favourite resort was Smithfield and the Haymarket.

The same evils which affect the tenantry, would be felt by small proprietors cultivating their own estates, and in a still greater degree, since not their profits only, but rent also would be diminished. And though in England this class of persons may not be very numerous, yet in arguing generally, they must be taken into account. Many of these could not even derive much benefit, if any, from the fall of money-wages likely to ensue sooner or later from the decline in the price of corn, as they rarely if ever employ any labour but that of their own family.

It is not, of course, my object here, to write a formal treatise on the corn laws. All that I wish to show is, that the evils which would result from a total abolition of restrictions in a country which has long been accustomed to them, would be greater than the advocates of such a measure seem generally to admit, and that instead of affecting rich landlords only, it would injure very much the important classes of agricultural labourers, tenants, and small proprietors. We have seen also, that it could not take place with-

out a considerable destruction of capital vested in the
soil, and a loss of much more unavoidable in changing
from one employment to another.   All these inconveniencies greatly diminish, at all events, the benefit
to be expected from throwing quite open the trade
in corn.   And though after a time this injury might
cease to be felt, and the amount of national wealth
increase beyond what it could have done under the
restrictive system, as would probably be the case, yet
it seems to me very doubtful how far this ought to
be considered a sufficient good to induce the legislature to create so great a present evil; particularly
when we consider that the above advantage must be
purchased by a still farther increase of the manufacturing population at the expense of the agricultural,
the former of which, by the supposition, is already so
numerous as to be not only a frequent source of misery to individuals, but even a cause of danger to the
State.

If then a plan can be devised, which, in keeping up
the present average price of corn, shall not entail upon the country those ruinous fluctuations which are
apt to occur wherever the value of that necessary of
life is generally much higher than in other kingdoms,
it will perhaps be well to adhere to such a system.
No doubt, this might be attained by granting a bounty
on exportation equal to the duty on importation, so
that in case of a superabundant crop, the farmers
might be relieved by sending it abroad.   This, however, would render necessary a considerable tax, to

which the country might not be very willing to submit. In lieu of this, the present corn law of England seems to have answered pretty well, as, ever since its enactment, the price of grain has been on the whole steady, and in general lower than in preceding years.

It seems scarcely necessary to add, that the same reasons which would induce me to combat any restrictions, were they now for the first time proposed, would prompt me strenuously to resist any addition to the duties already existing. Here general principles become again applicable. If, to retrace the steps we have already taken, be a course of very doubtful wisdom, at least let us not proceed farther in the same career. Such an attempt, besides being opposed to all sound ideas of Political Economy, could not fail to excite the passions of different classes of society against each other, and scatter the brands of civil discord throughout the community.

NOTE.

NOTE A.

Besides the advantages resulting from the Union, and the emancipation of the trade of Ireland connected with it, M. Storch attributes no small part of the rapid advance made by that country in productive industry at the commencement of the present century, to the continental blockade instituted by Bonaparte, by means of which it got the monopoly of the rich market of Great Britain. " The continental blockade," says he, " in placing the British isles in a state of outlawry with the other nations of the commercial world, announced to Ireland, that it was called upon to furnish exclusively, to England, Scotland, and even to the American isles, the agricultural products refused to them by other countries. That unexpected act of hostility made the Irish acquainted with the extent of their productive capabilities, and let England know of what utility to it is that island, of itself far more precious than all the empire of India." He then goes on to state, that from 1806 to 1808, the exportations of Ireland increased by nearly a *third*,* besides all the augmentation which had preceded that period, and that the importations had advanced in no less a proportion. Thus, the total value of all the manufactured goods imported into Ireland from England had increased from the Union up to 1808 from $11\frac{5}{10}$ million of roubles to $24\frac{9}{101}$, or in round numbers from about L.1,800,000 sterling to more than double that amount. The increase in the quantity imported of the most common articles of foreign and colonial produce was equally great, such as tea, sugar, rum, and wine. Of rum the consumption had augmented *eight fold*.

The above facts, and others of the same sort, are of very great importance in one point of view. They form an unanswerable argument against those who pretend to say that Ireland has *suffered* from its union with England. The reverse is the case in a most remarkable degree.

The source whence M. Storch has drawn these facts, is a publication by M. d'Ivernois, entitled " Effets du blocus Continental sur le commerce, les finances, le credit et la prospérité des isles Britanniques." London, 1810. See the note in the fourth volume of Storch.

---

* The continental blockade was ordained by Bonaparte for all the countries subject to his sway, at Berlin the 21st November 1806. Russia, Austria, and the other continental powers, agreed to the same towards the close of 1807.